Houghton Mifflin

Math Expressions

Volume 2

Developed by
The Children's Math Worlds
Research Project

PROJECT DIRECTOR AND AUTHOR

Dr. Karen C. Fuson

This material is based upon work supported by the
National Science Foundation
under Grant Numbers
ESI-9816320, REC-9806020, and RED-935373.

Any opinions, findings, and conclusions or recommendations expressed in this material are those of the author and do not necessarily reflect the views of the National Science Foundation.

HOUGHTON MIFFLIN BOSTON

Teacher Reviewers

Kindergarten
Patricia Stroh Sugiyama
Wilmette, Illinois

Barbara Wahle
Evanston, Illinois

Grade 1
Sandra Budson
Newton, Massachusetts

Janet Pecci
Chicago, Illinois

Megan Rees
Chicago, Illinois

Grade 2
Molly Dunn
Danvers, Massachusetts

Agnes Lesnick
Hillside, Illinois

Rita Soto
Chicago, Illinois

Grade 3
Jane Curran
Honesdale, Pennsylvania

Sandra Tucker
Chicago, Illinois

Grade 4
Sara Stoneberg Llibre
Chicago, Illinois

Sheri Roedel
Chicago, Illinois

Grade 5
Todd Atler
Chicago, Illinois

Leah Barry
Norfolk, Massachusetts

Special Thanks
Special thanks to the many teachers, students, parents, principals, writers, researchers, and work-study students who participated in the Children's Math Worlds Research Project over the years.

Credits
Cover art: (arctic fox) © Mike Macri/Masterfile. (bridge) © Photodisc/Getty Images
Illustrative art: Dave Klug
Technical art: Morgan-Cain & Associates

Printed in the U.S.A.

ISBN-13: 978-0-618-50989-8
ISBN-10: 0-618-50989-5

5 6 7 8 9 KDL 11 10 09 08 07

VOLUME 2 CONTENTS

Unit 4 Multi-Digit Division

Discover Long Division

1 Find the Unknown Factor 267
Going Further 270
FAMILY LETTER 271

2 Divide Thousands 273
Going Further 274

3 Divide by Numbers Other Than 5 . . 275
Going Further 276

4 Find Just-Under Quotient Digits . . . 277
Going Further 278

5 Estimate to Check Quotients 279
Going Further 280

Problem Solving and Division

6 Make Sense of Remainders 281

7 Problem Solving 285

8 Averages 287

UNIT 4 Test 291

Mini Unit D Polygons and Circles

1 Polygons 293
FAMILY LETTER 297

2 Circles 299

3 Explore Circle Graphs 301

4 The Passing of Time 305
Going Further 308

5 Graphing Day . . . . *

UNIT D Test 309

Unit 5 Fractions

Fractions With Like Denominators

1 Understand Fractions 311
FAMILY LETTER 315

2 Fraction Partners of One Whole . . . 317

3 Compare Fractions 319
Understand Fractions of One Whole 321

4 Fractions of Different-Size Wholes 323

5 Add and Subtract Fractions With Like Denominators 325
Work With Unit Fractions 327

6 Mixed Numbers and Improper Fractions 329
Understand Improper Fractions and Mixed Numbers 331

7 Add and Subtract Mixed Numbers With Like Denominators 333

8 Practice With Fractions 335

Fractions With Unlike Denominators

9 Simplify Fractions 337

10 Add Fractions with Unlike Denominators 343

11 Compare and Subtract Fractions With Unlike Denominators 349

12 Discover Probability 351

13 Probability Day . . . . *

14 Practice With Unlike Denominators 353

Multiplication With Fractions

15 Multiply a Fraction by a Whole Number 355

16 Fractions of Whole Numbers 357

17 Fraction Comparisons 361

18 Fractions on the Number Line 365

19 Practice With Fractions 367

UNIT 5 Test 369

*This lesson consists only of activities from the Teacher's Guide.

Unit E Three-Dimensional Figures

1 Spheres and Cubes 371
FAMILY LETTER 373
2 Prisms and Cylinders 375
Going Further. 378
3 Compare and Contrast Solids. 379
Going Further. 380
UNIT E Test 381

Unit 6 Decimal Numbers

Understand Decimal Numbers

1 Explore Decimal Numbers 383
FAMILY LETTER 385
2 Sequential Decimal Numbers 387
3 Relate Whole Numbers and Decimals 389
4 Number Lines and Rounding 391
5 Compare Decimal Numbers 393
Going Further. 395
6 Practice With Decimal Numbers. . . 397

Use Decimal Numbers

7 Add Decimal Numbers. 399
8 Subtract Decimal Numbers 401
9 Estimate With Decimal Numbers . . 403
Going Further. 405
10 Mixed Practice With Decimals 407
Going Further. 408
UNIT 6 Test 409

Unit F The U.S. Customary System

1 Length 411
Going Further. 414
FAMILY LETTER 415
2 Square and Cubic Measurement . . 417
3 Weight 419
4 Capacity 421
5 Time and Temperature 423
6 Estimation Day . . . . *
UNIT F Test 425

Glossary

Glossary S1

*This lesson consists only of activities from the Teacher's Guide.

4–1 Class Activity

Name ______________________________ Date ______________

Vocabulary
dividend
divisor
quotient

▶ Divide Hundreds

In mathematics, special words are used to describe parts of a problem.

Discuss these multiplication and division words.

Multiplication Words **Division Words**

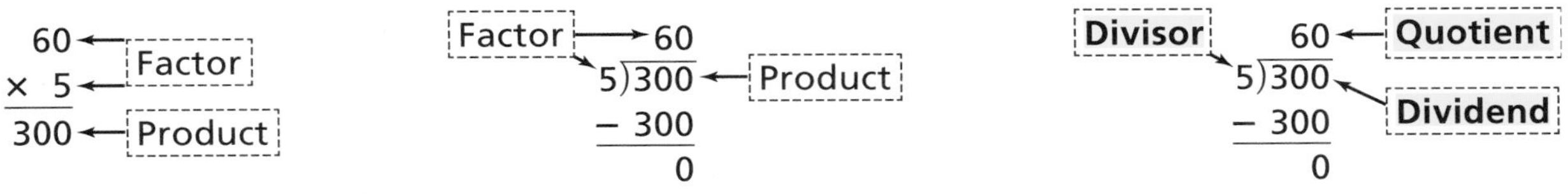

1. Describe the relationships among these 5 words in rectangles.

____

____

▶ Three Division Methods

The sidewalk crew knows that the sidewalk is 330 square feet. The sidewalk is 5 feet wide. How long is the sidewalk? Ellie, José, and Wanda each use a different method to find the answer.

Ellie's Rectangle Sections Method

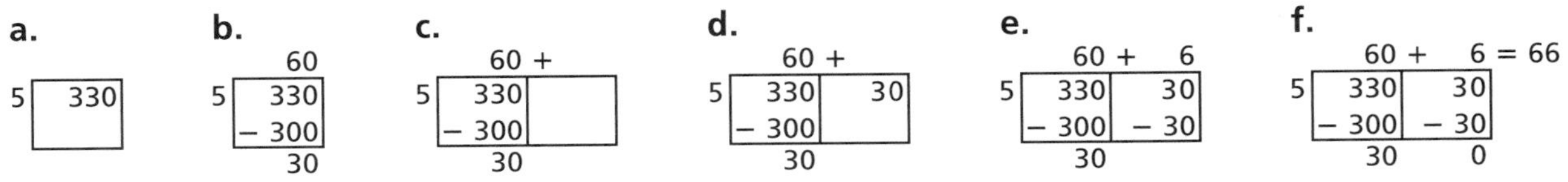

José's Expanded Notation Method

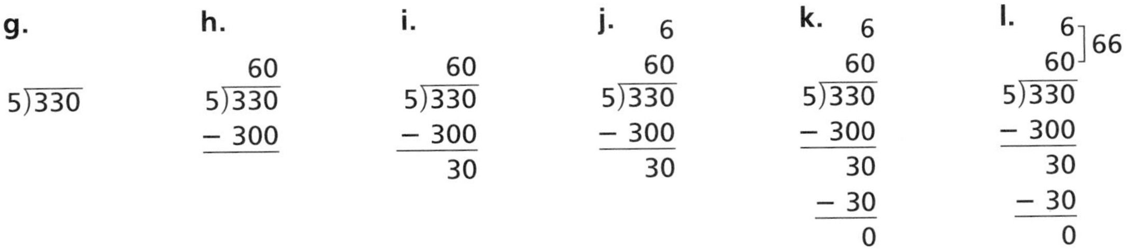

Name ______________________ Date ______________

Vocabulary
remainder

▶ Three Division Methods (Continued)

Wanda's Digit-by-Digit Method

```
m.          n.          o.          p.          q.          r.
                6           6           6          66          66
5)330       5)330       5)330       5)330       5)330       5)330
           − 30        − 30        − 30        − 30        − 30
                          3          30          30          30
                                                           − 30
                                                              0
```

Write the answer on a separate sheet of paper.

2. How are their methods alike?
3. How are their methods different?
4. What other methods do you know that could solve this problem?
5. How do the division methods relate to the multiplication methods below?

Rectangle Sections Method

	60 +	6
5	5 × 60 = 300	5 × 6 = 30

$$\begin{array}{r} 300 \\ +\ 30 \\ \hline 330 \end{array}$$

Expanded Notation Method

$$\begin{array}{lr} 66 = 60 & +\ 6 \\ \times\ 5 = & 5 \\ \hline 5 \times 60 = & 300 \\ 5 \times\ \ 6 = & 30 \\ \hline & 330 \end{array}$$

▶ Understand Remainders

We call the left over quantity in a division problem the **remainder**. We write an "R" before a remainder.

Discuss and compare this problem.

The school store sells pencils in 5-packs. The students who run the store have a box of 332 single pencils. They need to know how many 5-packs can be made from the box of single pencils.

6. How are this problem and the sidewalk problem on page 267 alike and how are they different?

Name ________________________ Date ____________

▶ Patterns in Remainders as Products Increase

Write the answer to each exercise, including any remainders.

7.	$5\overline{)30}$	$5\overline{)31}$	$5\overline{)32}$	$5\overline{)33}$	$5\overline{)34}$	$5\overline{)35}$
8.	$5\overline{)43}$	$5\overline{)44}$	$5\overline{)45}$	$5\overline{)46}$	$5\overline{)47}$	$5\overline{)48}$
9.	$5\overline{)300}$	$5\overline{)301}$	$5\overline{)302}$	$5\overline{)303}$	$5\overline{)304}$	$5\overline{)305}$
10.	$5\overline{)354}$	$5\overline{)355}$	$5\overline{)356}$	$5\overline{)357}$	$5\overline{)358}$	$5\overline{)359}$

Look for patterns in your remainders and answer the following questions.

11. What happens to the remainder part of the quotient as the dividend increases by 1?

____

12. What is the smallest number of single pencils the store could have and make exactly 66 five-packs?

____

13. What other numbers of single pencils could the store have and still make 66 but not 67 five-packs?

____

14. What numbers of single pencils could the store have and make 68 but not 69 five-packs?

____

15. How big can a remainder be? Why?

____

____

____

____

____

Name ______________________ Date ______________

▶ Division and Money

Suppose you and your four friends earn \$55 cutting grass. It is important for you to know how to divide so that you can share the money equally.

- Divide the ten-dollar bills into 5 equal groups.
- Divide the one-dollar bills into 5 equal groups.

$$\begin{array}{r} 1 \\ 10 \\ 5\overline{)55} \\ -\,50 \\ \hline 5 \\ -\,5 \\ \hline 0 \end{array} \quad \left.\right\} \$11$$

Next week, you and your friends earn \$65. How should you divide the extra ten-dollar bill?

- The ten-dollar bill would have to become 10 one-dollar bills.
- Each friend would get 2 more dollars.

$$\begin{array}{r} 3 \\ 10 \\ 5\overline{)65} \\ -\,50 \\ \hline 15 \\ -\,15 \\ \hline 0 \end{array} \quad \left.\right\} \$13$$

Here you change one \$10 for ten \$1 to get \$15 to share.

Show your work.

1. Amy earned \$100 in 5 days. If she earned the same amount of money each day, how much money did she earn in one day?

____

2. Chris made \$250 for 5 hours of work. How much did Chris earn per hour?

____

Family Letter

Dear Family,

Your child is familiar with multiplication from earlier units. Unit 4 of *Math Expressions* extends the concepts used in multiplication to teach your child division. The main goals of this unit are to:

- Learn methods for dividing whole numbers up to five digits.
- Use estimates to check the reasonableness of answers.
- Solve problems involving division and remainders.

Your child will learn and practice techniques such as the Rectangle Sections, Expanded Notation, and Digit-by-Digit methods to gain speed and accuracy in division. At first, your child will learn these methods using 5 as the divisor as most students have little difficulty with 5 count-bys. Later the methods are extended to divisors of 2, 3, 4, 6, 7, 8, and 9. Then your child will learn to divide when there is a zero in the quotient or dividend and to watch out for potential problems involving these situations.

Examples of Division Methods:

Your child may use whatever method he or she chooses as long as he or she can explain it. Some children like to use different methods.

Rectangle Sections Method

	60 +	6 = 66
5	330	30
	− 300	− 30
	30	0

Expanded Notation Method

$$\begin{array}{r} 6 \\ 60 \end{array}\Big]\,66 \qquad \begin{array}{r} 5\overline{)330} \\ -\,300 \\ \hline 30 \\ -\,30 \\ \hline 0 \end{array}$$

Digit-by-Digit Method

$$\begin{array}{r} 66 \\ 5\overline{)330} \\ -\,30 \\ \hline 30 \\ -\,30 \\ \hline 0 \end{array}$$

Your child will also learn to interpret remainders in the context of the problem being solved, for example, as fractions of a whole or as decimal amounts of money.

Finally, your child will apply this knowledge to solve mixed problems with one or more steps and using all four operations.

If you have questions or problems, please contact me.

Sincerely,
Your child's teacher

Carta a la familia

Estimada familia:

En unidades anteriores su niño se ha familiarizado con la multiplicación. La Unidad 4 de *Math Expressions* amplía los conceptos usados en la multiplicación para que su niño aprenda la división. Los objetivos principales de esta unidad son:

- aprender métodos para dividir números enteros de hasta cinco dígitos.
- usar la estimación para comprobar si las respuestas son razonables.
- resolver problemas que requieran división y residuos.

Su niño aprenderá y practicará técnicas como áreas de rectángulos, notación extendida y dígito por dígito, para adquirir rapidez y precisión en la división. Al principio, su niño aprenderá estos métodos usando 5 como divisor, ya que la mayoría de los estudiantes tienen poca dificultad cuando cuentan de 5 en 5. Más adelante los métodos se extenderán al uso de los divisores 2, 3, 4, 6, 7, 8 y 9. Luego, su niño aprenderá a dividir cuando haya un cero en el cociente o en el dividendo, y a detectar problemas que pueden surgir en esas situaciones.

Ejemplos de métodos de división:

Método del área de rectángulos

	60 +	6 = 66
5	330	30
	– 300	– 30
	30	0

Método de notación extendida

```
  6 ⎤
 60 ⎦ 66
5)330
– 300
   30
 – 30
    0
```

Método de dígito por dígito

```
   66
5)330
– 30
   30
 – 30
    0
```

Su niño puede usar el método que elija siempre y cuando pueda explicarlo. A algunos niños les gusta usar métodos diferentes.

Su niño también aprenderá a interpretar los residuos en el contexto del problema que se esté resolviendo; por ejemplo, como fracciones de un entero o como cantidades decimales de dinero.

Por último, su niño aplicará este conocimiento para resolver problemas mixtos de uno o más pasos, usando las cuatro operaciones.

Si tiene alguna pregunta o comentario, por favor comuníquese conmigo.

Atentamente,
El maestro de su niño

Name ____________________ Date ____________

▶ Division With Four-Digit Dividends

Wanda, Ellie, and José each use their favorite method to solve 1,194 ÷ 5.

1. Discuss how their methods are alike and how they are different.

Ellie's Rectangle Sections Method

```
      200    + 30   + 8 = 238 R4
5 |  1,194 |  194 |  44 |
  |– 1,000 |– 150 |– 40 |
      194     44     4
```

José's Expanded Notation Method

```
       8 ┐
      30 │238
     200 ┘R4
 5)1,194
 – 1,000
     194
   – 150
      44
    – 40
       4
```

Wanda's Digit-by-Digit Method

```
   238 R4
 5)1,194
 – 1 0
     19
   – 15
     44
   – 40
      4
```

On a separate sheet of paper, rewrite each problem in long division format. Solve using any method.

2. 3,248 ÷ 5 = ______

3. 4,873 / 5 = ______

Find the product *P* for each problem.

4. $5\overline{)\,P\,}$ with quotient 1,000

   5 × 1,000 = *P*

   P = ______

5. $5\overline{)\,P\,}$ with quotient 3,000

   5 × 3,000 = *P*

   P = ______

6. $5\overline{)\,P\,}$ with quotient 6,000

   5 × 6,000 = *P*

   P = ______

7. $5\overline{)\,P\,}$ with quotient 8,000

   5 × 8,000 = *P*

   P = ______

Solve using any method.

8. 8,435 ÷ 5 = ______

9. 18,435 ÷ 5 = ______

10. 37,265 ÷ 5 = ______

11. 44,714 / 5 = ______

Name ____________________ Date ____________

Vocabulary
partial-quotients method

▶ Estimate Quotients to Solve Division

When you divide, you ask, "How many groups of a given size are there in the total amount?" With each step, you estimate and try to find the closest answer.

In the **partial-quotients method**, you make a series of estimates and then add them up at the end. This method is similar to the Expanded Notation Method, but the partial quotients are written next to the division problem instead of above it. Beginning with tens is an easy way to start.

- Start with 10 × 8 = 80 to solve 8)178. This works, but maybe 20 × 8 is closer to 178.
- Try 20 × 8. The product of 20 and 8 is 160, which is closer to 178, so we use 20 as our partial quotient. Write 20 to the side as shown.
- Next ask, "How many 8s are in the remaining 18?"
- Write 2 to the side as shown and then subtract 16 from 18.
- Finally, add the two partial quotients, 20 and 2. The final result is this sum along with whatever was left over as the remainder.

8)178	
– 160	20
18	
– 16	2
2	22
22 R2	

Solve on a separate sheet of paper. Use partial-quotients division.

1. 6)132
2. 7)189
3. 12)157
4. 5)1,035
5. 8)977
6. 9)285

▶ Solve Problems Using Partial Quotients

Solve.

7. Sonja has 175 stamps in her collection. There are an equal number of stamps on each of the first 7 pages of her collector's book. How many stamps are on each page?

____

Name ______________________ Date __________

▶ Division Word Problems

1. A helper in the school store suggests selling notebooks in packages of 4. How many packages of 4 can be made from 192 notebooks?

2. Another student suggests selling notebooks in packages of 6. How many packages of 6 notebooks can be made from 192 single notebooks?

3. The store will sell packages of notebooks for $3.00 each. Would packages of 4 or packages of 6 be a better deal for students?

4. Which package size would make more money for the store?

Another helper suggests making packages of 7 or 8 notebooks and selling them for $6.00 each.

5. How many packages of 7 notebooks can be made from 192 notebooks?

6. How many packages of 8 notebooks can be made from 192 notebooks?

7. Would you rather buy a 7-pack or an 8-pack? Why?

8. Would 7-packs or 8-packs make more money for the store?

▶ Division Exercises

Use any method to solve.

9. $3\overline{)2{,}061}$

10. $9\overline{)432}$

11. $2\overline{)1{,}476}$

Name ________________________ Date ____________

▶ Mental Math

Look for patterns with zero when dividing multiples of 10 or 100 by 10.

20 ÷ 10 = 2	200 ÷ 10 = 20
50 ÷ 10 = 5	500 ÷ 10 = 50
30 ÷ 10 = 3	300 ÷ 10 = 30
90 ÷ 10 = 9	900 ÷ 10 = 90
110 ÷ 10 = 11	1,100 ÷ 10 = 110

20 ÷ 10

$$2 \times \underbrace{10 \div 10}_{1} = 2 \times 1 = 2$$

200 ÷ 10

$$20 \times \underbrace{10 \div 10}_{1} = 20 \times 1 = 20$$

1. What happens when you divide a multiple of 10 by 10?

____

____

2. What happens when you divide a multiple of 100 by 10?

____

____

▶ Apply Patterns With Zeros to Division

Divide mentally.

3. 40 ÷ 10 = ______
4. 600 ÷ 10 = ______
5. 310 ÷ 10 = ______
6. 800 ÷ 10 = ______
7. 10 ÷ 10 = ______
8. 670 ÷ 10 = ______

Solve.

9. Dwight saved 100 pennies. If he splits his pennies evenly among himself and his 9 friends, how many pennies will each person get?

____

10. The sports stadium can seat 900 people. There are 10 equal sections of seats in the stadium. How many seats are in each section?

____

Name ______________________ Date ______________

▶ Puzzled Penguin Problem

The Puzzled Penguin started to solve this division problem. He knew he had a problem, so, his friends suggested different ways to fix it.

$$\begin{array}{r} 7 \\ 4\overline{)3{,}476} \\ -\ 28 \\ \hline 6 \end{array}$$

Jacob suggested he erase the 7 and write 8 in its place. He would also need to erase the calculations and do them over. $\begin{array}{r} 8 \\ 4\overline{)3{,}476} \\ -\ 32 \\ \hline 2 \end{array}$	Fred told him to cross out the 7 and write 8 above it. He would then subtract one more 4. $\begin{array}{r} 8 \\ \not{7} \\ 4\overline{)3{,}476} \\ -\ 28 \\ \hline 6 \\ -\ 4 \\ \hline \end{array}$
Amad showed him that if he used the Expanded Notation Method, he could just keep going. $\begin{array}{r} 100 \\ 700 \\ 4\overline{)3{,}476} \\ -\ 2{,}800 \\ \hline 676 \\ -\ 400 \\ \hline 276 \end{array}$	Kris showed him how, with the Rectangle Sections Method, he could add another section. $\begin{array}{c\|r\|r\|} & 700\ + & 100 \\ \hline 4 & 3{,}476 & 676 \\ & -\ 2{,}800 & -\ 400 \\ \hline & 676 & 276 \end{array}$

1. What was the Puzzled Penguin's problem?

____

2. Discuss the solutions above. Which friend was right?

____

▶ Zeros in Quotients

Solve. Discuss why a zero is needed in the quotient.

3. $6\overline{)1{,}842}$

4. $8\overline{)5{,}125}$

Name ______________________ Date ______________

▶ Choose Between Calculation and Mental Math

Some problems have numbers that are easy to work with mentally. Other problems are easier to solve using pencil and paper or a calculator.

Use Mental Math

Some problems may contain numbers that are easy to work with mentally.

Example: There are 150 ribbons to be handed out at the school Field Day. There are 30 events, and the same number of ribbons will be awarded at each event. How many ribbons will be given out at each event?

The numbers in this problem are multiples of 10.
Think: 150 ÷ 30 is the same as 15 ÷ 3, so the anwer is 5.
Also, 30 × 5 = 150.

Use Calculation

If the problem asks for an exact answer and there is no noticeable pattern, then you will have to do the calculation.

Example: Last month Mandy was in school for 132 hours. She spent 6 hours in school each day. How many days did she go to school?

We need to find 132 ÷ 6. This is difficult to do mentally, so use paper and pencil or a calculator: 132 ÷ 6 = 22.

Solve. Then write the method you used.

1. Altogether, the members of the exercise club drink 900 bottles of water each month. Each member drinks 10 bottles. How many members are there?

____

2. Juan ran 270 minutes in 6 days. He ran the same number of minutes each day. How many minutes did he run each day?

____

4–5 **Class Activity**

Name ______________________ Date ______________

► Check Quotients With Rounding and Estimation

Rounding and estimating can be used to check answers. Review your rounding skills and then apply what you know to division problems.

Use rounding and estimating to decide whether each quotient makes sense.

1. $\begin{array}{r} 18 \text{ R2} \\ 3\overline{)56} \end{array}$
2. $\begin{array}{r} 92 \text{ R3} \\ 5\overline{)463} \end{array}$
3. $\begin{array}{r} 928 \\ 6\overline{)5{,}568} \end{array}$
4. $\begin{array}{r} 129 \text{ R4} \\ 7\overline{)907} \end{array}$

Solve using any method. Then check your answer by rounding and estimating.

5. $3\overline{)29}$
6. $6\overline{)34}$
7. $7\overline{)59}$
8. $3\overline{)72}$
9. $6\overline{)83}$
10. $7\overline{)88}$
11. $9\overline{)67}$
12. $9\overline{)95}$
13. $6\overline{)375}$
14. $2\overline{)257}$
15. $3\overline{)298}$
16. $7\overline{)384}$
17. $2\overline{)457}$
18. $3\overline{)470}$
19. $7\overline{)540}$
20. $7\overline{)628}$
21. $8\overline{)683}$
22. $9\overline{)717}$
23. $7\overline{)805}$
24. $8\overline{)869}$
25. $9\overline{)914}$
26. $6\overline{)593}$
27. $6\overline{)706}$
28. $6\overline{)969}$
29. $6\overline{)1{,}723}$
30. $2\overline{)2{,}986}$
31. $7\overline{)8{,}574}$
32. $6\overline{)4{,}652}$
33. $2\overline{)5{,}235}$
34. $7\overline{)7{,}310}$

Name ______________________________ Date ______________

▶ Choose Between an Estimate and an Exact Answer

Some problems require an exact answer. For others, you only need an estimate.

Exact Answer If a problem asks for an exact answer then you will have to do the calculation.	**Estimate** If a problem asks for a *close* answer and uses *about, approximately, almost*, and *nearly*, then you can estimate.
Example: The school cafeteria prepares 3,210 lunches each week. The same numbers of lunches are prepared 5 days per week. How many lunches are prepared each day?	**Example:** Milo has to read a 229 page book. He has 8 days to finish it. About how many pages should he read each day?
Discuss why you think this problem requires an exact answer.	Discuss why an estimate and not an exact answer is appropriate.

Decide whether you need an exact answer or an estimate. Then find the answer.

1. Sam bought a board that was 72 inches long to make bookshelves. He wants to cut the board into three equal pieces and use each one for a shelf. How long will each shelf be?

   ____

2. Sam's mother baked 62 muffins for his class. There are 18 people in Sam's class, including the teacher. About how many muffins should each person get?

   ____

3. Each 24-inch shelf can hold about 10 books. Approximately how many inches wide is each book?

   ____

4. Malcom wants to buy 3 concert tickets. Each ticket costs $45.50. How much money will he need?

   ____

Name ________________________________ Date ____________

▶ Different Kinds of Remainders

Remainders in division have different meanings depending upon the type of problem you solve.

$$\begin{array}{r} 2\text{ R}1 \\ 4\overline{)9} \\ -\ 8 \\ \hline 1 \end{array}$$

The same numeric solution shown at the right works for the following five problems. Discuss why the remainder means something different each time.

A. **The remainder is not part of the question.** Thomas has one 9-foot pine board. He needs to make 4-foot shelves for his books. How many shelves can he cut?

B. **The remainder causes the answer to be rounded up.** Nine students are going on a field trip. Parents have offered to drive. If each parent can drive 4 students, how many parents need to drive?

C. **The remainder is a fractional part of the answer.** One Monday Kim brought 9 apples to school. She shared them equally among herself and 3 friends. How many apples did each person get?

D. **The remainder is a decimal part of the answer.** Raul bought 4 toy cars for $9.00. Each car costs the same amount. How much did each car cost?

E. **The remainder is the only part needed to answer the question.** Nine students have signed up to run a relay race. If each relay team can have 4 runners, how many students cannot run in the race?

Name ______________________________ Date ____________

▶ Remainders as Fractions

Discuss situation C from page 281.

One Monday, Kim brought 9 apples to school. She shared them equally among herself and 3 friends. How many apples did each person get?

Kim's apples were very tasty, so every week more friends wanted to share them.

1. The next Monday, Kim brought 13 apples to share equally among herself and 5 friends. How many apples did each person get?

   ____

2. The next Monday after that, Kim brought 17 apples to share equally among herself and 7 friends. How many apples did each person get?

   ____

3. Write the numeric solutions to all three apple-sharing problems. Each time, write the answer first with a whole number remainder. Then on the line after the equals sign, write each answer using a fraction. Remember that a unit fraction $\left(\frac{1}{d}\right)$ means 1 of *d* equal parts of a whole.

   $4\overline{)9}$ = ______ $6\overline{)13}$ = ______ $8\overline{)17}$ = ______

4. From week to week, did Kim get more or less apples? Why?

   ____

   ____

Name ____________________ Date ____________

▶ Decimal Remainders

Discuss situation D from page 281.

Raul bought 4 toy cars for $9.00. Each car cost the same amount. How much did each car cost?

5. Describe how the Digit-by-Digit solution steps show how we can write a money division problem as dollars and cents.

Step A	Step B	Step C	Step D
$\begin{array}{r} \$2 \\ 4\overline{)\$9.00} \\ -\ 8 \\ \hline 1 \end{array}$	$\begin{array}{r} \$2 \\ 4\overline{)\$9.00} \\ -\ 8 \\ \hline 1.0 \end{array}$	$\begin{array}{r} \$2.2 \\ 4\overline{)\$9.00} \\ -\ 8 \\ \hline 1.0 \\ -\ 0.8 \\ \hline 0.2 \end{array}$	$\begin{array}{r} \$2.25 \\ 4\overline{)\$9.00} \\ -\ 8 \\ \hline 1.0 \\ -\ 0.8 \\ \hline 0.20 \\ -\ 0.20 \\ \hline 0 \end{array}$
How many dollars are in the answer? ______	How many dimes are in the left over dollar? ______	How many dimes are in the answer? ______	How many pennies are in the left over dimes? ______
How many dollars are left over? ______		How many dimes are left over? ______	How many pennies are in the answer? ______

6. Compare the numeric solutions to the apple problem and the toy-car problem. How are they different?

____

____

____

7. What makes them numerically equal?

____

8. If Raul had paid $7.00 for the cars, how much would each car have cost?

____

Name ______________________ Date ______________

▶ Real-World Division Problems

Solve. Then discuss the meaning of the remainder.

9. Maddie tried to divide 160 stickers equally among herself and 5 friends. There were some stickers left over, so she kept them. How many stickers did Maddie get?

10. Kendra bought a bag of 200 cheese crackers for her class. If each student gets 7 crackers, how many students are there? How many crackers are left over?

11. Jerry has $36.00 in his bank. He wants to give the same amount of money to each of his 8 cousins. How much money will each of Jerry's cousins get?

12. Racheed had 87 pennies. He divided them equally among his 4 sisters. How many pennies did Racheed have after he gave his sisters their shares?

13. Mara wants to buy some new pencil boxes for her pencil collection at the store. She has 47 pencils. If each pencil box can hold 9 pencils, how many pencil boxes does Mara need to buy?

14. Henry's coin bank takes only nickels. Henry takes $4.42 to the bank to change for nickels. How many nickels will he get?

15. On a separate sheet of paper, make up a problem where the remainder is a fraction. Use $36 \div 5$.

Name ______________________ Date ______________

▶ Mixed One-Step Word Problems

The fourth and fifth grade classes at Jackson School held a Just-for-Fun Winter Carnival. All of the students in the school were invited.

Discuss what operation you need to use to solve each problem. Then solve the problem.

1. Two students from each fourth and fifth grade class were on the planning committee. If Jackson School has 14 fourth and fifth grade classes in all, how many students planned the carnival?

   ____

2. To advertise the carnival, students decorated 4 hallway bulletin boards. They started with 2,025 pieces of colored paper. When they finished they had 9 pieces left. How many pieces of paper did they use?

   ____

3. The parents ordered pizzas to serve at the carnival. Each pizza was cut into 8 slices. How many pizzas had to be ordered so that 1,319 people could each have one slice?

   ____

4. 825 students signed up to run in timed races. If exactly 6 students ran in each race, how many races were there?

   ____

5. At the raffle booth, 364 fourth graders each bought one ticket to win a new school supply set. Only 8 fifth graders each bought a ticket. How many students bought raffle tickets altogether?

   ____

6. Altogether, 1,263 students were enrolled in the first through fifth grades at Jackson School. On the day of the carnival, 9 students were absent. How many students could have participated in the carnival activities?

   ____

Name ______________________ Date ______________

▶ Mixed Multi-Step Word Problems

Solve these problems about Pine Street School's Olympic Games.

7. At the start of the games, 193 fourth graders were separated into three events. 87 students participated in the first event. The rest of the students were evenly divided between the other 2 events. How many students participated in the last event?

8. Cup Pyramids: Three teams built pyramids of paper cups. Each team had exactly 176 cups to use. Team 1 used exactly half of their cups. Team 2 used 4 times as many cups as Team 3. Team 3 used 32 cups. Which team stacked the most cups?

9. The Parents' Club provided 357 celery sticks, 676 carrot sticks, and 488 apple slices. If each student took 3 snack pieces, how many students got a snack?

10. 75 first graders and 84 second graders skipped around the gym. After a while, only 8 students were still skipping. How many students had stopped skipping?

11. Basket Dunk: A team from each school had 250 foam balls and a bucket. The Jackson team dunked 6 fewer balls than the Pine Street team. The Pine Street team dunked all but 8 of their balls. How many balls did the two teams dunk in all?

12. When the day was over, everybody had earned at least 1 medal, and 32 students each got 2 medals. In all, 194 each of gold, silver, and bronze medals were given out. How many students played in the games?

Name ____________________ Date __________

Vocabulary
mean

▶ Calculate the Mean

The **mean** of a set of data is a number that describes the size of each of *n* equal groups made from *n* data values. You can find the mean by adding the values and dividing that sum by the number of values.

1. Davis made 4 clay pots on Friday, 7 clay pots on Saturday, and 4 clay pots on Sunday. What is the mean number of pots he made each day? Make a drawing to show how the pots for each day can be redistributed to find the mean.

   ____

2. Serena, Marco, and Ray each have a fish tank. Serena has 5 fish. Marco has 6 fish. Ray has 10 fish. What is the mean number of fish that the three friends have? Make a drawing to show how they can move fish so each person has an equal share.

   ____

Find the mean.

Show your work.

3. 2, 3, 5, 7, 8 Mean: ________
4. 1, 6, 13, 4, 12, 3, 10 Mean: ________
5. 29, 35, 18, 62 Mean: ________
6. 165, 917, 443, 212, 218 Mean: ________

Name ____________________ Date ____________

► Word Problems With Mean

Last week, the town of Midville hosted a county fair. Solve these problems about the fair.

7. The fair organizers kept track of the high temperature each day. It was 67° on Monday, 71° on Tuesday, 75° on Wednesday, 69° on Thursday, and 78° on Friday. What was the mean high temperature during the five days of the fair?

8. The organizers recorded the attendance each weekday. What was the mean attendance?

Day	Attendance
Monday	874
Tuesday	658
Wednesday	723
Thursday	796
Friday	909

9. Because the fair was so popular, the organizers decided to extend it one more day. On Saturday, 954 people attended the fair. What was the mean attendance over the 6 days?

10. The Johnson family attended the fair. The ticket prices for the fair are listed below.

Adults	$5.00
Teens (13–18 years old)	$4.00
Children (under 13)	$3.00

There are 2 adults and 2 teens in the Johnson family. What was the mean ticket price for the family?

Name ______________________________ Date ______________

Vocabulary
measures of central tendency
median
mode

► Word Problems With Mode and Median

The mode and median are also measures for a set of data. The mean, median, and mode are sometimes called **measures of central tendency**.

The **median** of a set of data is the middle value when the values are listed in order from least to greatest.

14, 25, 27, 32, 32
The median is 27.

If there are two middle values, the median is the mean of the two middle values (it is halfway between them).

14, 25, 32, 32
The median is the mean of 25 and 32, which is 28.5.

The **mode** of a set of data is the value that appears most often. A set of data can have one mode, several modes, or no mode (when no data value is repeated).

14, 25, 27, 32, 32
The mode is 32.

14, 25, 27, 32
There is no mode.

Solve.

Show your work.

11. There was a Guess-Your-Age booth at the fair. One afternoon, the ages of the visitors to the booth were 22, 33, 22, 30, 33, 27, and 22. Find the mean, median, and mode of the ages.

mean: ________

median: ________

mode: ________

12. One more person came to the booth. His age was 67 years. Find the new mean, median, and mode of the visitors' ages.

mean: ________

median: ________

mode: ________

4–8 Class Activity

Name ______ Date ______

▶ Choose the Best Measure

The mean, median, and mode are all measures of the typical value in a set of data. In some cases, one measure may be better than another to represent a set of data.

For each situation, find the mean, median, and mode of the set of data. Then decide which best represents the data.

13. Mr. Garcia's store sells cereal in 12, 18, and 22 ounce boxes. One week, he sold boxes that were 12, 18, 12, 22, 18, 22, 12, and 12 ounce sizes.

Mean: ______

Median: ______

Mode: ______

14. Last week, it rained for 5 days. It rained 11 mm on Monday, 8 mm on Tuesday, 22 mm on Wednesday, 9 mm on Thursday, and 10 mm on Friday.

Mean: ______

Median: ______

Mode: ______

15. Aliya's friends spent 300, 250, 300, 750, 200, 300, 250, 350, and 900 minutes on homework.

Mean: ______

Median: ______

Mode: ______

16. John took five math tests this term. His scores were 81, 75, 69, 81, and 54.

Mean: ______

Median: ______

Mode: ______

17. **Math Journal** Write and solve a word problem that involves finding the mean, median, or mode of a data set.

Name ____________________ Date ____________

Solve.

1. $8\overline{)25}$

2. $7\overline{)56}$

3. $6\overline{)216}$

4. $4\overline{)306}$

5. $3\overline{)927}$

6. $2\overline{)5{,}309}$

7. $5\overline{)3{,}025}$

8. $9\overline{)75{,}298}$

Use rounding and estimation to decide whether each answer makes sense. Explain your work.

Show your work.

9. $\begin{array}{r}18 \text{ R1}\\ 3\overline{)46}\end{array}$ ____________________

____

10. $\begin{array}{r}49 \text{ R3}\\ 6\overline{)297}\end{array}$ ____________________

____

11. $\begin{array}{r}36\\ 7\overline{)182}\end{array}$ ____________________

____

Solve.

12. The science club is renting vans for a trip. Six students can ride in each van. The club will fill as many vans as possible, and the remaining students will ride in other cars. If 28 students are going on the trip, how many students will ride in other cars?

____

13. Mr. Walsh cut a 31-foot-long board into 5-foot pieces. How long was each piece?

____

Name ______________________ Date __________

Solve.

Show your work.

14. Tara worked for 4 hours and earned $15.00. How much did she earn each hour?

____

15. How many packages of 8 buns would Mr. Johnson need for 233 hamburgers?

____

16. The school store started with 3,250 notebooks to sell on Monday. At the end of the day, they had 712 notebooks left. How many did they sell?

____

17. Mrs. Suarez wants to give 3 crackers to each of her 27 students. If there are 6 crackers in a package, how many packages will she need?

____

____

18. Janeka bought 319 apples. She used 175 of them to make applesauce. She plans to use the rest to make 18 apple pies. How many apples will be used in each pie?

____

19. On her first four math tests, Clara scored 80, 83, 79, and 86. What was her mean test score?

____

20. **Extended Response** If she scores 87 on her final test, will Clara's mean score go up or down? Explain.

____

____

____

Name ________________ Date ________

Vocabulary
polygon
closed
regular
congruent

▶ What Are Polygons?

The prefix *poly-* means "many," and the suffix *-gon* refers to angles. A **polygon** has "many angles."

A polygon has only straight line segments that do not cross each other. A polygon is **closed**. That means it has no endpoints.

1. Circle the figures that are polygons.

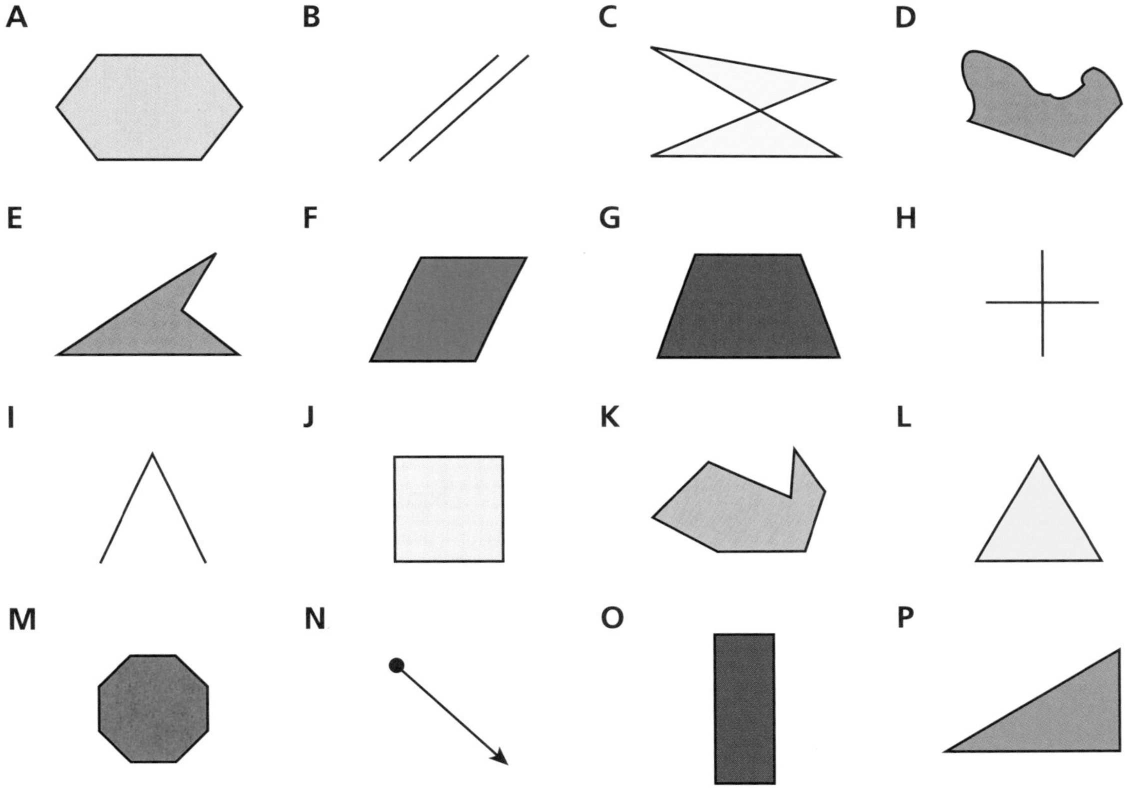

2. Why must a polygon have three or more sides and angles?

____

____

All sides and angles of a **regular** polygon are **congruent**.

3. Which of the polygons above look regular?

____

D–1 Class Activity

Name ____________________ Date ____________

Vocabulary
convex
concave

▶ Convex and Concave Polygons

Polygons can be convex or concave. In concave polygons there exists a line segment with endpoints inside the polygon and a point on the line segment that is outside the polygon. A convex polygon has no such line segment. Which polygons are convex and which are concave?

4. 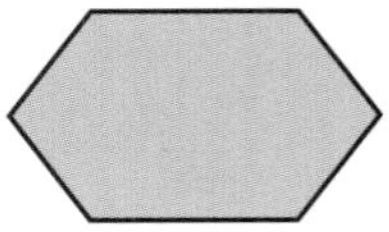

____

5. 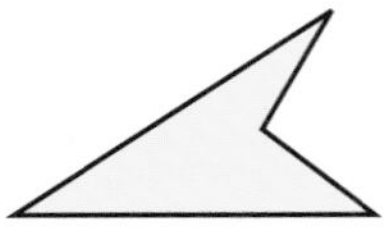

____

6. 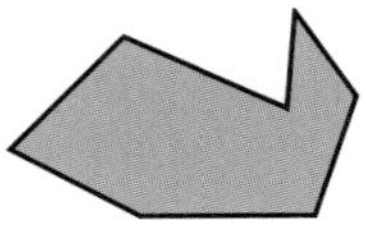

____

7. 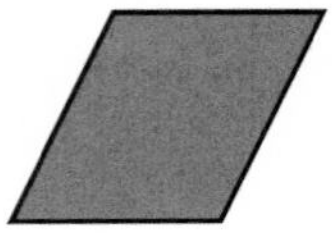

____

8. How can you remember the meaning of the words concave and convex?

____

____

____

____

9. Can a concave polygon be a regular polygon? Explain.

____

____

____

____

10. Can a triangle be concave? Explain.

____

____

____

11. What is the common name for a regular 4-sided polygon? ______________

12. What is the common name for a regular 3-sided polygon? ______________

____

D–1 Class Activity

Name ____________________ Date __________

Vocabulary
triangle
quadrilateral
pentagon

► Name Polygons

Polygons have special names that tell how many sides and angles they have. Some names of polygons are **triangle**, **quadrilateral**, and **pentagon**.

Write a prefix to match each number.

13. three ________ 14. four ________ 15. five ________

16. six ________ 17. seven ________ 18. eight ________

19. nine ________ 20. ten ________ 21. twelve ________

Name each polygon.

22.
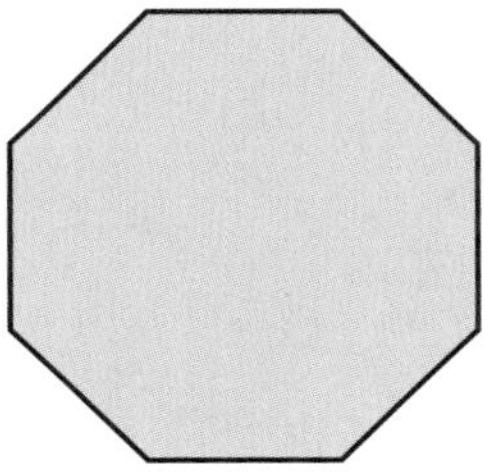
____

23.
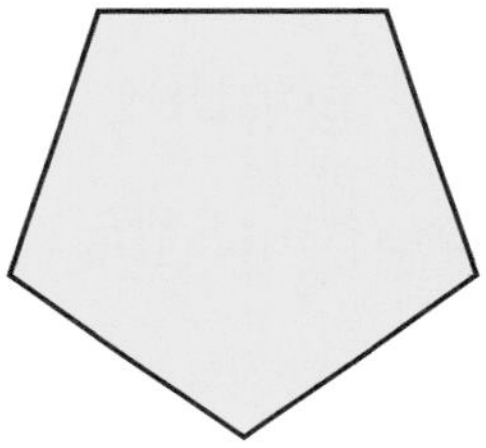
____

24.
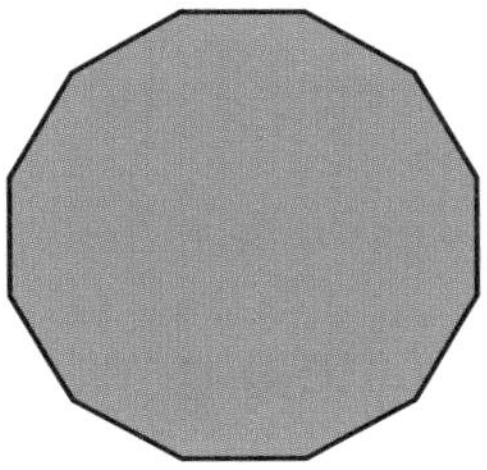
____

25.
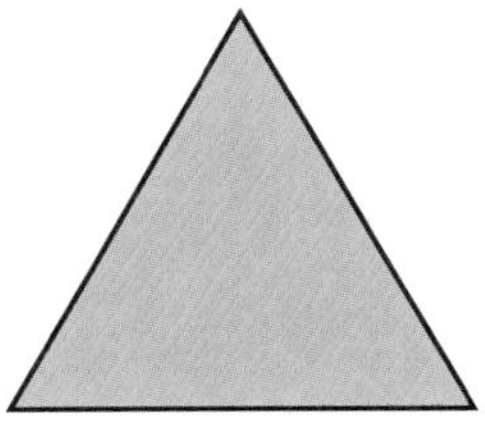
____

26.
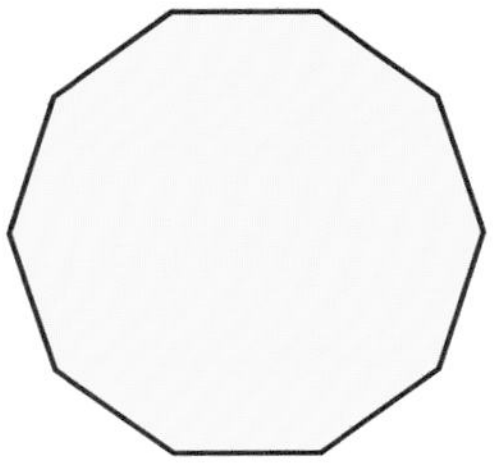
____

27.
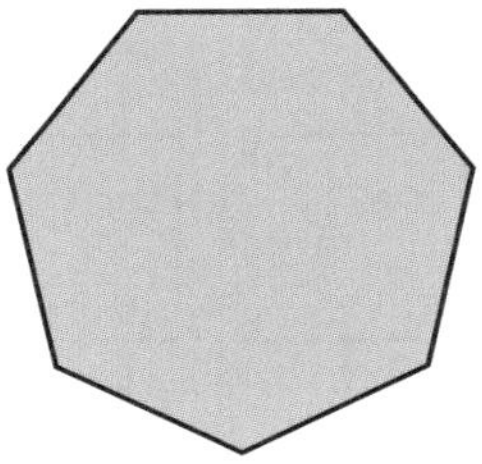
____

28.
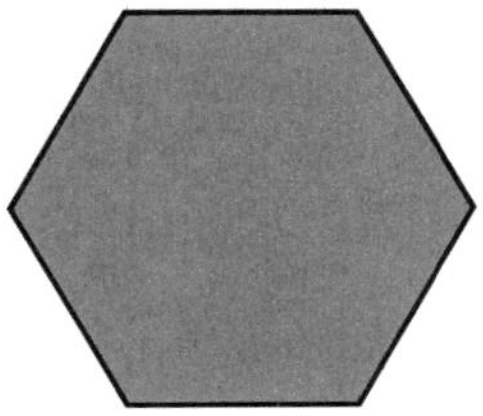
____

29.

____

30.
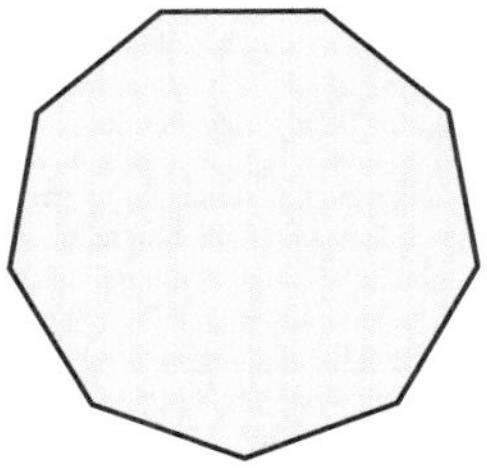
____

D–1 Class Activity

Name ______________________________ Date ______________

► Find Perimeter of Polygons

Use multiplication to write a general equation for the perimeter of each regular polygon. Use *P* to represent perimeter.

31. equilateral triangle

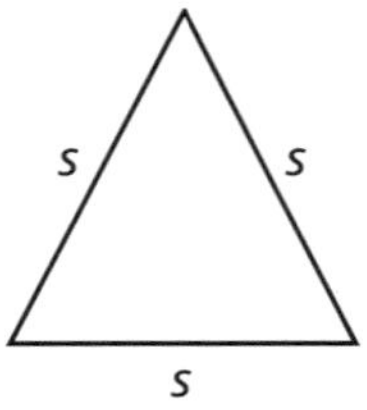

____

32. square

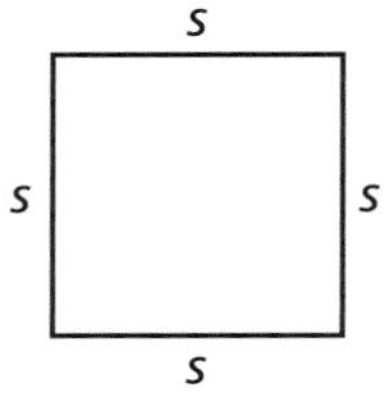

____

33. regular pentagon

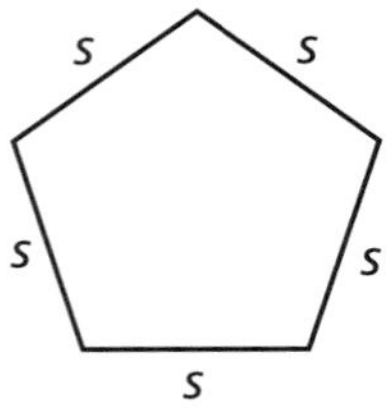

____

34. a regular hexagon with sides of length *s* ______________

35. a regular dodecagon with sides of length *s* ______________

36. Write a general equation for any regular polygon with *n* sides of length *s*. ______________

What is the total perimeter of each group of regular polygons?

37. 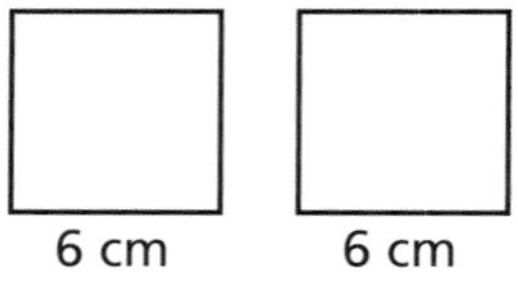

____

38. 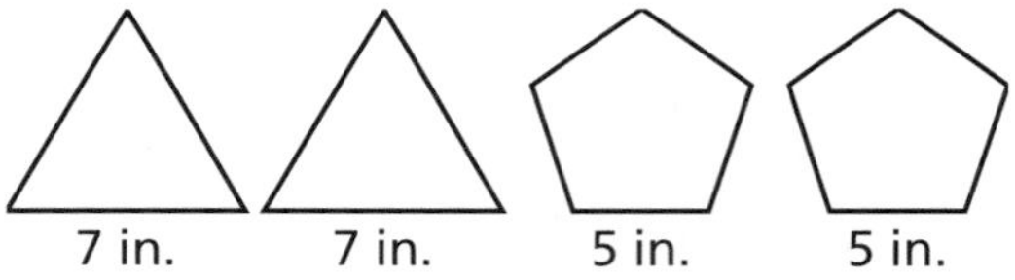

____

39. 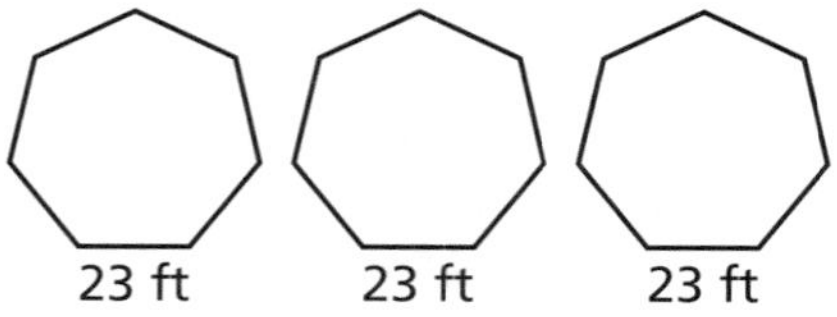

____

40. 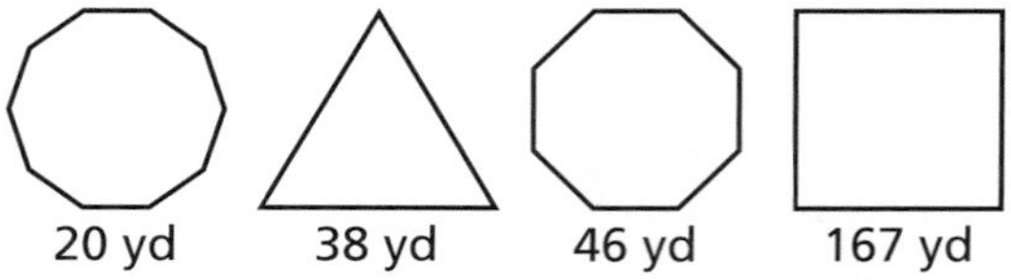

____

Family Letter

Dear Family,

This unit is about polygons, circles, circle graphs, and measuring time. The goals for this unit are for students:

- to know about polygons and how they are named

A polygon is any shape that has three or more sides and angles and whose sides are connected to each other. Here are a few polygons.

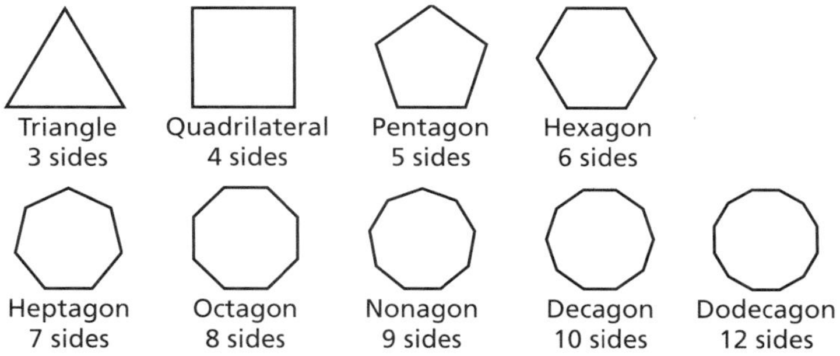

- to know the parts of circles, such as *center, circumference, diameter,* and *radius*

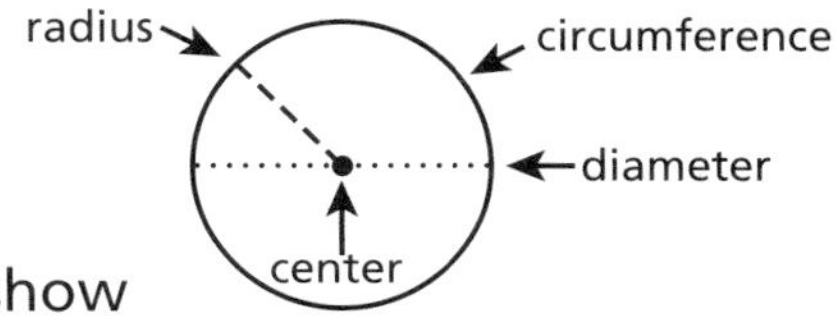

- to understand how we use circles to show parts of wholes, such as in circle graphs and in telling time on a clock

How I Spend My Allowance

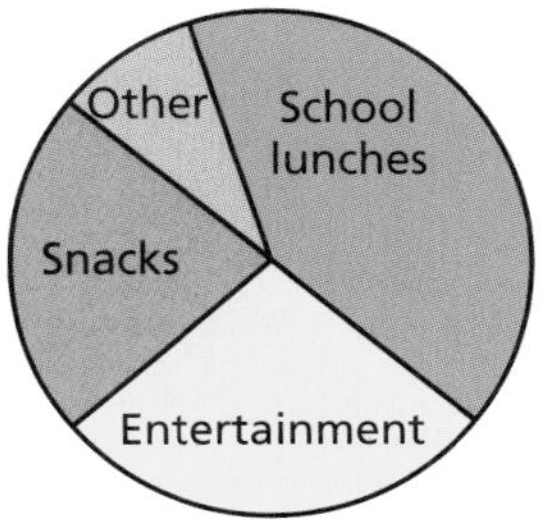

Each different part of a circle graph represents a part of the topic of the graph. The portion of a clock between the start and end point of the minute hand shows what part of an hour has passed.

Our next unit is about division. If your child does not know all the basic divisions, please arrange regular practice time at home. If you need practice materials for division or if you have any questions or comments, please call or write to me.

Sincerely,
Your child's teacher

Carta a la familia

Estimada familia:

Esta unidad trata los polígonos, los círculos, las gráficas circulares y la medición del tiempo. Los objetivos de esta unidad pretenden que los estudiantes:

- aprendan los nombres y las características de los polígonos

Un polígono es toda figura de tres o más lados y ángulos, cuyos lados están conectados entre sí. Éstos son algunos polígonos.

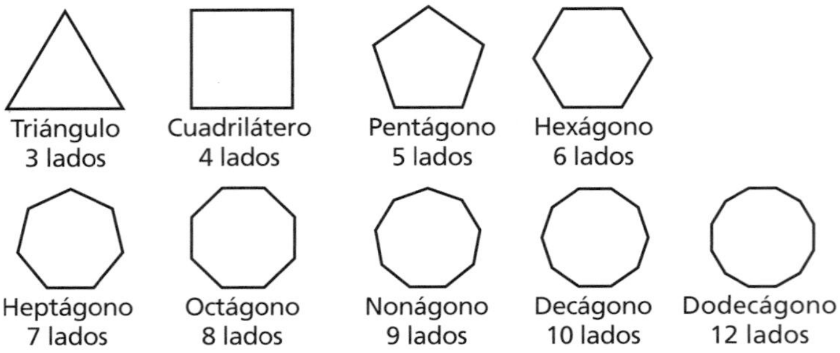

- identifiquen las partes de un círculo, como el *centro,* la *circunferencia,* el *diámetro* y el *radio*

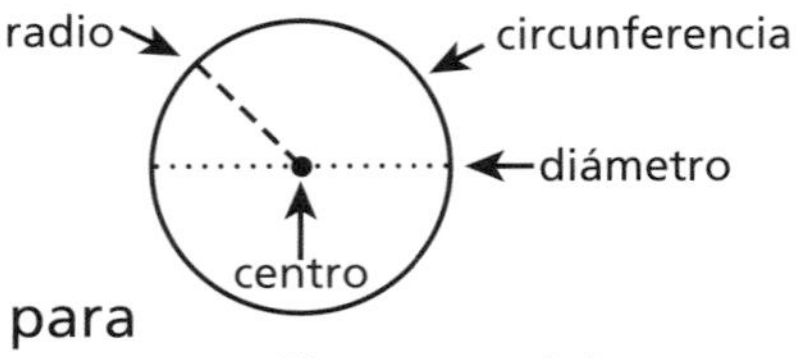

- comprendan cómo usamos los círculos para mostrar partes de enteros, como en las gráficas circulares y al decir la hora al mirar el reloj

Cómo gasto el dinero de mi mesada

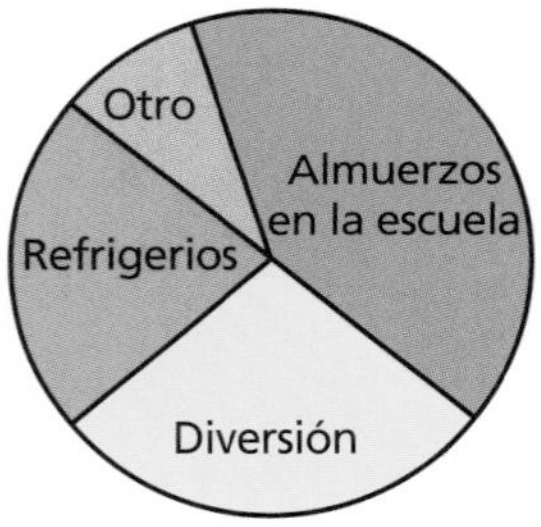

Cada una de las partes de una gráfica circular representa una parte del tema de la gráfica. La distancia en el reloj entre el punto donde comienza y donde termina el minutero, muestra qué parte de una hora ha pasado.

La siguiente unidad trata la división. Si su niño no sabe todas las divisiones básicas, por favor establezca un horario para practicar en casa. Si necesita materiales para practicar la división o si tiene alguna pregunta o comentario, por favor comuníquese conmigo.

Atentamente,
El maestro de su niño

Name ____________________ Date ____________

Vocabulary
center
radius
diameter

▶ Compare Polygons and Circles

Name each regular polygon.

1. 
____

2. 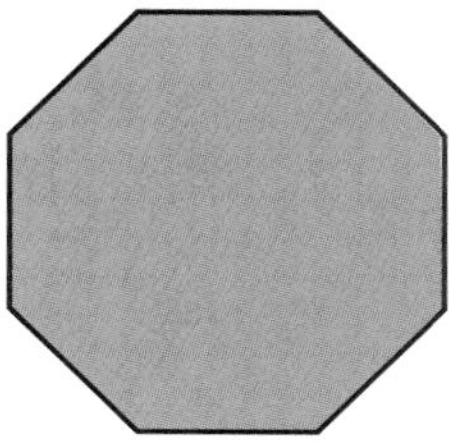
____

3. 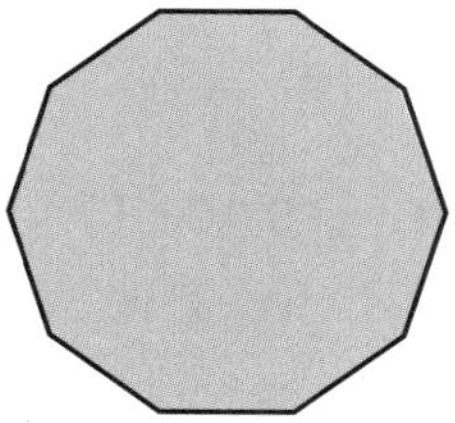
____

4. 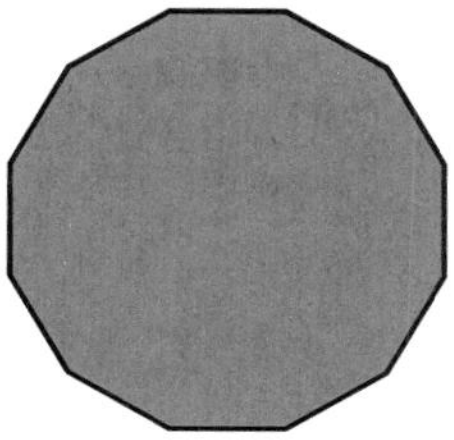
____

5. What happens to the angles of regular polygons as they have more and more sides?

____

____

6. What is the name of a smooth curved line around the outside of a regular polygon everywhere equidistant from the center?

____

▶ Radius and Diameter

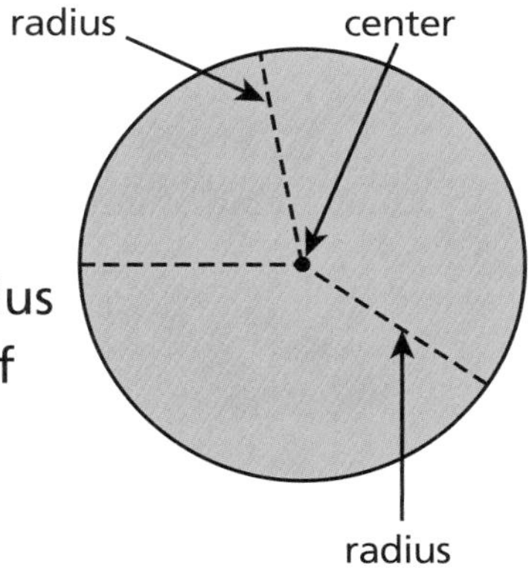

A line segment joining the **center** of a circle to any point on its perimeter is called a **radius**. For any circle, every radius has the same length. That length is also called the radius of the circle. A line segment drawn through the center of a circle is called its **diameter**. Its length is also called the diameter of the circle.

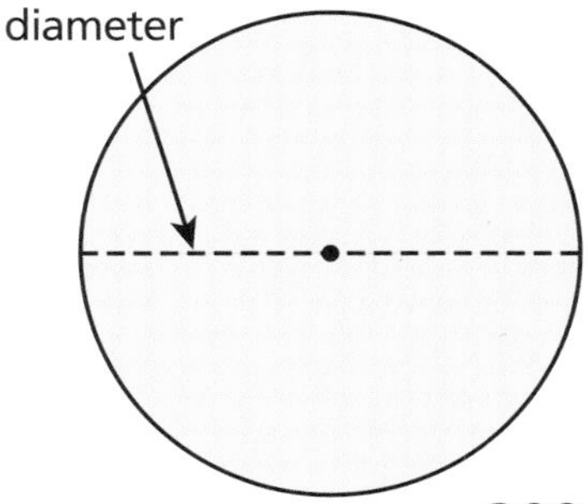

7. What is the radius of this circle? ____________

8. What is the diameter? ____________

9. How can knowing about radius help you draw a circle?

____

____

D–2 Class Activity

Name ____________________ Date ________

Vocabulary
circumference
pi

▶ Explore Circumference

The curved line around the edge or perimeter of a circle is its **circumference**. The length of that line is also called the circumference of the circle.

If you divide the circumference (C) of a circle by its diameter (d), you always get the same number. The number is called ***pi*** and it is written with the Greek letter π, *pi*.

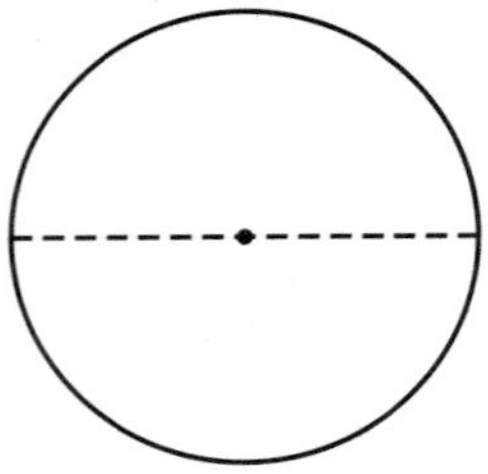

$C \div d = \pi$

Pi is about 3.14 or $\frac{22}{7}$.

10. If you know the product and one factor of any division, how can you find the other factor? $\frac{C}{d} = \pi$

____

____

11. If you know the diameter of a circle and you know π, how can you find the circumference of the circle?

____

____

12. What is the general equation for finding the circumference of a circle?

$C =$ ________

13. Fill in the name of each part of the circle.

D–3 Class Activity

Name ______________________ Date ______________

▶ Divide a Circle

We can divide a whole circle into equal parts. We can show this with a round pizza.

What part of the whole pizza does one slice show?

1. 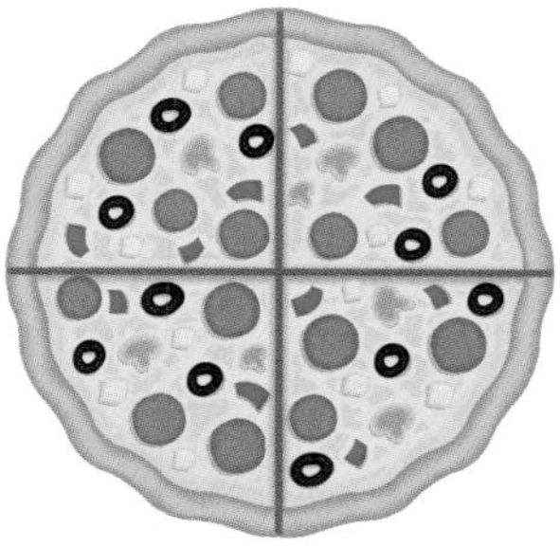

____

2. 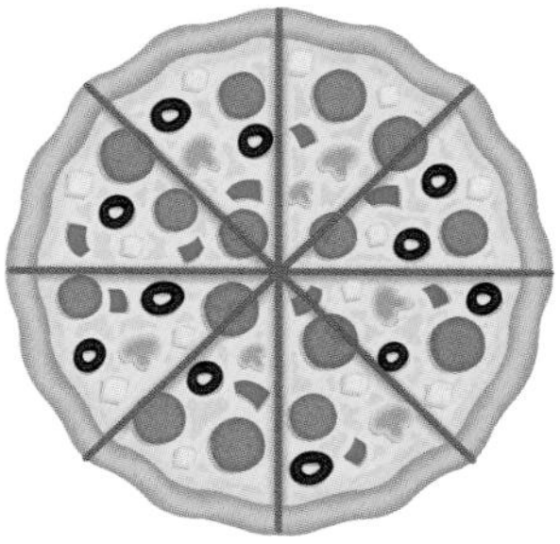

____

3. 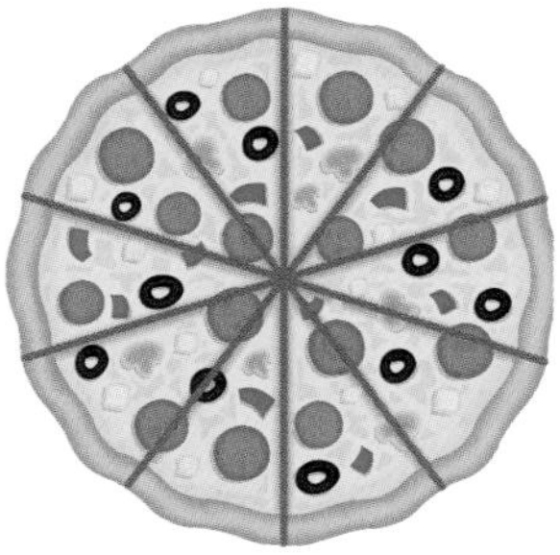

____

Mark the largest part with an L and the smallest parts with an S. Place a check mark (✓) beside the parts of equal size.

4. 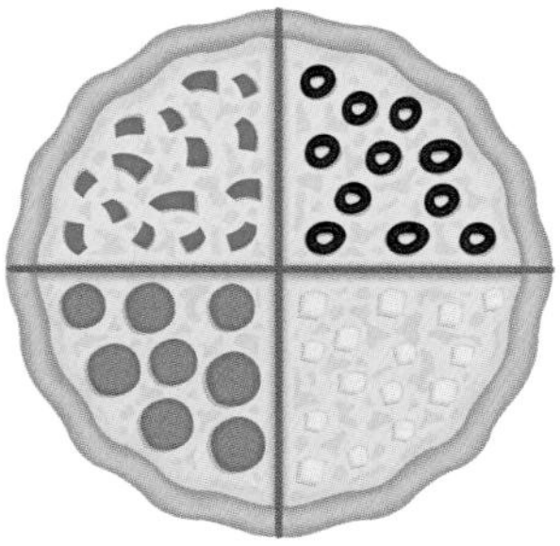

5. 

6. 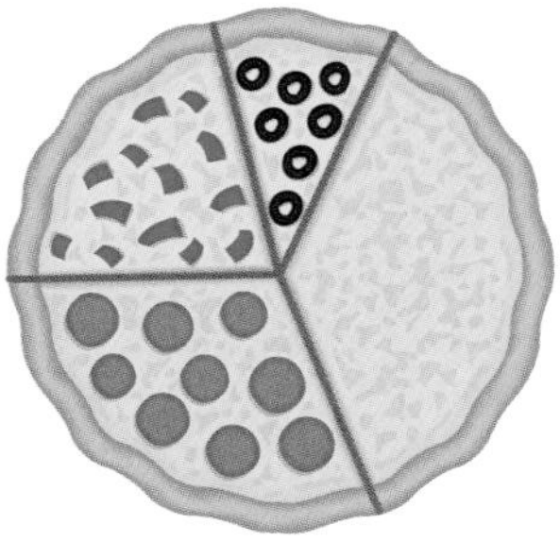

7. How can you tell the relative sizes of the parts of the pizzas in exercises 5 and 6?

____

____

____

____

____

Name ____________________ Date ____________

Vocabulary
circle graph

▶ Read Circle Graphs

A **circle graph** can show parts of any kind of whole.

Cleon gets $10.00 from his parents each week. The circle graph shows how Cleon spent his money last week.

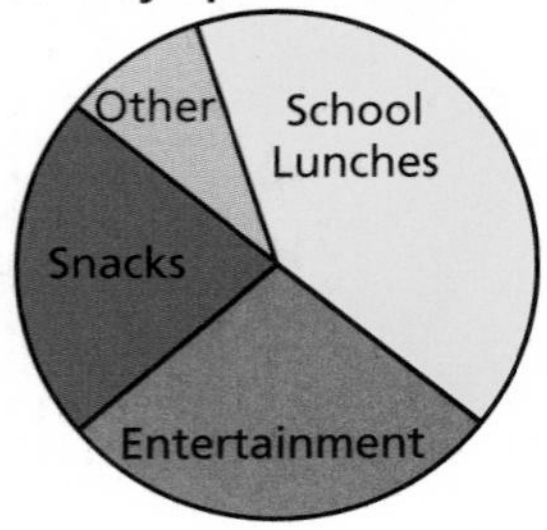

8. What do the sizes of the parts of the circle tell about how Cleon spent his money?

9. On what did Cleon spend the most money? On what did he spend the least money? How do you know?

10. If Cleon spent $1.00 on "Other" things, how much did he probably spend on lunches at school? Explain your thinking.

11. How much did Cleon probably spend on snacks last week?

12. What is probably the most Cleon could have spent to go to the school movie night with his friends last week?

D–3 Class Activity

Name ______________________ Date ____________

► Compare Circle Graphs

You can use a circle graph to compare parts of equal-sized wholes.

The circle graph to the right shows how Cleon spent his $10.00 this week.

Money Spent Last Week

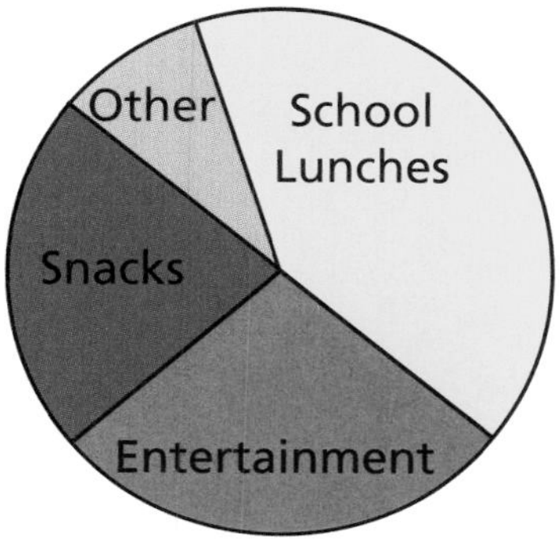

Money Spent This Week

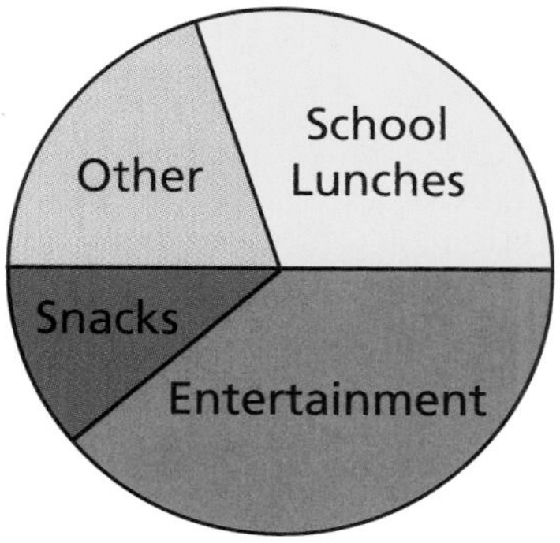

13. What is the whole for both circle graphs?

____

14. How much did Cleon spend this week on School Lunches? on Snacks? on Other?

____

15. On what did Cleon spend more this week than last week? On what did he spend less? Explain how you know.

____

____

____

____

16. How much could Cleon have spent on a computer game this week?

____

Name ______________________ Date ______________

▶ Circle Graphs Showing Percents

Circle graphs are a good way to show percents because the circle represents one whole, or 100%.

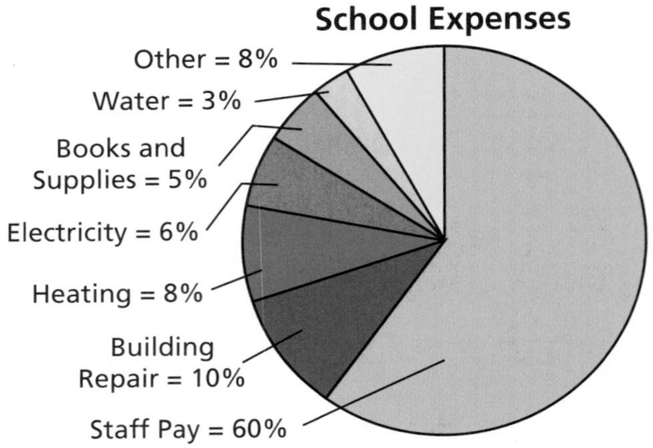

17. What information does the graph give?

____

18. What information doesn't it give?

____

19. What is the largest expense for the school?

____

20. Which expense costs the school 5% of its budget?

____

21. Does the school spend more on Heating or on Water?

____

22. What is the difference in percents between Heating and Water?

____

23. Write two more questions about the circle graph.

____

____

D–4 Class Activity

Name ____________________ Date ____________

Vocabulary
analog
digital

► Tell Time on Different Clocks

An **analog** clock has a face, a shorter hour hand, and a longer minute hand.

1. Discuss how to remember which hand is which and what is the clockwise direction.
2. Write the 5s count-bys around the outside of the green clock to see minutes.

Write the time.

3. 

____

4. 

____

5. 

____

A **digital** clock shows the hour and minutes with numbers.

On a separate sheet of paper, draw an analog clock to show the time on the digital clock.

6. 

7. 

8. 

9. What does a digital clock usually tell us that an analog clock does not show?

____

10. Draw digital clocks for the clocks shown in exercises 3, 4, and 5 in the space below. Give times as A.M. or P.M.

Name ____________________ Date ____________

▶ Read Elapsed Time

You can imagine the hands moving to tell how much time has passed.

How many hours have passed since 12:00 on each clock? How many minutes?

11.

____

____

12.

____

____

13.

____

____

How many hours and how many minutes does the clock show? Write the time that the clock shows.

14.

________ hours

________ minutes

____

15.

________ hours

________ minutes

____

16.

________ hours

________ minutes

____

How many hours and minutes have passed between the times shown in:

17. exercises 14 and 15

____

____

18. exercises 15 and 16

____

____

19. exercises 14 and 16

____

____

Name ____________________ Date ____________

► Regroup Minutes

Show your work.

20. What operation lets you find the difference between two times numerically?

____

21. How many minutes will pass between 8:15 A.M. and 8:47 A.M.?

____

22. How many minutes will pass between 8:15 A.M. and 9:47 A.M.?

____

23. If you started your homework at 4:15 P.M. and finished at 5:08 P.M., how much time did you spend on your homework?

____

____

24. If you start something at 11:15 A.M. and finish at 2:30 P.M., how can you find the elapsed time?

____

____

25. You need to be at school at 8:30 A.M. and it takes you 45 minutes to get there. What time should you leave home to get there on time?

____

26. You practice your musical instrument for 35 minutes every day. If you start at 4:42 P.M., at what time will you finish? Why can the answer not be 4:77? What do you have to do to fix the answer?

____

____

Name _______________ Date _______________

Vocabulary
rule
function table

▶ Calculate Change Over Time

When something changes steadily over time, the change can be expressed by a **rule**. **Function tables** can help you see the rule.

1. A tree grows 4 feet a year. Complete the function table to show how much it will grow in 5 years.

Year	Feet
1	4
2	8
3	
4	
5	

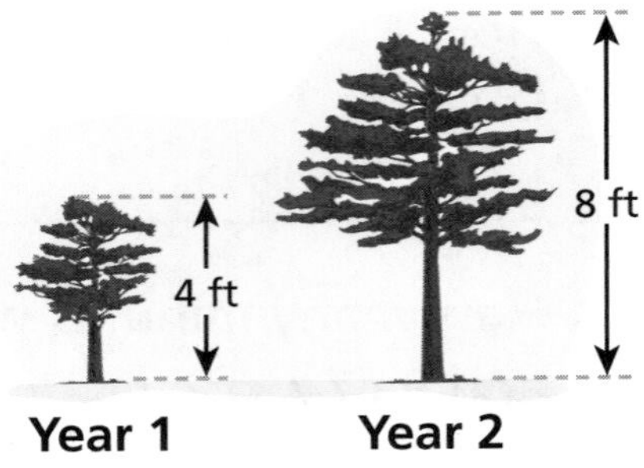

2. If you know how many years the tree has grown, what rule tells you how many feet it has grown in that time?

____

____

3. A gray whale calf gains about 30 pounds each day. How much will it gain in one week?

____

Day	Pounds
1	30
2	60
3	
4	
5	
6	
7	

4. If you know how many days have passed, what rule tells you how many pounds the calf has gained in that time? Use the rule to find out how many pounds the whale will gain in 20 days.

____

____

____

____

UD–Test Unit Test

Name ____________________ Date ____________

Name each regular polygon and find the perimeter.

1. 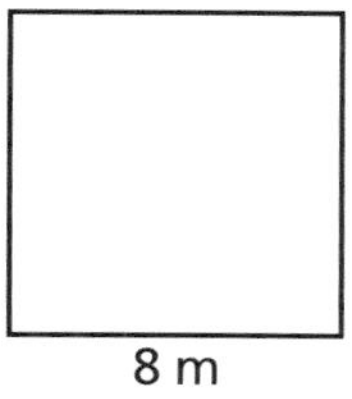

____

____

2. 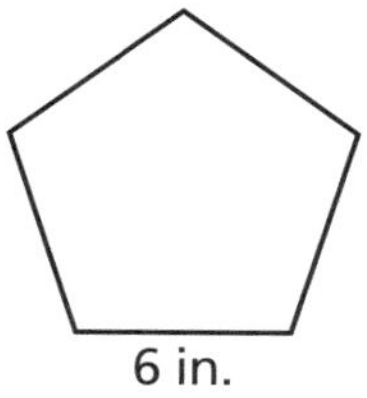

____

____

3. 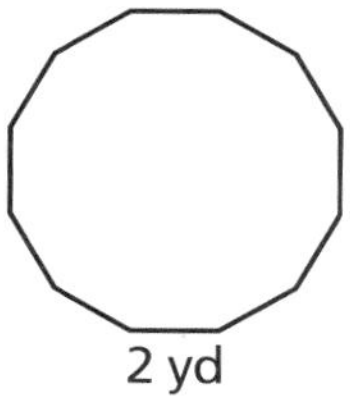

____

____

Use the circle graph to answer the questions. Show your work.

Pet Preferences for a Grade 4 Class

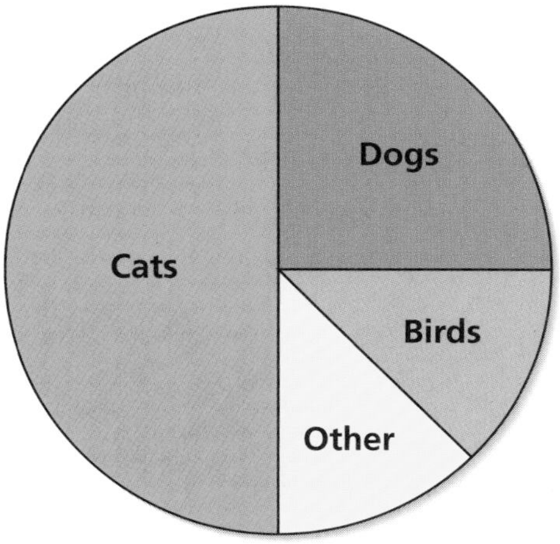

4. There are 24 students in the class. How many students prefer each type of pet?

Cats _______________

Dogs _______________

Birds _______________

Other _______________

5. How many more students prefer cats or dogs than birds?

____

____

Name ______________________ Date ____________

6. Label each part of the circle.

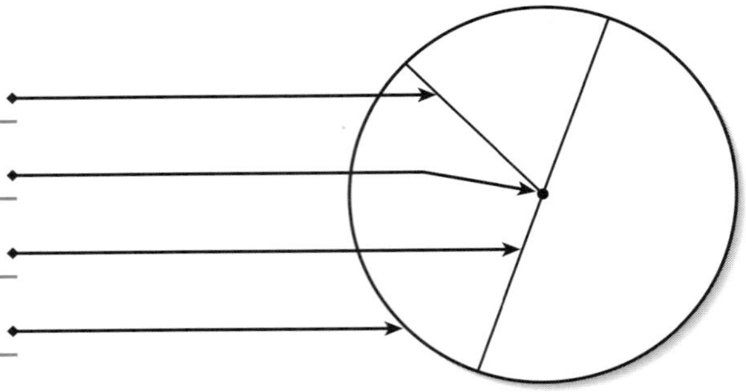

____

____

____

____

7. If you know the radius of a circle, how can you find its diameter?

____

8. Look at the digital clock to the right. How many hours have passed since 6:00 P.M.?

____

9. Keith wants to practice his speech for 30 minutes. The analog clock shows the time now. What time will he be finished?

____

10. **Extended Response** Jorgia's paper route takes 65 minutes to complete. If she wants to finish by 7:30, what is the latest time she should start? Explain.

____

____

____

____

Name ________________________________ Date ____________

Vocabulary
- fraction
- denominator
- numerator
- unit fraction

▶ Understand Unit Fractions

A **fraction** is a quantity made from equal parts of a whole.

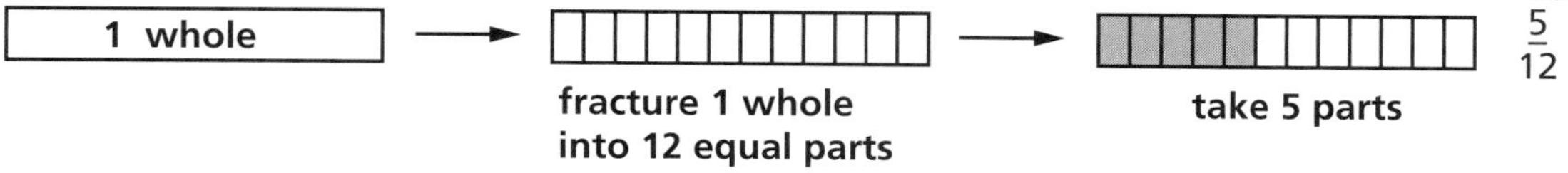

$\frac{n}{d}$ $\frac{\text{numerator}}{\text{denominator}}$ $\frac{\text{number of equal parts in this fraction}}{\text{total equal divided parts in the whole}}$

A **unit fraction** is a fraction whose numerator is 1. It shows one $\frac{1}{d}$ of d equal parts of a whole.

Fold your fraction strips to show each chain of unit fractions. Then name and write the fraction that each chain represents.

1. $\frac{1}{3} + \frac{1}{3} =$ ________

2. $\frac{1}{8} + \frac{1}{8} + \frac{1}{8} + \frac{1}{8} + \frac{1}{8} =$ ________

3. $\frac{1}{6} + \frac{1}{6} + \frac{1}{6} + \frac{1}{6} =$ ________

4. $\frac{1}{12} + \frac{1}{12} + \frac{1}{12} + \frac{1}{12} + \frac{1}{12} + \frac{1}{12} =$ ________

5. $\frac{1}{4} + \frac{1}{4} =$ ________

6. $\frac{1}{12} + \frac{1}{12} + \frac{1}{12} + \frac{1}{12} + \frac{1}{12} + \frac{1}{12} + \frac{1}{12} + \frac{1}{12} =$ ________

7. $\frac{1}{6} + \frac{1}{6} =$ ________

8. $\frac{1}{8} + \frac{1}{8} + \frac{1}{8} + \frac{1}{8} + \frac{1}{8} + \frac{1}{8} + \frac{1}{8} =$ ________

5–1 Class Activity

Name ______________________ Date __________

▶ Patterns in Fraction Strips

9. Describe patterns and relationships you see in these fraction strips.

____

____

1										1
$\frac{1}{2}$	$\frac{1}{2}$									$\frac{2}{2}$
$\frac{1}{3}$	$\frac{1}{3}$	$\frac{1}{3}$								$\frac{3}{3}$
$\frac{1}{4}$	$\frac{1}{4}$	$\frac{1}{4}$	$\frac{1}{4}$							$\frac{4}{4}$
$\frac{1}{5}$	$\frac{1}{5}$	$\frac{1}{5}$	$\frac{1}{5}$	$\frac{1}{5}$						$\frac{5}{5}$
$\frac{1}{6}$	$\frac{1}{6}$	$\frac{1}{6}$	$\frac{1}{6}$	$\frac{1}{6}$	$\frac{1}{6}$					$\frac{6}{6}$
$\frac{1}{7}$	$\frac{1}{7}$	$\frac{1}{7}$	$\frac{1}{7}$	$\frac{1}{7}$	$\frac{1}{7}$	$\frac{1}{7}$				$\frac{7}{7}$
$\frac{1}{8}$	$\frac{1}{8}$	$\frac{1}{8}$	$\frac{1}{8}$	$\frac{1}{8}$	$\frac{1}{8}$	$\frac{1}{8}$	$\frac{1}{8}$			$\frac{8}{8}$
$\frac{1}{9}$	$\frac{1}{9}$	$\frac{1}{9}$	$\frac{1}{9}$	$\frac{1}{9}$	$\frac{1}{9}$	$\frac{1}{9}$	$\frac{1}{9}$	$\frac{1}{9}$		$\frac{9}{9}$
$\frac{1}{10}$	$\frac{1}{10}$	$\frac{1}{10}$	$\frac{1}{10}$	$\frac{1}{10}$	$\frac{1}{10}$	$\frac{1}{10}$	$\frac{1}{10}$	$\frac{1}{10}$	$\frac{1}{10}$	$\frac{10}{10}$

▶ Chains of Unit Fractions

Fold your fraction strips to show each fraction. Then say and write the chain of unit fractions that describes each fraction.

10. $\frac{3}{4}$ = ____________

11. $\frac{3}{8}$ = ____________

12. $\frac{8}{8}$ = ____________

13. $\frac{2}{12}$ = ____________

14. $\frac{3}{12}$ = ____________

15. $\frac{3}{6}$ = ____________

16. $\frac{5}{12}$ = ____________

17. $\frac{2}{3}$ = ____________

18. $\frac{6}{8}$ = ____________

19. $\frac{5}{6}$ = ____________

Name ____________________ Date ____________

▶ Fractions as Parts of a Whole

Jon made a large sandwich for the 6 people in his family. He asked his father to help him cut it into 6 equal pieces. To do this, they made a paper cutting guide as long as the sandwich. Jon folded the paper into 6 equal lengths, and his father used it to cut the sandwich into equal pieces.

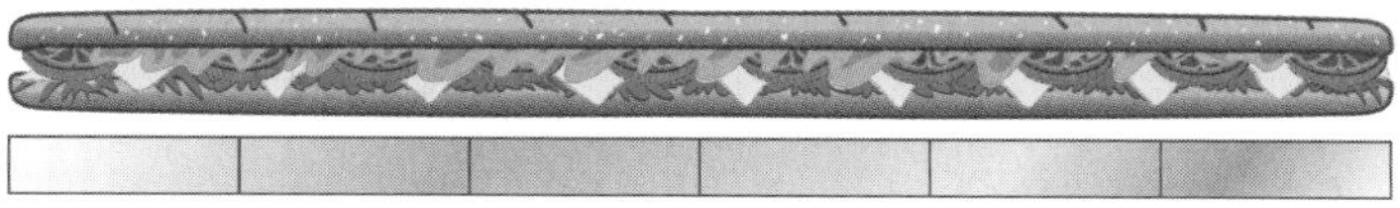

Solve.

20. If each person ate 1 piece of the sandwich, what fraction of the sandwich did each person eat? Fold your 6-part fraction strip to show the fraction of the whole sandwich that each person ate.

____

21. How many pieces of the whole sandwich did Jon's mother and father eat together? Fold your fraction strip to show the fraction of the whole sandwich Jon's mother and father ate in all. _______________

22. After Jon's mother and father got their pieces, what fraction of the sandwich was left?

____

23. If Jon and each of his sisters shared the remaining sandwich equally, how many sisters does Jon have?

____

24. What ideas about fractions did we use to answer the questions about Jon's sandwich?

____

25. **On the Back** Write a word problem in which you might need to divide a whole into equal parts.

Name Date

Family Letter

Dear Family,

Your child has experience with fractions through comparisons, measurements, and remainders in division. Unit 5 of *Math Expressions* builds on this experience. The main goals of this unit are to:

- understand the meaning of fractions
- compare fractions with like and unlike denominators
- add and subtract fractions and mixed numbers with like and unlike denominators
- multiply a fraction by a whole number and a whole number by a fraction

Your child will use fraction bars and fraction strips to gain a visual and conceptual understanding of fractions as parts of a whole. Later, your child will use these models to add and subtract fractions, convert between improper fractions and mixed numbers, and find equivalent fractions. Your child will also learn how to use a multiplication table to find equivalent fractions.

Examples of Fraction Bar Modeling:

Fraction Comparisons

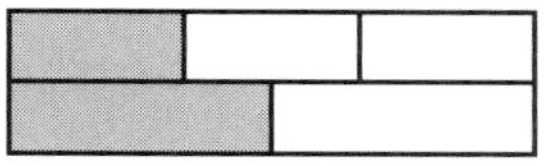

$\frac{1}{3} < \frac{1}{2}$

Fraction Subtraction

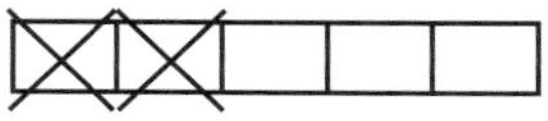

$\frac{5}{5} - \frac{2}{5} = \frac{3}{5}$

Equivalent Fractions

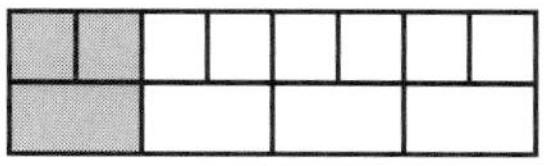

$\frac{2}{8} = \frac{1}{4}$

In later lessons of this unit, your child will be introduced to the number-line model for fractions. Students name fractions corresponding to given lengths on the number line and identify lengths corresponding to given fractions. They also see that there are many equivalent fraction names for any given length.

Your child will apply this knowledge about fractions and fraction operations to solve mixed word problems, including problems involving probability and comparisons.

If you have questions or problems, please contact me.

Sincerely,
Your child's teacher

Carta a la familia

Estimada familia:

Su niño ha usado fracciones al hacer comparaciones, mediciones y en los residuos de la división. La Unidad 5 de *Math Expressions* amplía esta experiencia. Los objetivos principales de la unidad son:

- comprender el significado de las fracciones
- comparar fracciones con denominadores iguales y distintos
- sumar y restar fracciones y números mixtos con denominadores iguales y distintos
- multiplicar una fracción por un número entero y un número entero por una fracción

Su niño usará barras y tiras de fracciones para comprender y visualizar el concepto de las fracciones como partes de un entero. Luego, usará estos modelos para sumar y restar fracciones, convertir fracciones impropias y números mixtos, y hallar fracciones equivalentes. También aprenderá a usar una tabla de multiplicación para hallar fracciones equivalentes.

Ejemplos de modelos con barras de fracciones:

Comparar fracciones

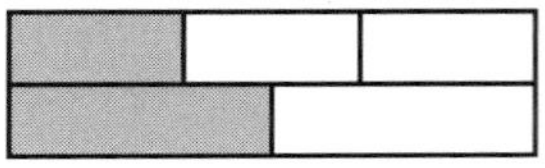

$\frac{1}{3} < \frac{1}{2}$

Restar fracciones

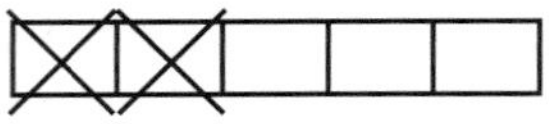

$\frac{5}{5} - \frac{2}{5} = \frac{3}{5}$

Fracciones equivalentes

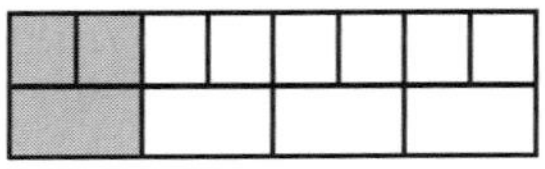

$\frac{2}{8} = \frac{1}{4}$

Más adelante en esta unidad, su niño verá el modelo de la recta numérica para las fracciones. Los estudiantes nombrarán las fracciones que correspondan a determinadas longitudes en la recta numérica e identificarán longitudes que corresponden a fracciones dadas. También observarán que hay muchos nombres de fracciones equivalentes para una longitud determinada.

Su niño aplicará este conocimiento de las fracciones y operaciones con fracciones para resolver problemas verbales variados, que incluyen problemas de probabilidad y comparaciones.

Si tiene alguna duda o comentario, por favor comuníquese conmigo.

Atentamente,
El maestro de su niño

Name ________________________ Date ____________

▶ Fifths That Add to 1

Every afternoon, student volunteers help the school librarian put returned books back on the shelves. The librarian puts the books in equal piles on a cart.

One day Jean and Maria found 5 equal piles on the return cart. They knew there were different ways they could share the job of reshelving the books. They drew fraction bars to help them find all the possibilities.

1. On each fifths bar, circle two groups of fifths to show one way the girls could share the work. (Each bar should show a different possibility.) Then complete the equation next to each bar to show their shares.

1 whole = all of the books				
$\frac{1}{5}$	$\frac{1}{5}$	$\frac{1}{5}$	$\frac{1}{5}$	$\frac{1}{5}$
$\frac{1}{5}$	$\frac{1}{5}$	$\frac{1}{5}$	$\frac{1}{5}$	$\frac{1}{5}$
$\frac{1}{5}$	$\frac{1}{5}$	$\frac{1}{5}$	$\frac{1}{5}$	$\frac{1}{5}$
$\frac{1}{5}$	$\frac{1}{5}$	$\frac{1}{5}$	$\frac{1}{5}$	$\frac{1}{5}$

1 whole		Jean's share		Maria's share
$\frac{5}{5}$	=	$\frac{\_}{5}$	+	$\frac{\_}{5}$
$\frac{5}{5}$	=	$\frac{\_}{5}$	+	$\frac{\_}{5}$
$\frac{5}{5}$	=	$\frac{\_}{5}$	+	$\frac{\_}{5}$
$\frac{5}{5}$	=	$\frac{\_}{5}$	+	$\frac{\_}{5}$

Name ____________________ Date ____________

▶ Sixths That Add to 1

The librarian put 6 equal piles of returned books on the cart for Liu and Henry to reshelf. They also drew fraction bars.

2. On each sixths bar, circle two groups of sixths to show one way that Liu and Henry could share the work. (Each bar should show a different possibility.) Then complete the equation next to each bar to show their shares.

1 whole = all of the books							1 whole		Liu's share		Henry's share
$\frac{1}{6}$	$\frac{1}{6}$	$\frac{1}{6}$	$\frac{1}{6}$	$\frac{1}{6}$	$\frac{1}{6}$		$\frac{6}{6}$	=	$\frac{\_}{6}$	+	$\frac{\_}{6}$
$\frac{1}{6}$	$\frac{1}{6}$	$\frac{1}{6}$	$\frac{1}{6}$	$\frac{1}{6}$	$\frac{1}{6}$		$\frac{6}{6}$	=	$\frac{\_}{6}$	+	$\frac{\_}{6}$
$\frac{1}{6}$	$\frac{1}{6}$	$\frac{1}{6}$	$\frac{1}{6}$	$\frac{1}{6}$	$\frac{1}{6}$		$\frac{6}{6}$	=	$\frac{\_}{6}$	+	$\frac{\_}{6}$
$\frac{1}{6}$	$\frac{1}{6}$	$\frac{1}{6}$	$\frac{1}{6}$	$\frac{1}{6}$	$\frac{1}{6}$		$\frac{6}{6}$	=	$\frac{\_}{6}$	+	$\frac{\_}{6}$
$\frac{1}{6}$	$\frac{1}{6}$	$\frac{1}{6}$	$\frac{1}{6}$	$\frac{1}{6}$	$\frac{1}{6}$		$\frac{6}{6}$	=	$\frac{\_}{6}$	+	$\frac{\_}{6}$

▶ Find the Unknown Partner

Write the fraction that will complete each equation.

3. $1 = \frac{7}{7} = \frac{1}{7} +$ ________

4. $1 = \frac{4}{4} = \frac{3}{4} +$ ________

5. $1 = \frac{8}{8} = \frac{3}{8} +$ ________

6. $1 = \frac{5}{5} = \frac{2}{5} +$ ________

7. $1 = \frac{3}{3} = \frac{2}{3} +$ ________

8. $1 = \frac{10}{10} = \frac{6}{10} +$ ________

9. $1 = \frac{6}{6} = \frac{2}{6} +$ ________

10. $1 = \frac{8}{8} = \frac{5}{8} +$ ________

Name ______________________ Date ____________

► Compare Fractions

1. Puzzled Penguin is trying to understand fractions. Discuss the patterns you see in the fraction bars he made.

1	$\frac{1}{1}$

$\frac{1}{2}$ | $\frac{1}{2}$ — $\frac{2}{2}$

$\frac{1}{3}$ | $\frac{1}{3}$ | $\frac{1}{3}$ — $\frac{3}{3}$

$\frac{1}{4}$ | $\frac{1}{4}$ | $\frac{1}{4}$ | $\frac{1}{4}$ — $\frac{4}{4}$

$\frac{1}{5}$ | $\frac{1}{5}$ | $\frac{1}{5}$ | $\frac{1}{5}$ | $\frac{1}{5}$ — $\frac{5}{5}$

$\frac{1}{6}$ | $\frac{1}{6}$ | $\frac{1}{6}$ | $\frac{1}{6}$ | $\frac{1}{6}$ | $\frac{1}{6}$ — $\frac{6}{6}$

$\frac{1}{7}$ | $\frac{1}{7}$ | $\frac{1}{7}$ | $\frac{1}{7}$ | $\frac{1}{7}$ | $\frac{1}{7}$ | $\frac{1}{7}$ — $\frac{7}{7}$

$\frac{1}{8}$ | $\frac{1}{8}$ | $\frac{1}{8}$ | $\frac{1}{8}$ | $\frac{1}{8}$ | $\frac{1}{8}$ | $\frac{1}{8}$ | $\frac{1}{8}$ — $\frac{8}{8}$

$\frac{1}{9}$ | $\frac{1}{9}$ | $\frac{1}{9}$ | $\frac{1}{9}$ | $\frac{1}{9}$ | $\frac{1}{9}$ | $\frac{1}{9}$ | $\frac{1}{9}$ | $\frac{1}{9}$ — $\frac{9}{9}$

$\frac{1}{10}$ | $\frac{1}{10}$ | $\frac{1}{10}$ | $\frac{1}{10}$ | $\frac{1}{10}$ | $\frac{1}{10}$ | $\frac{1}{10}$ | $\frac{1}{10}$ | $\frac{1}{10}$ | $\frac{1}{10}$ — $\frac{10}{10}$

$\frac{1}{11}$ | $\frac{1}{11}$ | $\frac{1}{11}$ | $\frac{1}{11}$ | $\frac{1}{11}$ | $\frac{1}{11}$ | $\frac{1}{11}$ | $\frac{1}{11}$ | $\frac{1}{11}$ | $\frac{1}{11}$ | $\frac{1}{11}$ — $\frac{11}{11}$

$\frac{1}{12}$ | $\frac{1}{12}$ | $\frac{1}{12}$ | $\frac{1}{12}$ | $\frac{1}{12}$ | $\frac{1}{12}$ | $\frac{1}{12}$ | $\frac{1}{12}$ | $\frac{1}{12}$ | $\frac{1}{12}$ | $\frac{1}{12}$ | $\frac{1}{12}$ — $\frac{12}{12}$

2. Puzzled Penguin knows that 4 is greater than 2, so he thinks that $\frac{1}{4}$ is greater than $\frac{1}{2}$. Is he right or wrong? Explain.

____

____

____

Name ____________________ Date ____________

▶ Practice Comparing Fractions

Circle the greater fraction. Use your fraction strips if you need to.

3. $\frac{1}{12}$ or $\frac{1}{2}$
4. $\frac{3}{8}$ or $\frac{1}{8}$
5. $\frac{2}{5}$ or $\frac{2}{7}$
6. $\frac{1}{3}$ or $\frac{1}{5}$
7. $\frac{4}{12}$ or $\frac{5}{12}$
8. $\frac{7}{9}$ or $\frac{5}{9}$
9. $\frac{1}{7}$ or $\frac{2}{7}$
10. $\frac{3}{6}$ or $\frac{3}{8}$

Write < or > to make each statement true.

11. $\frac{3}{10} \bigcirc \frac{3}{9}$
12. $\frac{3}{6} \bigcirc \frac{3}{5}$
13. $\frac{8}{16} \bigcirc \frac{8}{18}$
14. $\frac{2}{7} \bigcirc \frac{3}{7}$
15. $\frac{7}{15} \bigcirc \frac{7}{14}$
16. $\frac{5}{11} \bigcirc \frac{4}{11}$

17. Explain how to compare fractions with the same denominator but different numerators.

____

____

____

18. Explain how to compare fractions with the same numerator but different denominators.

____

____

____

Name ______________________ Date ____________

$\frac{1}{1}$	$\frac{1}{1}$
$\frac{1}{2}$ $\frac{1}{2}$	$\frac{2}{2}$
$\frac{1}{3}$ $\frac{1}{3}$ $\frac{1}{3}$	$\frac{3}{3}$
$\frac{1}{4}$ $\frac{1}{4}$ $\frac{1}{4}$ $\frac{1}{4}$	$\frac{4}{4}$
$\frac{1}{5}$ $\frac{1}{5}$ $\frac{1}{5}$ $\frac{1}{5}$ $\frac{1}{5}$	$\frac{5}{5}$
$\frac{1}{6}$ $\frac{1}{6}$ $\frac{1}{6}$ $\frac{1}{6}$ $\frac{1}{6}$ $\frac{1}{6}$	$\frac{6}{6}$
$\frac{1}{7}$ $\frac{1}{7}$ $\frac{1}{7}$ $\frac{1}{7}$ $\frac{1}{7}$ $\frac{1}{7}$ $\frac{1}{7}$	$\frac{7}{7}$
$\frac{1}{8}$ $\frac{1}{8}$ $\frac{1}{8}$ $\frac{1}{8}$ $\frac{1}{8}$ $\frac{1}{8}$ $\frac{1}{8}$ $\frac{1}{8}$	$\frac{8}{8}$
$\frac{1}{9}$ $\frac{1}{9}$ $\frac{1}{9}$ $\frac{1}{9}$ $\frac{1}{9}$ $\frac{1}{9}$ $\frac{1}{9}$ $\frac{1}{9}$ $\frac{1}{9}$	$\frac{9}{9}$
$\frac{1}{10}$ $\frac{1}{10}$ $\frac{1}{10}$ $\frac{1}{10}$ $\frac{1}{10}$ $\frac{1}{10}$ $\frac{1}{10}$ $\frac{1}{10}$ $\frac{1}{10}$ $\frac{1}{10}$	$\frac{10}{10}$
$\frac{1}{11}$ $\frac{1}{11}$ $\frac{1}{11}$ $\frac{1}{11}$ $\frac{1}{11}$ $\frac{1}{11}$ $\frac{1}{11}$ $\frac{1}{11}$ $\frac{1}{11}$ $\frac{1}{11}$ $\frac{1}{11}$	$\frac{11}{11}$
$\frac{1}{12}$ $\frac{1}{12}$ $\frac{1}{12}$ $\frac{1}{12}$ $\frac{1}{12}$ $\frac{1}{12}$ $\frac{1}{12}$ $\frac{1}{12}$ $\frac{1}{12}$ $\frac{1}{12}$ $\frac{1}{12}$ $\frac{1}{12}$	$\frac{12}{12}$
$\frac{1}{13}$ $\frac{1}{13}$ $\frac{1}{13}$ $\frac{1}{13}$ $\frac{1}{13}$ $\frac{1}{13}$ $\frac{1}{13}$ $\frac{1}{13}$ $\frac{1}{13}$ $\frac{1}{13}$ $\frac{1}{13}$ $\frac{1}{13}$ $\frac{1}{13}$	$\frac{13}{13}$
$\frac{1}{14}$ $\frac{1}{14}$ $\frac{1}{14}$ $\frac{1}{14}$ $\frac{1}{14}$ $\frac{1}{14}$ $\frac{1}{14}$ $\frac{1}{14}$ $\frac{1}{14}$ $\frac{1}{14}$ $\frac{1}{14}$ $\frac{1}{14}$ $\frac{1}{14}$ $\frac{1}{14}$	$\frac{14}{14}$
$\frac{1}{15}$ $\frac{1}{15}$ $\frac{1}{15}$ $\frac{1}{15}$ $\frac{1}{15}$ $\frac{1}{15}$ $\frac{1}{15}$ $\frac{1}{15}$ $\frac{1}{15}$ $\frac{1}{15}$ $\frac{1}{15}$ $\frac{1}{15}$ $\frac{1}{15}$ $\frac{1}{15}$ $\frac{1}{15}$	$\frac{15}{15}$
$\frac{1}{16}$ $\frac{1}{16}$ $\frac{1}{16}$ $\frac{1}{16}$ $\frac{1}{16}$ $\frac{1}{16}$ $\frac{1}{16}$ $\frac{1}{16}$ $\frac{1}{16}$ $\frac{1}{16}$ $\frac{1}{16}$ $\frac{1}{16}$ $\frac{1}{16}$ $\frac{1}{16}$ $\frac{1}{16}$ $\frac{1}{16}$	$\frac{16}{16}$
$\frac{1}{17}$ $\frac{1}{17}$ $\frac{1}{17}$ $\frac{1}{17}$ $\frac{1}{17}$ $\frac{1}{17}$ $\frac{1}{17}$ $\frac{1}{17}$ $\frac{1}{17}$ $\frac{1}{17}$ $\frac{1}{17}$ $\frac{1}{17}$ $\frac{1}{17}$ $\frac{1}{17}$ $\frac{1}{17}$ $\frac{1}{17}$ $\frac{1}{17}$	$\frac{17}{17}$
$\frac{1}{18}$ $\frac{1}{18}$ $\frac{1}{18}$ $\frac{1}{18}$ $\frac{1}{18}$ $\frac{1}{18}$ $\frac{1}{18}$ $\frac{1}{18}$ $\frac{1}{18}$ $\frac{1}{18}$ $\frac{1}{18}$ $\frac{1}{18}$ $\frac{1}{18}$ $\frac{1}{18}$ $\frac{1}{18}$ $\frac{1}{18}$ $\frac{1}{18}$ $\frac{1}{18}$	$\frac{18}{18}$
$\frac{1}{19}$ $\frac{1}{19}$ $\frac{1}{19}$ $\frac{1}{19}$ $\frac{1}{19}$ $\frac{1}{19}$ $\frac{1}{19}$ $\frac{1}{19}$ $\frac{1}{19}$ $\frac{1}{19}$ $\frac{1}{19}$ $\frac{1}{19}$ $\frac{1}{19}$ $\frac{1}{19}$ $\frac{1}{19}$ $\frac{1}{19}$ $\frac{1}{19}$ $\frac{1}{19}$ $\frac{1}{19}$	$\frac{19}{19}$
$\frac{1}{20}$ $\frac{1}{20}$ $\frac{1}{20}$ $\frac{1}{20}$ $\frac{1}{20}$ $\frac{1}{20}$ $\frac{1}{20}$ $\frac{1}{20}$ $\frac{1}{20}$ $\frac{1}{20}$ $\frac{1}{20}$ $\frac{1}{20}$ $\frac{1}{20}$ $\frac{1}{20}$ $\frac{1}{20}$ $\frac{1}{20}$ $\frac{1}{20}$ $\frac{1}{20}$ $\frac{1}{20}$ $\frac{1}{20}$	$\frac{20}{20}$

Name ______________________ Date ______________

▶ Compare Fractions of Different-Size Wholes

Jon and his five friends want sandwiches. They make two different kinds: one on a short loaf of bread and one on a longer loaf. Jon cuts each sandwich into 6 pieces. His friends think the pieces are not the same size.

1. Are Jon's friends correct? Explain.

2. What can Jon do to make sure everyone gets the same amount of food?

Hattie's dad orders one small, one medium, and one large pizza. He divides each pizza into 8 equal pieces. Hattie takes $\frac{1}{8}$ of the small pizza and her friend takes $\frac{1}{8}$ of the large pizza.

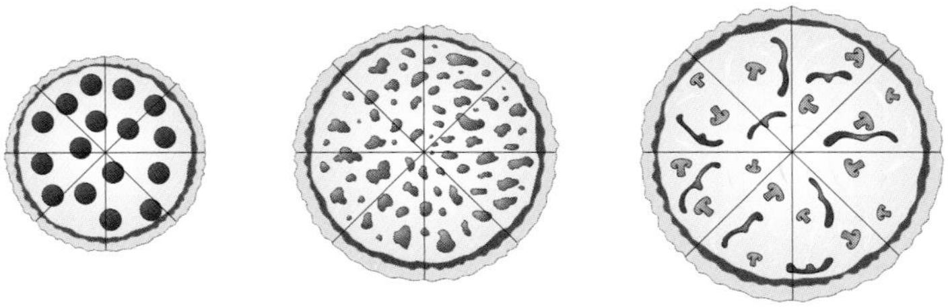

3. Hattie says she has less pizza than her friend. Is she correct? Explain.

4. What do these problems tell us about fractions?

Name ______________________ Date ____________

▶ Fraction Word Problems

Solve.

Show your work.

5. A shelter had 4 spaniel puppies and 6 beagle puppies. Jack adopted $\frac{1}{2}$ of the spaniel puppies, and Carmen adopted $\frac{1}{2}$ of the beagle puppies. Who adopted more puppies? How do you know?

____

____

6. Julio planted 16 daisies and 10 sunflowers. His neighbor's goat ate 5 daisies and 5 sunflowers. Did the goat eat a larger fractional part of the daisies or the sunflowers? Explain.

____

____

____

____

7. A fruit market sells two different packages of oranges. Bags contain 12 oranges, and boxes contain 15 oranges. Both packages cost $3.00. Which package is a better buy? Why?

____

____

8. The fourth grade has three running teams. Each team has 12 runners. In a race, $\frac{1}{4}$ of Team A, $\frac{1}{3}$ of Team B, and $\frac{1}{6}$ of Team C passed the first water stop at the same time. Which team had the most runners at the first water stop at that time? Explain.

____

____

5–5 Class Activity

Name ____________________ Date ____________

▶ Add and Subtract Fractions

The circled parts of this fraction bar show an addition problem.

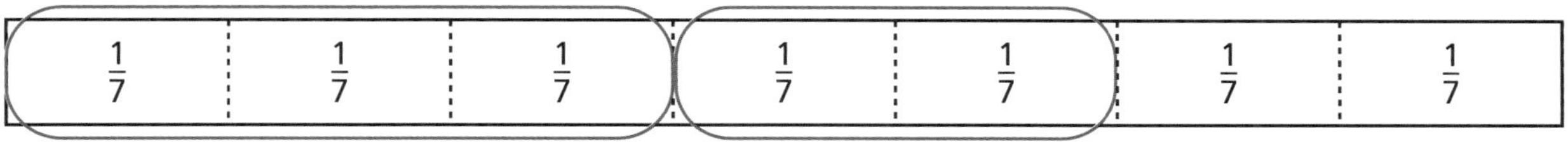

1. Write the numerators that will complete the addition equation.

$\frac{\_\_}{7} + \frac{\_\_}{7} = \frac{\_\_ + \_\_}{7} = \frac{\_\_}{7}$

Solve each problem. Write the correct numerator to complete each equation.

2. $\frac{3}{9} + \frac{4}{9} = \frac{\_\_ + \_\_}{9} = \frac{\_\_}{9}$

3. $\frac{1}{5} + \frac{3}{5} = \frac{\_\_ + \_\_}{5} = \frac{\_\_}{5}$

4. $\frac{2}{8} + \frac{5}{8} = \frac{\_\_ + \_\_}{8} = \frac{\_\_}{8}$

5. What happens to the numerators in each problem?

____

6. What happens to the denominators in each problem?

____

The circled and crossed-out parts of this fraction bar show a subtraction problem.

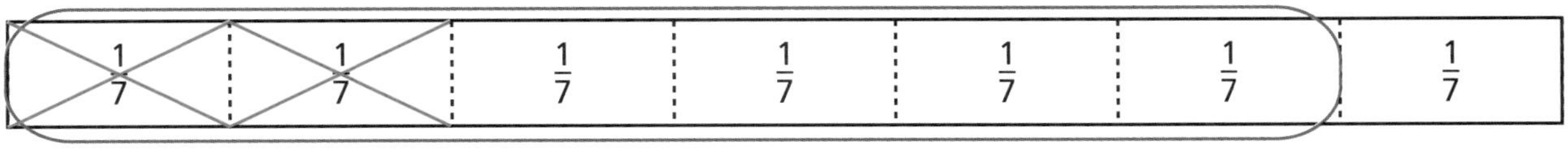

7. Write the numerators that will complete the subtraction equation.

$\frac{\_\_}{7} - \frac{\_\_}{7} = \frac{\_\_ - \_\_}{7} = \frac{\_\_}{7}$

Name ______________________________ Date ______________

▶ Add and Subtract Fractions (continued)

Solve each problem. Write the correct numerators to complete each sentence.

8. $\frac{5}{6} - \frac{4}{6} = \frac{\_\_ - \_\_}{6} = \frac{\_\_}{6}$ 9. $\frac{9}{10} - \frac{5}{10} = \frac{\_\_ - \_\_}{10} = \_\_$ 10. $\frac{14}{16} - \frac{9}{16} = \frac{\_\_ - \_\_}{16} = \_\_$

11. What happens to the numerators in each problem?

____

12. How is subtraction of fractions with like denominators similar to addition of fractions with like denominators?

____

____

▶ Mixed Practice With Addition and Subtraction

Puzzled Penguin knows that if he catches 3 fish and then catches 2 more fish, he has 5 fish. He also knows that if he catches 4 fish and eats 3 of his fish, he has 1 fish left. This is what he wrote:

$\frac{3}{5} + \frac{2}{5} = \frac{5}{10}$ $\frac{4}{5} - \frac{3}{5} = \frac{1}{0}$

13. What part of his work is not correct? ______________________________

14. What can you tell him that will help him understand how to add and subtract fractions with like denominators properly? ______________________________

____

____

Solve each problem. Include the "circled" step.

15. $\frac{1}{4} + \frac{2}{4} =$ 16. $\frac{3}{9} + \frac{5}{9} =$ 17. $\frac{12}{6} - \frac{2}{6} =$

18. $\frac{4}{10} + \frac{5}{10} =$ 19. $\frac{2}{5} + \frac{4}{5} =$ 20. $\frac{8}{12} - \frac{3}{12} =$

21. $\frac{5}{7} + \frac{3}{7} =$ 22. $\frac{7}{11} - \frac{4}{11} =$ 23. $\frac{9}{8} - \frac{5}{8} =$

5–5 Class Activity

Name ______________________________ Date ______________

▶ Work With Unit Fractions

one whole										$\frac{1}{1}$
$\frac{1}{2}$	$\frac{1}{2}$									$\frac{2}{2}$
$\frac{1}{3}$	$\frac{1}{3}$	$\frac{1}{3}$								$\frac{3}{3}$
$\frac{1}{4}$	$\frac{1}{4}$	$\frac{1}{4}$	$\frac{1}{4}$							$\frac{4}{4}$
$\frac{1}{5}$	$\frac{1}{5}$	$\frac{1}{5}$	$\frac{1}{5}$	$\frac{1}{5}$						$\frac{5}{5}$
$\frac{1}{6}$	$\frac{1}{6}$	$\frac{1}{6}$	$\frac{1}{6}$	$\frac{1}{6}$	$\frac{1}{6}$					$\frac{6}{6}$
$\frac{1}{7}$	$\frac{1}{7}$	$\frac{1}{7}$	$\frac{1}{7}$	$\frac{1}{7}$	$\frac{1}{7}$	$\frac{1}{7}$				$\frac{7}{7}$
$\frac{1}{8}$	$\frac{1}{8}$	$\frac{1}{8}$	$\frac{1}{8}$	$\frac{1}{8}$	$\frac{1}{8}$	$\frac{1}{8}$	$\frac{1}{8}$			$\frac{8}{8}$
$\frac{1}{9}$	$\frac{1}{9}$	$\frac{1}{9}$	$\frac{1}{9}$	$\frac{1}{9}$	$\frac{1}{9}$	$\frac{1}{9}$	$\frac{1}{9}$	$\frac{1}{9}$		$\frac{9}{9}$
$\frac{1}{10}$	$\frac{1}{10}$	$\frac{1}{10}$	$\frac{1}{10}$	$\frac{1}{10}$	$\frac{1}{10}$	$\frac{1}{10}$	$\frac{1}{10}$	$\frac{1}{10}$	$\frac{1}{10}$	$\frac{10}{10}$

5–6 **Class Activity**

Name ______________________________ Date ______________

Vocabulary
improper fraction
mixed number

▶ Real-World Uses of Mixed Numbers

Mellie's Deli makes sandwiches. This is the price list.

Mellie's Deli

Regular (serves 2)	$3.00
Friendship (serves 4)	$5.00
Super (serves 10)	$12.00
Magna (serves 18)	$20.00

Nineteen friends decide to camp in the park. They order two Super sandwiches. Each camper eats 1 serving.

Solve.

1. How many campers does one Super sandwich serve?

   ____

2. What fraction of the second sandwich is needed to serve the rest of the campers?

   ____

3. What fraction of the second sandwich is left over?

   ____

4. What number tells how many Super sandwiches the campers ate in all?

   ____

▶ Define Mixed Number and Improper Fraction

An **improper fraction** is a fraction that has a numerator greater than or equal to its denominator.	$\frac{10}{6}$ $\frac{19}{5}$ $\frac{3}{3}$
A **mixed number** is a number that consists of a whole number and a fraction.	$1\frac{4}{6}$ $3\frac{4}{5}$

Name ______________________ Date ______________________

▶ Convert Between Mixed Numbers and Improper Fractions

Change each mixed number to an improper fraction and each improper fraction to a mixed number.

5. $5\frac{2}{3} =$

6. $3\frac{3}{7} =$

7. $6\frac{6}{10} =$

8. $9\frac{1}{4} =$

9. $2\frac{7}{8} =$

10. $4\frac{5}{9} =$

11. $8\frac{3}{5} =$

12. $7\frac{4}{6} =$

13. $\frac{40}{6} =$

14. $\frac{11}{2} =$

15. $\frac{23}{7} =$

16. $\frac{28}{3} =$

17. $\frac{22}{4} =$

18. $\frac{25}{8} =$

19. $\frac{29}{7} =$

20. $6\frac{4}{8} =$

21. $4\frac{6}{9} =$

22. $\frac{16}{3} =$

5–6 Class Activity

Name Date

▶ Understand Improper Fractions and Mixed Numbers

1 whole

$\frac{1}{8}$	$\frac{1}{8}$	$\frac{1}{8}$	$\frac{1}{8}$	$\frac{1}{8}$	$\frac{1}{8}$	$\frac{1}{8}$	$\frac{1}{8}$
$\frac{1}{8}$	$\frac{1}{8}$	$\frac{1}{8}$	$\frac{1}{8}$	$\frac{1}{8}$	$\frac{1}{8}$	$\frac{1}{8}$	$\frac{1}{8}$
$\frac{1}{8}$	$\frac{1}{8}$	$\frac{1}{8}$	$\frac{1}{8}$	$\frac{1}{8}$	$\frac{1}{8}$	$\frac{1}{8}$	$\frac{1}{8}$
$\frac{1}{8}$	$\frac{1}{8}$	$\frac{1}{8}$	$\frac{1}{8}$	$\frac{1}{8}$	$\frac{1}{8}$	$\frac{1}{8}$	$\frac{1}{8}$
$\frac{1}{8}$	$\frac{1}{8}$	$\frac{1}{8}$	$\frac{1}{8}$	$\frac{1}{8}$	$\frac{1}{8}$	$\frac{1}{8}$	$\frac{1}{8}$
$\frac{1}{8}$	$\frac{1}{8}$	$\frac{1}{8}$	$\frac{1}{8}$	$\frac{1}{8}$	$\frac{1}{8}$	$\frac{1}{8}$	$\frac{1}{8}$
$\frac{1}{8}$	$\frac{1}{8}$	$\frac{1}{8}$	$\frac{1}{8}$	$\frac{1}{8}$	$\frac{1}{8}$	$\frac{1}{8}$	$\frac{1}{8}$

$\frac{1}{5}$	$\frac{1}{5}$	$\frac{1}{5}$	$\frac{1}{5}$	$\frac{1}{5}$
$\frac{1}{5}$	$\frac{1}{5}$	$\frac{1}{5}$	$\frac{1}{5}$	$\frac{1}{5}$
$\frac{1}{5}$	$\frac{1}{5}$	$\frac{1}{5}$	$\frac{1}{5}$	$\frac{1}{5}$
$\frac{1}{5}$	$\frac{1}{5}$	$\frac{1}{5}$	$\frac{1}{5}$	$\frac{1}{5}$
$\frac{1}{5}$	$\frac{1}{5}$	$\frac{1}{5}$	$\frac{1}{5}$	$\frac{1}{5}$
$\frac{1}{5}$	$\frac{1}{5}$	$\frac{1}{5}$	$\frac{1}{5}$	$\frac{1}{5}$
$\frac{1}{5}$	$\frac{1}{5}$	$\frac{1}{5}$	$\frac{1}{5}$	$\frac{1}{5}$

Name Date

1 whole

1 whole
1 whole
1 whole
1 whole
1 whole
1 whole
1 whole

1 whole
1 whole
1 whole
1 whole
1 whole
1 whole
1 whole

5–7 Class Activity

Name ______________________ Date ______________

▶ Practice Addition and Subtraction With Improper Fractions

Add or subtract.

1. $\frac{8}{5} + \frac{3}{5} =$ ______
2. $\frac{6}{9} + \frac{12}{9} =$ ______
3. $\frac{10}{7} - \frac{3}{7} =$ ______
4. $\frac{10}{8} + \frac{7}{8} =$ ______
5. $\frac{9}{6} - \frac{4}{6} =$ ______
6. $\frac{16}{10} - \frac{7}{10} =$ ______

▶ Add Mixed Numbers With Like Denominators

Add.

7. $2\frac{3}{5} + 1\frac{1}{5}$
8. $1\frac{2}{5} + 3\frac{4}{5}$
9. $3\frac{5}{8} + 1\frac{3}{8}$
10. $5\frac{2}{3} + 2\frac{2}{3}$

▶ Subtract Mixed Numbers With Like Denominators

Subtract.

11. $5\frac{6}{8} - 3\frac{3}{8}$
12. $6\frac{2}{8} - 4\frac{5}{8}$
13. $4\frac{1}{5} - 1\frac{3}{5}$
14. $5\frac{1}{6} - 3\frac{4}{6}$

Explain each solution.

15. $\overset{5}{\cancel{6}}\,\frac{\overset{7+2=9}{\cancel{2}}}{7} = 5\frac{9}{7}$

$- 1\frac{5}{7} = 1\frac{5}{7}$

$4\frac{4}{7}$

16. $\overset{5}{\cancel{6}}\,\frac{\overset{6+2=8}{\cancel{2}}}{6} = 5\frac{8}{6}$

$- 1\frac{5}{6} = 1\frac{5}{6}$

$4\frac{3}{6}$

17. $\overset{5}{\cancel{6}}\,\frac{\overset{11+2=13}{\cancel{2}}}{11} = 5\frac{13}{11}$

$- 1\frac{5}{11} = 1\frac{5}{11}$

$4\frac{\cancel{8}}{11}$

5–7 Class Activity

Name ______________________________ Date ______________

▶ Puzzled Penguin

Dear Math Students:

Here is a subtraction problem that I tried to solve.

$$\begin{array}{r} 7\frac{3}{8} \\ -\ 1\frac{5}{8} \\ \hline 6\frac{2}{8} \end{array}$$

Is my answer correct? If not, please help me understand why it is wrong.

Thank you,
Puzzled Penguin

18. ____

____

____

▶ Compare and Subtract

Compare each pair of mixed numbers. Then subtract the smaller one from the larger.

19. $3\frac{2}{5}$; $1\frac{4}{5}$ ______________

20. $\frac{8}{9}$; $2\frac{2}{9}$ ______________

21. $\frac{14}{11}$; $1\frac{6}{11}$ ______________

22. $4\frac{1}{8}$; $2\frac{7}{8}$ ______________

23. $3\frac{2}{6}$; $4\frac{3}{6}$ ______________

24. $10\frac{1}{3}$; $7\frac{2}{3}$ ______________

Name ______________________ Date ____________

▶ Compare, Add, and Subtract Fractions

Practice what you know.

Circle the greater fraction.

1. $\frac{4}{6}$ or $\frac{4}{5}$
2. $\frac{8}{10}$ or $\frac{7}{10}$
3. $\frac{6}{9}$ or $\frac{6}{10}$
4. $\frac{2}{3}$ or $\frac{2}{4}$
5. $\frac{5}{7}$ or $\frac{5}{8}$
6. $\frac{7}{8}$ or $\frac{6}{8}$

Compare each pair of fractions. Then add them to find the total and subtract the smaller one from the larger one to find the difference.

7. $\frac{6}{10}$; $\frac{3}{10}$ ____________________
8. $\frac{4}{6}$; $\frac{5}{6}$ ____________________
9. $\frac{2}{7}$; $\frac{5}{7}$ ____________________
10. $\frac{4}{5}$; $\frac{2}{5}$ ____________________
11. $\frac{7}{9}$; $\frac{3}{9}$ ____________________
12. $\frac{7}{8}$; $\frac{4}{8}$ ____________________

Add or subtract.

13. $\frac{3}{6} + \frac{2}{6} =$ ______
14. $\frac{4}{7} + \frac{1}{7} =$ ______
15. $\frac{5}{8} - \frac{4}{8} =$ ______
16. $\frac{4}{9} + \frac{4}{9} =$ ______
17. $\frac{3}{4} - \frac{2}{4} =$ ______
18. $\frac{8}{10} - \frac{3}{10} =$ ______

Compare each pair of mixed numbers. Then find the total and the difference.

19. $2\frac{3}{4}$; $3\frac{1}{4}$ ____________________
20. $1\frac{5}{12}$; $5\frac{3}{12}$ ____________________

On the Back Write four improper fractions. Write each one as a mixed number. Write four mixed numbers. Write each one as an improper fraction.

Name Date

Name ________________________ Date ____________

▶ Equivalent Fractions

Read and discuss the problem situation.

Luis works summers at Maria's Fruit Farm. One day, Maria agreed to give Luis extra pay if he could sell $\frac{2}{3}$ of her supply of peaches. They started with 15 bags of peaches, and Luis sold 10 of them.

1. Luis said to Maria, "Ten bags is $\frac{10}{15}$ of the 15 bags you wanted to sell. I think $\frac{2}{3}$ is the same as $\frac{10}{15}$. I can show you why." Luis made this drawing. Did Luis earn his pay?

____

____

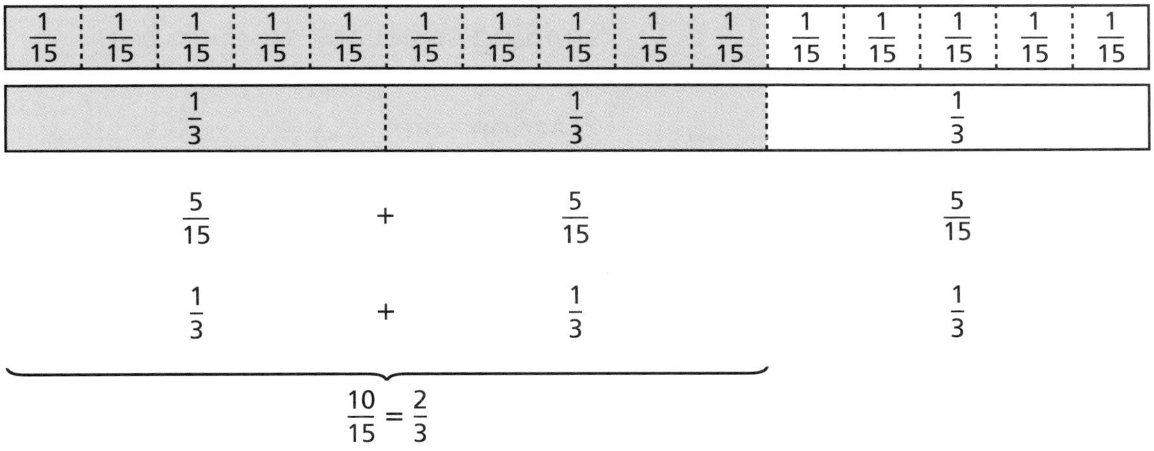

2. Maria said, "You are just making groups of 5 fifteenths. You can show what you did using numbers." Here's what Maria wrote:

$$\frac{10}{15} = \frac{10 \div 5}{15 \div 5} = \frac{2}{3}$$

Discuss what Maria did. How does dividing the numerator and denominator by 5 affect the fraction?

____

____

5–9 Class Activity

Name ______________________ Date ______________________

Vocabulary
equivalent fractions
simplify
simplest form

▶ Simplify Fractions

Two fractions that represent the same part of a whole are **equivalent fractions**. The fractions $\frac{10}{15}$ and $\frac{2}{3}$ are equivalent.

Simplifying a fraction means finding an equivalent fraction with a smaller numerator and denominator.

A fraction is in **simplest form** if there is no whole number (other than 1) that divides evenly into both the numerator and denominator.

3. Maria had 12 boxes of apricots. She sold 10 of the boxes. Write the fraction of the boxes sold, and lightly shade the twelfths fraction bar to show this fraction.

Fraction sold: ______________

4. Group the twelfths to form an equivalent fraction with a smaller denominator. Show the new fraction by dividing, labeling, and lightly shading the blank fraction bar.

Fraction sold: ______________

$\frac{1}{12}$	$\frac{1}{12}$	$\frac{1}{12}$	$\frac{1}{12}$	$\frac{1}{12}$	$\frac{1}{12}$	$\frac{1}{12}$	$\frac{1}{12}$	$\frac{1}{12}$	$\frac{1}{12}$	$\frac{1}{12}$	$\frac{1}{12}$

5. In problem 4, you formed groups of twelfths to get a larger unit fraction. How many twelfths are in each group? In other words, what is the *group size*?

____

6. Show how you can find the equivalent fraction by dividing the numerator and denominator by the group size.

$\frac{10}{12} = \frac{10 \div }{12 \div } = -$

5–9 Class Activity

Name ______________________ Date ____________

▶ Simplify Fractions (continued)

Shade the bar to show the fraction of items sold. Group the unit fractions to form an equivalent fraction in simplest form. Show your work numerically.

7. Maria had 12 bags of grapes. She sold 9 bags. What fraction did she sell?

$\frac{1}{12}$	$\frac{1}{12}$	$\frac{1}{12}$	$\frac{1}{12}$	$\frac{1}{12}$	$\frac{1}{12}$	$\frac{1}{12}$	$\frac{1}{12}$	$\frac{1}{12}$	$\frac{1}{12}$	$\frac{1}{12}$	$\frac{1}{12}$

Group size: ____________ Fraction of bags sold: $\frac{9 \div \_\_}{12 \div \_\_} = \frac{\_\_}{\_\_}$

8. Maria had 15 crates of apples. She sold 6 crates. What fraction did she sell?

$\frac{1}{15}$	$\frac{1}{15}$	$\frac{1}{15}$	$\frac{1}{15}$	$\frac{1}{15}$	$\frac{1}{15}$	$\frac{1}{15}$	$\frac{1}{15}$	$\frac{1}{15}$	$\frac{1}{15}$	$\frac{1}{15}$	$\frac{1}{15}$	$\frac{1}{15}$	$\frac{1}{15}$	$\frac{1}{15}$

Group size: ____________ Fraction of crates sold: $\frac{6 \div \_\_}{15 \div \_\_} = \frac{\_\_}{\_\_}$

9. Maria had 16 jars of cherry jam. She sold 10 jars. What fraction did she sell?

$\frac{1}{16}$	$\frac{1}{16}$	$\frac{1}{16}$	$\frac{1}{16}$	$\frac{1}{16}$	$\frac{1}{16}$	$\frac{1}{16}$	$\frac{1}{16}$	$\frac{1}{16}$	$\frac{1}{16}$	$\frac{1}{16}$	$\frac{1}{16}$	$\frac{1}{16}$	$\frac{1}{16}$	$\frac{1}{16}$	$\frac{1}{16}$

Group size: ____________ Fraction of jars sold: $\frac{10 \div \_\_}{16 \div \_\_} = \frac{\_\_}{\_\_}$

5–9 Class Activity

Name _______________ Date _______________

▶ Use Fraction Bars to Find Equivalent Fractions

10. Look at the thirds bar. Circle enough unit fractions on each of the other bars to equal $\frac{1}{3}$.

$\frac{1}{18}$	$\frac{1}{18}$	$\frac{1}{18}$	$\frac{1}{18}$	$\frac{1}{18}$	$\frac{1}{18}$	$\frac{1}{18}$	$\frac{1}{18}$	$\frac{1}{18}$	$\frac{1}{18}$	$\frac{1}{18}$	$\frac{1}{18}$	$\frac{1}{18}$	$\frac{1}{18}$	$\frac{1}{18}$	$\frac{1}{18}$	$\frac{1}{18}$	$\frac{1}{18}$

$\frac{1}{15}$	$\frac{1}{15}$	$\frac{1}{15}$	$\frac{1}{15}$	$\frac{1}{15}$	$\frac{1}{15}$	$\frac{1}{15}$	$\frac{1}{15}$	$\frac{1}{15}$	$\frac{1}{15}$	$\frac{1}{15}$	$\frac{1}{15}$	$\frac{1}{15}$	$\frac{1}{15}$	$\frac{1}{15}$

$\frac{1}{12}$	$\frac{1}{12}$	$\frac{1}{12}$	$\frac{1}{12}$	$\frac{1}{12}$	$\frac{1}{12}$	$\frac{1}{12}$	$\frac{1}{12}$	$\frac{1}{12}$	$\frac{1}{12}$	$\frac{1}{12}$	$\frac{1}{12}$

$\frac{1}{9}$	$\frac{1}{9}$	$\frac{1}{9}$	$\frac{1}{9}$	$\frac{1}{9}$	$\frac{1}{9}$	$\frac{1}{9}$	$\frac{1}{9}$	$\frac{1}{9}$

$\frac{1}{6}$	$\frac{1}{6}$	$\frac{1}{6}$	$\frac{1}{6}$	$\frac{1}{6}$	$\frac{1}{6}$

$\frac{1}{3}$	$\frac{1}{3}$	$\frac{1}{3}$

11. Discuss how the parts of the fraction bars you circled show this fraction chain. Explain how each different group of unit fractions is equal to $\frac{1}{3}$.

$$\frac{6}{18} = \frac{5}{15} = \frac{4}{12} = \frac{3}{9} = \frac{2}{6} = \frac{1}{3}$$

12. Write the group size for each fraction in the fraction chain. The first one is done for you.

__6__ ______ ______ ______ ______ ______

13. Complete each equation by showing how you use group size to simplify. The first is done for you.

$\frac{6 \div 6}{18 \div 6} = \frac{1}{3}$ $\frac{5 \div \_\_}{15 \div \_\_} = \frac{1}{3}$ $\frac{4 \div \_\_}{12 \div \_\_} = \frac{1}{3}$

$\frac{3 \div \_\_}{9 \div \_\_} = \frac{1}{3}$ $\frac{2 \div \_\_}{6 \div \_\_} = \frac{1}{3}$

5–9 Class Activity

Name ______________________ Date ______________

► Use a Multiplication Table to Find Equivalent Fractions

The table on the right shows part of the multiplication table at the left. You can make a chain of fractions equivalent to $\frac{1}{3}$ by using the products in the rows for the factors 1 and 3.

×	1	2	3	4	5	6	7	8	9	10
1	1	2	3	4	5	6	7	8	9	10
2	2	4	6	8	10	12	14	16	18	20
3	3	6	9	12	15	18	21	24	27	30
4	4	8	12	16	20	24	28	32	36	40
5	5	10	15	20	25	30	35	40	45	50
6	6	12	18	24	30	36	42	48	54	60
7	7	14	21	28	35	42	49	56	63	70
8	8	16	24	32	40	48	56	64	72	80
9	9	18	27	36	45	54	63	72	81	90
10	10	20	30	40	50	60	70	80	90	100

× 6

×	1	2	3	4	5	6	7	8	9	10
1	(1)	2	3	4	5	(6)	7	8	9	10
3	(3)	6	9	12	15	(18)	21	24	27	30

Complete each fraction equation. Look in the top row to find the multiplier or the divider.

14. $\frac{1 \times \_\_\_}{3 \times \_\_\_} = \frac{4}{12}$

15. $\frac{1 \times \_\_\_}{3 \times \_\_\_} = \frac{9}{27}$

16. $\frac{8 \div \_\_\_}{24 \div \_\_\_} = \frac{1}{3}$

17. $\frac{10 \div \_\_\_}{30 \div \_\_\_} = \frac{1}{3}$

Name ______________________ Date ______________

▶ Use a Multiplication Table to Find Equivalent Fractions (continued)

Here are two more rows from the multiplication table moved together. These rows can be used to generate a chain of fractions equivalent to $\frac{4}{7}$.

×	1	2	3	4	5	6	7	8	9	10
4	4	8	12	16	20	24	28	32	36	40
7	7	14	21	28	35	42	49	56	63	70

Complete each equation.

18. $\frac{4 \times \quad}{7 \times \quad} =$

19. $\frac{4 \times \quad}{7 \times \quad} =$

20. $\frac{20 \div \quad}{35 \div \quad} =$

21. $\frac{36 \div \quad}{63 \div \quad} =$

22. $\frac{12 \div \quad}{21 \div \quad} =$

23. $\frac{24 \div \quad}{42 \div \quad} =$

▶ Practice Simplifying Fractions

Simplify each fraction.

24. $\frac{4 \div \quad}{20 \div \quad} =$

25. $\frac{14 \div \quad}{35 \div \quad} =$

26. $\frac{3 \div \quad}{12 \div \quad} =$

27. $\frac{25 \div \quad}{40 \div \quad} =$

28. $\frac{8 \div \quad}{24 \div \quad} =$

29. $\frac{6 \div \quad}{54 \div \quad} =$

30. $\frac{12 \div \quad}{18 \div \quad} =$

31. $\frac{20 \div \quad}{30 \div \quad} =$

Name ______________________ Date ______________

▶ Find a Common Unit Fraction Using Fraction Bars

Read and discuss the Puzzled Penguin problem.

On Monday, Puzzled Penguin and his parents each ate $\frac{1}{3}$ of a fish. On Tuesday, they and Puzzled Penguin's friend each ate $\frac{1}{4}$ of a fish. Both fish were the same size. Puzzled Penguin wanted to know what fraction of a fish he ate on both Monday and Tuesday.

This is what Puzzled Penguin wrote: $\frac{1}{3} + \frac{1}{4} = \frac{2}{7}$

1. How did Puzzled Penguin add $\frac{1}{3}$ and $\frac{1}{4}$?

____

2. Is Puzzled Penguin's addition correct? Use the fraction strips below if needed.

____

Fish 1	$\frac{1}{3}$	$\frac{1}{3}$	$\frac{1}{3}$				
Fish 2	$\frac{1}{4}$	$\frac{1}{4}$	$\frac{1}{4}$	$\frac{1}{4}$			
Total	$\frac{1}{7}$	$\frac{1}{7}$	$\frac{1}{7}$	$\frac{1}{7}$	$\frac{1}{7}$	$\frac{1}{7}$	$\frac{1}{7}$

Discuss how the twelfths fraction bar can help Puzzled Penguin with his addition.

	Fish 1	Fish 2
	$\frac{1}{3}$	$\frac{1}{4}$

Total	$\frac{1}{12}$	$\frac{1}{12}$	$\frac{1}{12}$	$\frac{1}{12}$	$\frac{1}{12}$	$\frac{1}{12}$	$\frac{1}{12}$	$\frac{1}{12}$	$\frac{1}{12}$	$\frac{1}{12}$	$\frac{1}{12}$	$\frac{1}{12}$

3. Use the fraction bars to rename $\frac{1}{3}$ and $\frac{1}{4}$ using the unit fraction $\frac{1}{12}$.

$\frac{1}{3} = \frac{\_\_}{12}$ and $\frac{1}{4} = \frac{\_\_}{12}$

4. Add the renamed fractions.

$\frac{1}{3} + \frac{1}{4} = \frac{\_\_}{12} + \frac{\_\_}{12} = \frac{\_\_ + \_\_}{12} = \frac{\_\_}{12}$

5–10 Class Activity

Name ______________________________ Date ______________________

Vocabulary
common denominator

▶ Find a Common Unit Fraction Numerically

5. Show how we could rename $\frac{1}{3}$ and $\frac{1}{4}$ numerically so that they have the same unit fraction.

$$\frac{1\times}{3\times} = \frac{\quad}{12} \qquad \frac{1\times}{4\times} = \frac{\quad}{12}$$

6. How is the denominator of the new unit fraction, $\frac{1}{12}$, related numerically to the denominators of $\frac{1}{3}$ and $\frac{1}{4}$?

____

▶ Add Fractions With Unlike Denominators

To add unlike fractions, you need to rewrite the fractions so they have a **common denominator**. A common denominator is a number that is a multiple of both denominators. For $\frac{1}{3}$ and $\frac{1}{4}$, 12 is a common denominator because it is a multiple of both 3 and 4.

7. Three runners are running in a relay race. The first runner goes $\frac{3}{10}$ of the total distance. The second runner goes $\frac{2}{5}$ of the total distance. Using the fraction bars or a numerical method, find the fraction of the distance the first two runners complete together.

$\frac{1}{5}$	$\frac{1}{5}$	$\frac{1}{5}$	$\frac{1}{5}$	$\frac{1}{5}$

$\frac{1}{10}$	$\frac{1}{10}$	$\frac{1}{10}$	$\frac{1}{10}$	$\frac{1}{10}$	$\frac{1}{10}$	$\frac{1}{10}$	$\frac{1}{10}$	$\frac{1}{10}$	$\frac{1}{10}$

$$\frac{2\times}{5\times} = \frac{\quad}{10}$$

$$\frac{3}{10} + \frac{2}{5} = \frac{3}{10} + \frac{\quad}{10} = \frac{\quad + \quad}{10} = \frac{\quad}{10}$$

Name ____________________ Date ____________

Vocabulary
least common denominator

▶ Add Fractions With Unlike Denominators (continued)

In problem 7, you used 10 as the common denominator for $\frac{3}{10}$ and $\frac{2}{5}$. We say that 10 is the **least common denominator** of $\frac{3}{10}$ and $\frac{2}{5}$ because it is the smallest number that is a multiple of both 10 and 5. Using the least common denominator will give you fractions with smaller numbers that are easier to work with.

8. Lanny's parents brought two same-size cakes to the Parents' Club meeting at school. Lanny's mother served $\frac{3}{4}$ of her cake. Lanny's father served $\frac{5}{6}$ of his cake. Using the fraction bars or a numerical method, find the fraction of cake served in all.

$\frac{1}{4}$	$\frac{1}{4}$	$\frac{1}{4}$	$\frac{1}{4}$

$\frac{1}{12}$	$\frac{1}{12}$	$\frac{1}{12}$	$\frac{1}{12}$	$\frac{1}{12}$	$\frac{1}{12}$	$\frac{1}{12}$	$\frac{1}{12}$	$\frac{1}{12}$	$\frac{1}{12}$	$\frac{1}{12}$	$\frac{1}{12}$

$\frac{1}{6}$	$\frac{1}{6}$	$\frac{1}{6}$	$\frac{1}{6}$	$\frac{1}{6}$	$\frac{1}{6}$

$\frac{3 \times \underline{\quad}}{4 \times \underline{\quad}} = \frac{\underline{\quad}}{12}$ $\qquad$ $\frac{5 \times \underline{\quad}}{6 \times \underline{\quad}} = \frac{\underline{\quad}}{12}$

$\frac{3}{4} + \frac{5}{6} = \frac{\underline{\quad}}{12} + \frac{\underline{\quad}}{12} = \frac{\underline{\quad} + \underline{\quad}}{12} = \frac{\underline{\quad}}{12}$

9. Below are the additions you did in problems 4–8. Describe how the strategies you used to find fractions with like denominators in the following problems were alike and different.

$\frac{1}{3} + \frac{1}{4}$ $\qquad$ $\frac{3}{10} + \frac{2}{5}$ $\qquad$ $\frac{3}{4} + \frac{5}{6}$

____

____

____

____

____

Name ____________________ Date ____________________

▶ Find Equivalent Fractions With Fraction Bars

10. How do these fraction bars show equivalent fractions for $\frac{1}{3}$?

____

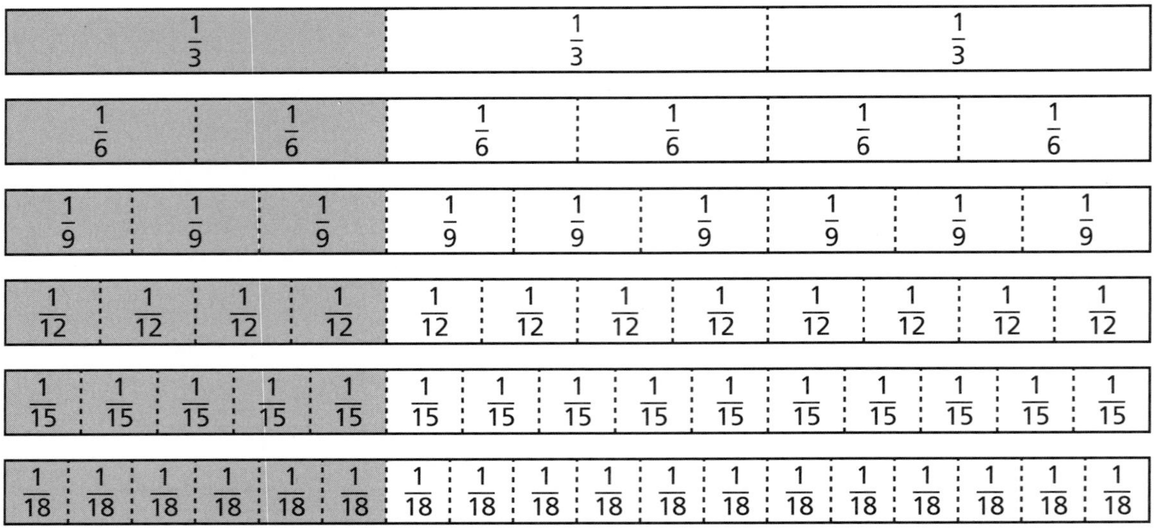

11. You can show how to find fractions equivalent to $\frac{1}{3}$ numerically. Fill in the blanks and finish the equations. Then explain how these fraction equations show equivalent fractions.

2 equal parts	3 equal parts	4 equal parts	___ equal parts	___ equal parts
$\times\ 2$	$\times\ 3$	$\times$ ___	$\times$ ___	$\times$ ___
$\frac{1 \times 2}{3 \times 2} = \frac{2}{6}$	$\frac{1 \times \_\_}{3 \times \_\_} = \frac{\_\_}{9}$	$\frac{1 \times \_\_}{3 \times \_\_} = \frac{\_\_}{12}$	$\frac{1 \times \_\_}{3 \times \_\_} = \frac{\_\_}{15}$	$\frac{1 \times \_\_}{3 \times \_\_} = \frac{\_\_}{18}$

____

____

____

____

Name ______________________________ Date ______________

▶ Find Equivalent Fractions With the Multiplication Table

Multiplication table rows show relationships among equivalent fractions.

12. What happens to the fractions as you move from right to left? How does the size of the unit fraction change? How does the number of unit fractions change?

____

____

____

×	1	2	3	4	5	6	7	8	9	10
1	(1)	2	3	4	(5)	6	7	8	9	10
3	(3)	6	9	12	(15)	18	21	24	27	30

Simplify fractions.

13. What happens to the fractions as you move from left to right? How does the size of the unit fraction change? How does the number of unit fractions change?

____

____

____

×	1	2	3	4	5	6	7	8	9	10
1	(1)	2	3	4	(5)	6	7	8	9	10
3	(3)	6	9	12	(15)	18	21	24	27	30

Unsimplify fractions to get a common denominator to add, subtract, or compare them.

5–10 Class Activity

Name ____________________ Date ____________

► Add Unlike Fractions

Find a common denominator. Then add.

	Find the common denominator.		**Add the fractions.**
14. $\frac{1}{4} + \frac{3}{8}$	$\frac{1 \times 2}{4 \times 2} = \frac{2}{\square}$	$\frac{3 \times 1}{8 \times 1} = \frac{3}{\square}$	$\frac{2}{\square} + \frac{3}{\square} = \frac{2 + 3}{\square} = \frac{5}{\square}$
15. $\frac{1}{6} + \frac{3}{8}$	$\frac{1 \times 4}{6 \times 4} = \frac{4}{\square}$	$\frac{3 \times 3}{8 \times 3} = \frac{9}{\square}$	$\frac{4}{\square} + \frac{9}{\square} = \frac{4 + 9}{\square} = \frac{13}{\square}$

16. $\frac{2}{5} + \frac{3}{8}$ ____________________ ____________________

17. $\frac{1}{4} + \frac{7}{10}$ ____________________ ____________________

18. $\frac{5}{12} + \frac{2}{3}$ ____________________ ____________________

19. $\frac{5}{6} + \frac{3}{4}$ ____________________ ____________________

20. $\frac{4}{7} + \frac{5}{6}$ ____________________ ____________________

21. $\frac{2}{5} + \frac{4}{15}$ ____________________ ____________________

Name ____________________ Date ____________

▶ Find Equivalent Fractions

On Monday, Puzzled Penguin and his parents each ate $\frac{1}{3}$ of a fish. On Tuesday, they and Puzzled Penguin's friend each ate $\frac{1}{4}$ of a fish. Both fish were the same size. Puzzled Penguin wanted to know which day he ate more fish. He also wanted to know how much more fish he ate on that day.

1. Use fraction bars to answer Puzzled Penguin's questions. Which day did he eat more fish? How much more?

   ____

2. Complete the numeric solution under the fraction bars. What number goes in the ⬚ boxes?

   ____

Monday	$\frac{1}{3}$ (shaded)				$\frac{1}{3}$				$\frac{1}{3}$			
Tuesday	$\frac{1}{4}$ (shaded)			$\frac{1}{4}$			$\frac{1}{4}$			$\frac{1}{4}$		
Total	$\frac{1}{12}$	$\frac{1}{12}$	$\frac{1}{12}$	$\frac{1}{12}$	$\frac{1}{12}$	$\frac{1}{12}$	$\frac{1}{12}$	$\frac{1}{12}$	$\frac{1}{12}$	$\frac{1}{12}$	$\frac{1}{12}$	$\frac{1}{12}$

Find equivalent fractions.

$\frac{1 \times 4}{3 \times 4} = \frac{4}{\square} \quad \frac{1 \times 3}{4 \times 3} = \frac{3}{\square}$

Compare.

$\frac{1}{3} \bigcirc \frac{1}{4} \quad \frac{4}{12} \bigcirc \frac{3}{12}$

Subtract.

$\frac{4}{12} - \frac{3}{12} = \frac{4-3}{12} = \frac{1}{12}$

3. Here is how Puzzled Penguin solved his problem. What mistakes did he make? Why is his solution wrong?

   $\frac{1}{4} - \frac{1}{3} = \frac{0}{1} = 0$

   ____

   ____

▶ Compare Fractions

4. Sue ate $\frac{3}{8}$ of a melon. Ron ate $\frac{2}{5}$ of a melon that was the same size. Who ate more?

   ____

Show your work.

5–11 **Class Activity**

Name ______________________ Date ____________

▶ Solve Problems With Unlike Fractions

Solve.

Show your work.

5. On Monday, Roberto read $\frac{1}{5}$ of a novel. On Tuesday, he read $\frac{3}{7}$ of the novel. How much of the novel did he read in the two days?

____

6. Alyssa ate $\frac{3}{5}$ of a box of raisins, and Lou ate $\frac{1}{6}$ of the box. What fraction of the box was left?

____

7. Paul jogged for $\frac{2}{10}$ of an hour. Inez jogged for $\frac{5}{8}$ of an hour. Who jogged for a longer period of time? How much longer?

____

For each pair of fractions, find equivalent fractions with a common denominator. Then compare, add, and subtract.

Fractions	Equivalent Fractions		Compare.
8. $\frac{2}{3}$ $\frac{4}{5}$	$\frac{2 \times}{3 \times} = \frac{\square}{\square}$	$\frac{4 \times}{5 \times} = \frac{\square}{\square}$	$\frac{2}{3} \bigcirc \frac{4}{5}$

Add.

$\frac{\square}{\square} + \frac{\square}{\square} = \frac{\quad + \quad}{\square} = \frac{\square}{\square}$

Subtract.

$\frac{\square}{\square} - \frac{\square}{\square} = \frac{\quad - \quad}{\square} = \frac{\square}{\square}$

Fractions	Equivalent Fractions		Compare.
9. $\frac{3}{4}$ $\frac{2}{5}$	$\frac{3 \times}{4 \times} = \frac{\square}{\square}$	$\frac{2 \times}{5 \times} = \frac{\square}{\square}$	$\frac{3}{4} \bigcirc \frac{2}{5}$

Add.

$\frac{\square}{\square} + \frac{\square}{\square} = \frac{\quad + \quad}{\square} = \frac{\square}{\square}$

Subtract.

$\frac{\square}{\square} - \frac{\square}{\square} = \frac{\quad - \quad}{\square} = \frac{\square}{\square}$

Order the fractions from greatest to least.

10. $\frac{1}{2}, \frac{1}{4}, \frac{3}{8}$ ______________________

11. $\frac{2}{3}, \frac{5}{6}, \frac{4}{9}$ ______________________

5–12 Class Activity

Name ______________________ Date ______________

Vocabulary
equally likely
probability

▶ Coin Toss Experiment

When you toss a coin, heads and tails are **equally likely** results. This means they have the same chance of occurring.

A **probability** is a number between 0 and 1 that tells you how likely something is to happen. When you toss a coin, you can expect to get heads about half the time, or on about 1 out of every 2 tosses. The probability of getting heads is $\frac{1}{2}$.

1. Toss a coin ten times and keep a tally.

Heads	Tails

Did you get heads for half of your tosses? __________

2. Find the total number of heads and the total number of tails tossed by everyone in your group.

Group results: __________ Heads __________ Tails

Did your group get heads on half of its tosses? __________

3. Work with your teacher to combine the results for everyone in your class.

Class results: __________ Heads __________ Tails

Did your class get heads on half of its tosses? __________

4. If the probability of getting heads is $\frac{1}{2}$, why didn't everyone get heads on half their tosses?

____

____

Name ______________________ Date ______________________

▶ Solve Probability Problems

5. Misha puts 15 glass marbles and 10 metal marbles in a bag. If she pulls 1 marble without looking, what is the probability it will be metal? ____________

6. Three of Misha's glass marbles are green. If she puts all 15 glass marbles in a bag and picks one, what is the probability she will get a green marble? ____________

7. Of the 10 metal marbles, 7 are brass and 3 are steel. If Misha puts the metal marbles in the bag and chooses one, what is the probability it will be brass? ____________

▶ Analyze a Spinner

Suppose you spin this spinner once. Solve each problem.

8. What is the probability the arrow will land in a space with dots?

____

9. What is the probability the spinner will land in a space with stars?

____

10. What is the probability the spinner will land in a space with stripes?

____

11. Use one of the divided circles below to design your own spinner. Ask your partner probability questions about your spinner.

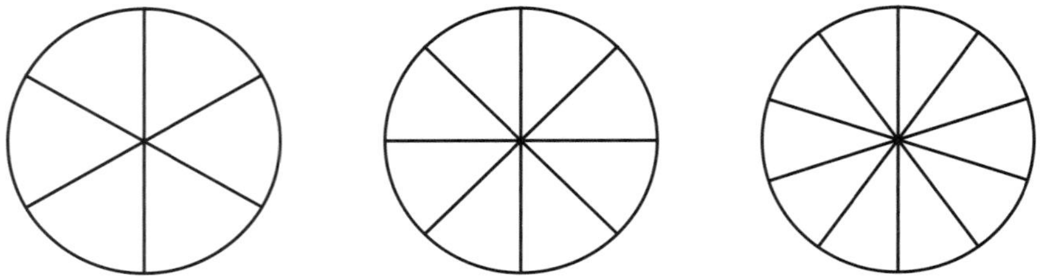

Name ______________________________ Date ____________

► Compare, Add, and Subtract Fractions

For each pair of fractions, find an equivalent fraction. Then compare the fractions, add them, and subtract the smaller fraction from the larger one. An example is shown below for $\frac{1}{2}$ and $\frac{5}{7}$.

Find equivalent fractions.	Compare.	Add.	Subtract.
$\frac{1}{2} = \frac{7}{14}$ $\quad \frac{5}{7} = \frac{10}{14}$	$\frac{1}{2} < \frac{5}{7}$	$\frac{1}{2} + \frac{5}{7} = \frac{17}{14}$	$\frac{5}{7} - \frac{1}{2} = \frac{3}{14}$

1. $\frac{3}{5}, \frac{5}{7}$

2. $\frac{5}{6}, \frac{2}{3}$

3. $\frac{1}{4}, \frac{3}{8}$

4. $\frac{3}{5}, \frac{9}{12}$

5. $\frac{3}{4}, \frac{2}{3}$

6. $\frac{1}{2}, \frac{5}{8}$

7. $\frac{11}{12}, \frac{5}{6}$

8. $\frac{5}{8}, \frac{4}{7}$

Name ______________________ Date __________

▶ Solve Problems With Fractions

Solve each problem.

Show your work.

9. At Kim's family reunion, a large cake was served for dessert. The children ate $\frac{2}{3}$ of the cake. The adults ate $\frac{1}{4}$ of the cake. Did the family eat all of the cake? Explain your thinking.

____

____

10. Maria's grandmother lives $\frac{5}{8}$ of the distance from Maria's home to Maria's school. Maria's uncle lives $\frac{7}{12}$ of the distance from Maria's home to her school. Who lives closer to Maria? How much closer?

____

11. Greta has a bag of 60 green and blue marbles. One at a time, she pulls out 6 marbles, returning each marble to the bag when she pulls it out. She gets 2 green marbles and 4 blue marbles. She says, "Now I know my bag contains 20 green and 40 blue marbles." Is she right or wrong? Explain your thinking.

____

____

12. Jerome and Sherry are playing a game. They roll a number cube to see who goes first. Jerome rolls a 6. Sherry also rolls a 6. Jerome thinks Sherry cheated because a 6 should come up only 1 out of 6 times. Is he right or wrong? Explain your thinking.

____

____

____

Name ______________________________ Date ____________

► A Whole Number Times a Unit Fraction

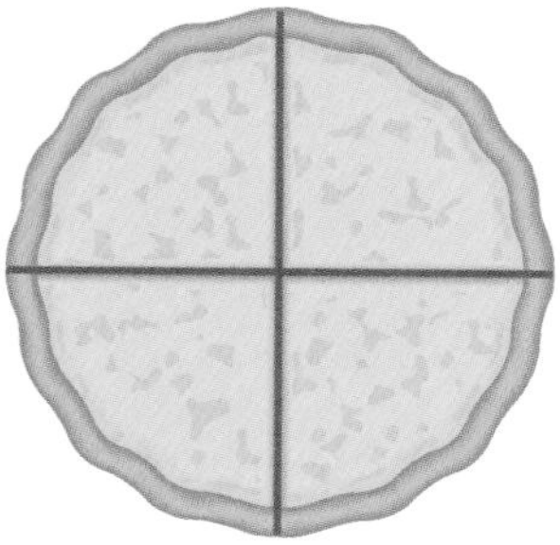

The lunchroom at Mandy's school serves pizza every Friday. Each slice is $\frac{1}{4}$ of a pizza. Mandy eats one slice every week.

Solve each problem, first by adding and then by multiplying. Show your work.

1. What fraction of a pizza does Mandy eat in 3 weeks?

____

2. What fraction of a pizza does Mandy eat in 5 weeks?

____

3. What fraction of a pizza does Mandy eat in 11 weeks?

____

____

► Practice and Generalize

Draw, shade, and label shapes to show the solution to each problem. You can use long bars if you want.

4. $2 \times \frac{1}{3}$

5. $6 \times \frac{1}{5}$

6. $10 \times \frac{1}{8}$

7. $3 \times \frac{1}{4}$

8. $8 \times \frac{1}{3}$

9. $14 \times \frac{1}{7}$

5–15 Class Activity

Name ____________________ Date ____________

▶ A Whole Number Times a Non-Unit Fraction

At Joe's school, the lunchroom serves sub sandwiches every Thursday. Each piece is $\frac{1}{6}$ of a whole sub. Joe eats 2 pieces every Thursday.

Solve each problem, first by adding and then by multiplying.

Show your work.

10. How much of a sub sandwich does Joe eat every Thursday?

____

11. What fraction of a sub does Joe eat in 3 weeks?

____

12. What fraction of a sub does Joe eat in 5 weeks?

____

▶ Practice and Generalize

Solve.

13. $8 \times \frac{3}{4} =$

14. $18 \times \frac{2}{3} =$

15. $10 \times \frac{5}{6} =$

16. $4 \times \frac{5}{7} =$

17. $4 \times \frac{3}{8} =$

18. $15 \times \frac{3}{10} =$

19. $3 \times \frac{4}{5} =$

20. $7 \times \frac{8}{9} =$

Name ______________________ Date ______________

▶ A Unit Fraction *of* a Whole Number

The librarian put 30 books on the shelves in 6 equal piles.

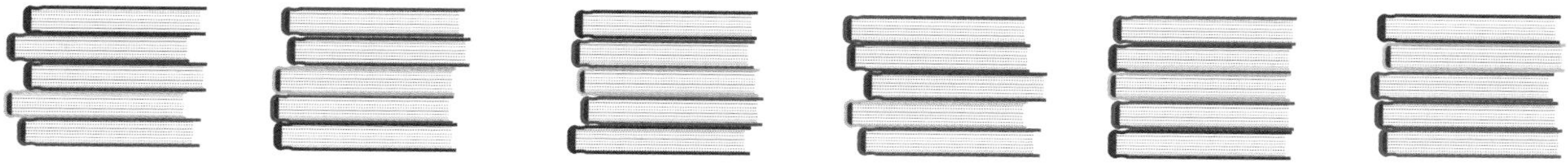

1. What fraction of the 30 books does each pile show? __________

2. Write a division equation that shows the number of books in each pile. ____________________

3. You can also write a multiplication equation to show the number of books in each pile. Discuss the equations below.

   of means *times*
   6 groups *of* 5 = 30
   $6 \times 5 = 30$

   of means *times*
   a $\frac{1}{6}$ group *of* 30 = 5
   $\frac{1}{6} \times 30 = 5$

4. Discuss the relationship between division by a whole number and multiplication by a unit fraction.

   30 books ÷ 6 equal piles = 5 books per pile $30 \div 6 = 5$

   $\frac{1}{6}$ of 30 books = $\frac{1}{6}$ of 30 = 5 books $\frac{1}{6} \times 30 = 5$

Find the unit fraction $\frac{1}{d}$ *of* each whole number by making *d* equal shares.

Examples: $\frac{1}{3} \times 15 = 15 \div 3 = \frac{15}{3} = 5$ $\frac{1}{4} \times 28 = 28 \div 4 = \frac{28}{4} = 7$

5. $\frac{1}{7} \times 14 =$ ______________

6. $\frac{1}{8} \times 40 =$ ______________

7. $\frac{1}{3} \times 12 =$ ______________

8. $\frac{1}{6} \times 60 =$ ______________

9. $\frac{1}{9} \times 63 =$ ______________

10. $\frac{1}{3} \times 27 =$ ______________

11. $\frac{1}{4} \times 10 =$ ______________

12. $\frac{1}{5} \times 19 =$ ______________

Name ______________________ Date ____________

▶ A Fraction *of* a Whole Number

Jim, Tina, and Maurice shelved the piles of library books.

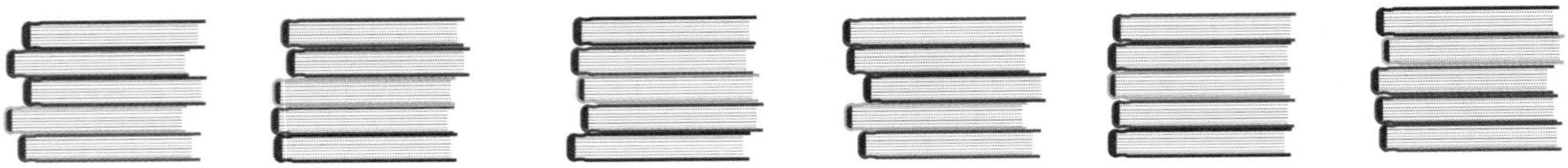

______ ______ ______ ______ ______ ______

Jim reshelved 1 of the piles.

13. What fraction of the books did Jim shelve? ______

14. How many books did he shelve? ______

15. Circle the books Jim shelved and write his name under them.

Tina reshelved 2 of the piles.

16. What fraction of the books did Tina shelve? ______

17. How many books did she shelve? ______

18. How many times as many books did Tina shelve as Jim? ______

19. Circle the books Tina shelved and write her name under them.

Maurice reshelved 3 of the piles.

20. What fraction of the books did Maurice shelve? ______

21. How many books did he shelve? ______

22. How many times as many books did Maurice shelve as Jim? ______

23. Circle the books Maurice shelved and write his name under them.

24. Have the three students shelved all the books? How do you know?

____

Name ______________________ Date ____________

► Any Fraction of a Whole Number

Find the fraction of each whole number. Use 5 to 12 if they help.

Examples: $\frac{2}{3} \times 15 = 2 \times (\frac{1}{3} \times 15) = 2 \times (\frac{15}{3}) = 2 \times 5 = 10$

25. $\frac{2}{7} \times 14 =$ ____________

26. $\frac{7}{8} \times 40 =$ ____________

27. $\frac{2}{3} \times 12 =$ ____________

28. $\frac{3}{6} \times 60 =$ ____________

29. $\frac{4}{9} \times 63 =$ ____________

30. $\frac{2}{3} \times 27 =$ ____________

31. $\frac{3}{4} \times 10 =$ ____________

32. $\frac{2}{5} \times 19 =$ ____________

► Solve Word Problems

Show your work.

33. Carlo saw 35 fish at the aquarium. $\frac{1}{5}$ of them were clownfish. How many fish were clownfish?

____

34. Gayle has 36 marbles. $\frac{2}{6}$ of the marbles are green. How many marbles are green?

____

35. Hayden is stacking 24 books into piles. He is putting $\frac{2}{8}$ of the books into each pile. How many books are in each pile?

____

36. Sarah had 54 carrot sticks. She put $\frac{2}{9}$ of the carrot sticks onto each plate. How many carrot sticks are on each plate?

____

37. **On the Back** Explain in your own words how to find a fraction of a whole number. Give an example.

Name Date

5–17 Class Activity

Name ____________________ Date ____________

▶ Compare Lengths

Asha made a long thin snake out of clay. Her little brother Sam made a short fat snake.

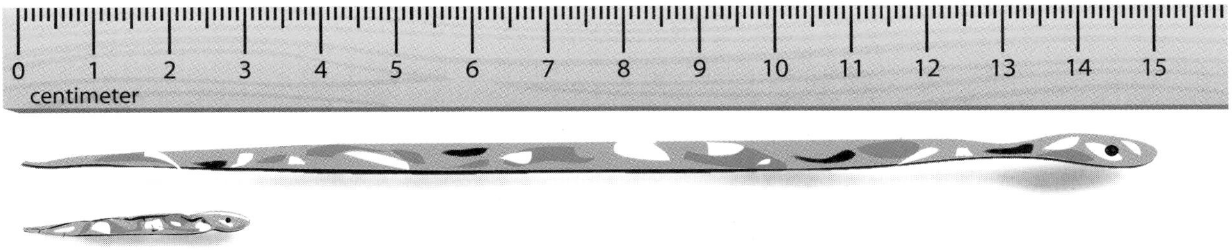

Complete these addition comparison statements. In the second blank, insert the word *shorter* or *longer*.

1. Asha's snake is ________ cm ________ than Sam's snake.

2. Sam's snake is ________ cm ________ than Asha's snake.

Now complete these statements to compare the snakes with multiplication.

3. Asha's snake is ________ as long as Sam's snake.

4. Sam's snake is ________ as long as Asha's snake.

5. Draw comparison bars to show the multiplication comparisons.

Name ______________________ Date ______________

▶ Bar Graphs

The bar graph below shows how many people went on the seven most popular rides at an amusement park.

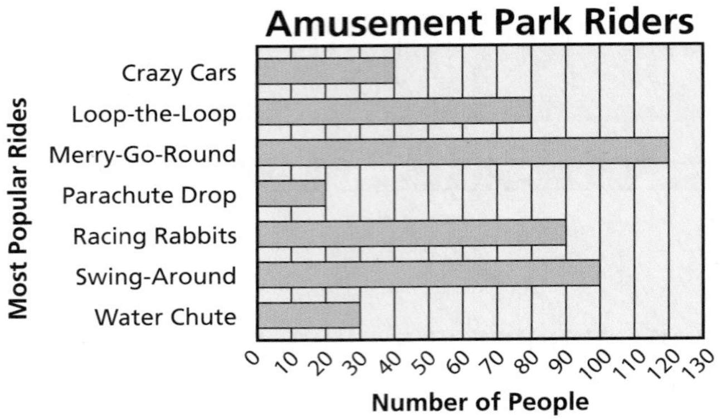

6. Find two pairs of values on the graph that are exact multiples of each other. For each pair, draw and label comparison bars and write two equations (with letters) to show the comparison. An example is shown below:

Loop-the-Loop (l)

Crazy Cars (c)

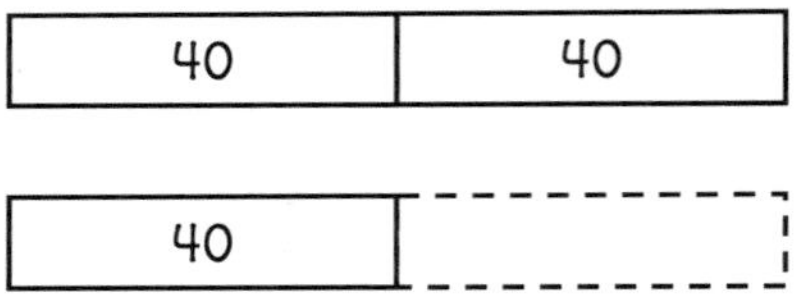

$l = 2 \times c$ $80 = 2 \times 40$

$c = \frac{1}{2} \times l$ $40 = \frac{1}{2} \times 80$

Name ______________________________ Date ____________

▶ Leading and Misleading Language

To solve comparison word problems, first decide which is the large amount and which is the small amount.

There are 7 fiddle players at the country music festival. There are $\frac{1}{5}$ as many fiddle players as guitar players. How many guitar players are there?

7. Draw comparison bars to see the problem. Then write the other multiplication comparison sentence.

   There are ______ guitar players.

   ____

   ____

   ____

8. Solve the problems on page 364. Then write your own multiplication comparison word problem with misleading language.

   ____

   ____

   ____

   ____

   ____

Name ______________________ Date ______________

▶ Other Comparison Problems

Solve. Draw comparison bars if you need to. Then write the other multiplication comparison sentence.

Show your work.

9. Frank made 10 goals at the hockey game. He made 5 times as many goals as Josie made. How many goals did Josie make?

   Josie made ______ goals.

   ____

   ____

10. Su-Lin has $15. Zane has $\frac{1}{3}$ as much money as Su-Lin. How much money does Zane have?

    Zane has ______.

    ____

    ____

11. On a cattle ranch, 32 calves were born this year. That was 4 times as many calves as were born last year. How many calves were born last year?

    ______ calves were born last year.

    ____

    ____

    ____

12. Ella practiced piano 3 hours this week. She spent $\frac{1}{6}$ as much time practicing as Ramón did. How many hours did Ramón practice?

    Ramón practiced ______ hours this week.

    ____

    ____

5–18 Class Activity

Name ______________________________ Date ____________

▶ Discuss Number Lines

The number line below shows the fourths between 0 and 1. Discuss how the number line is like and unlike the fraction bar above it.

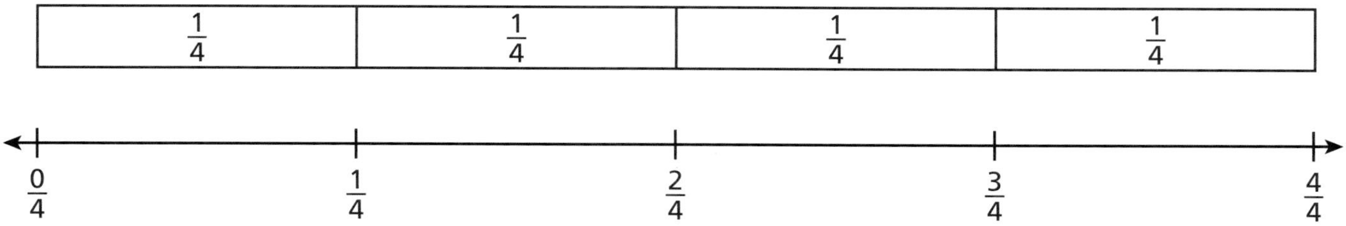

These number lines are divided to show different fractions.

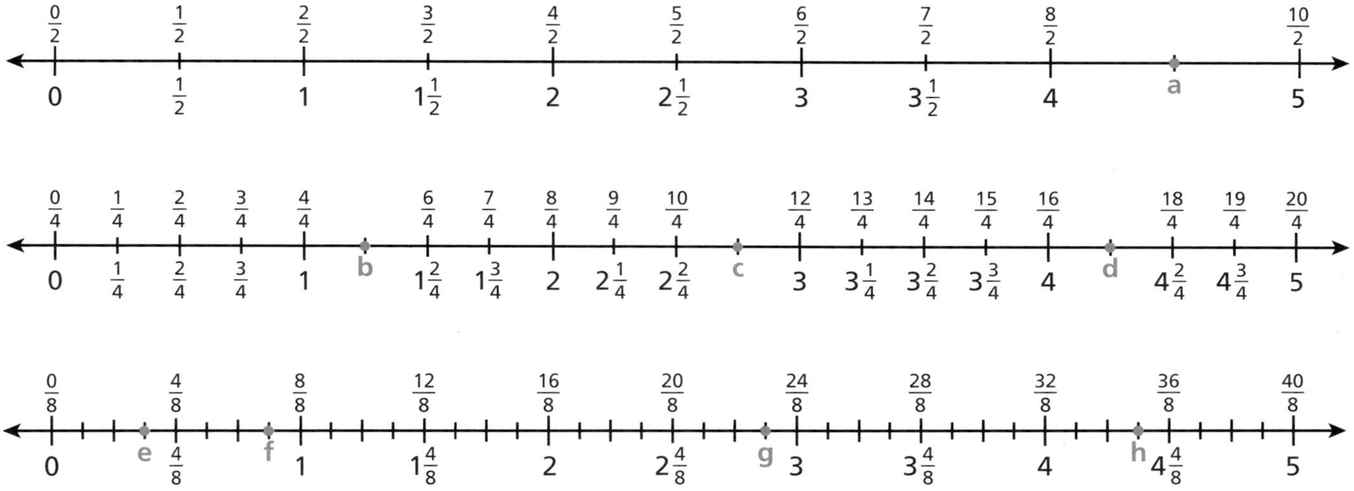

Complete the equivalent fraction equations.

1. $\frac{1}{2} = \frac{}{4}$
2. $\frac{1}{4} = \frac{}{8}$
3. $\frac{6}{8} = \frac{}{4}$
4. $\frac{2}{4} = \frac{}{8}$

▶ Identify Points

5. Write the fraction or mixed number for each lettered point above.

a. ________ b. ________ c. ________ d. ________

e. ________ f. ________ g. ________ h. ________

5–18 Class Activity

Name ________________________ Date ____________

▶ Number Lines for Thirds, Sixths, and Ninths

Tell how many equal parts are between zero and 1. Then write fraction labels above the equal parts.

6. ______

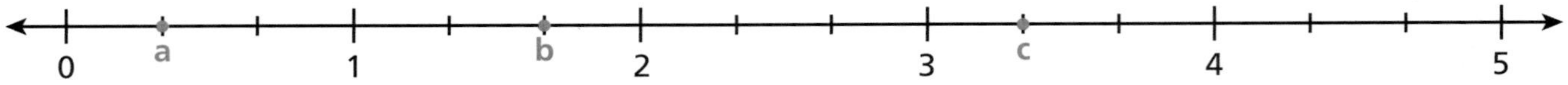

7. ______

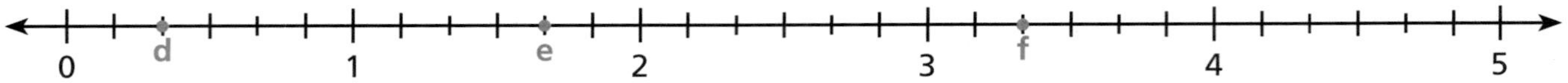

8. ______

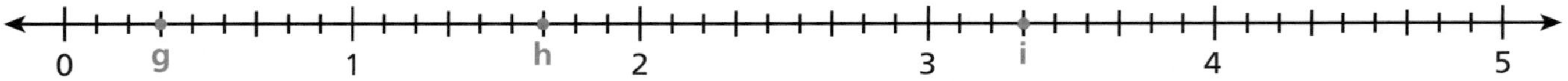

▶ Identify Points

9. Write the fraction or mixed number for each lettered point above. Describe any patterns you see with the class.

a. ______ b. ______ c. ______

d. ______ e. ______ f. ______

g. ______ h. ______ i. ______

For each fraction or mixed number, label that point on the number line with its letter.

10. 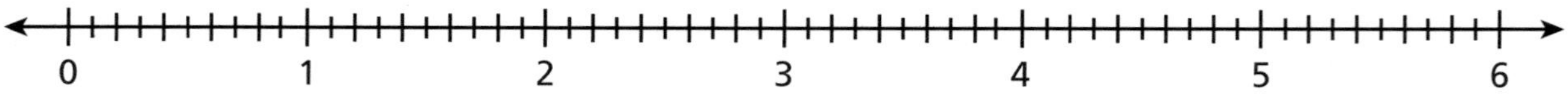

a. $\frac{1}{5}$ b. $\frac{7}{10}$ c. $1\frac{2}{5}$ d. $2\frac{1}{2}$

e. $3\frac{3}{10}$ f. $4\frac{2}{5}$ g. $4\frac{9}{10}$ h. $5\frac{1}{2}$

Name ______________________________ Date ______________

▶ Compare and Order Fractions

Write >, <, or = to make each statement true.

1. $\frac{3}{8}$ ◯ $\frac{1}{4}$
2. $\frac{4}{9}$ ◯ $\frac{1}{2}$
3. $\frac{2}{6}$ ◯ $\frac{3}{9}$
4. $\frac{5}{6}$ ◯ $\frac{11}{12}$
5. $\frac{1}{4}$ ◯ $\frac{}{6}$
6. $\frac{3}{7}$ ◯ $\frac{3}{5}$
7. $\frac{1}{9}$ ◯ $\frac{1}{8}$
8. $\frac{6}{7}$ ◯ $\frac{6}{8}$

Write the fractions in order from largest to smallest.

9. $\frac{1}{7}, \frac{1}{2}, \frac{1}{5}$ ____________
10. $\frac{3}{8}, \frac{3}{6}, \frac{3}{10}$ ____________
11. $\frac{5}{9}, \frac{5}{6}, \frac{5}{7}$ ____________
12. $\frac{1}{9}, \frac{1}{4}, \frac{1}{7}$ ____________

▶ Add and Subtract Fractions

Add each pair of fractions. Then subtract the smaller fraction from the larger fraction.

13. $\frac{4}{7}, \frac{2}{7}$
14. $\frac{2}{6}, \frac{3}{6}$
15. $\frac{2}{3}, \frac{4}{5}$
16. $\frac{3}{8}, \frac{3}{4}$
17. $5\frac{1}{3}, 2\frac{5}{6}$
18. $4\frac{3}{5}, 9\frac{1}{2}$

▶ Simplify Fractions

Write the simplest equivalent fraction.

19. $\frac{21}{28} =$ ________
20. $\frac{12}{36} =$ ________
21. $\frac{42}{48} =$ ________
22. $\frac{10}{45} =$ ________
23. $\frac{8}{18} =$ ________
24. $\frac{24}{30} =$ ________

Name ________________________ Date ____________

► Multiply Fractions and Whole Numbers

Multiply.

25. $\frac{1}{7} \times 21 =$ ______
26. $25 \times \frac{3}{5} =$ ______
27. $56 \times \frac{3}{8} =$ ______
28. $\frac{1}{4} \times 36 =$ ______
29. $36 \times \frac{5}{9} =$ ______
30. $\frac{2}{3} \times 27 =$ ______

Solve each problem.

Show your work.

31. Mario has 18 pencils. He sharpens $\frac{1}{6}$ of them before class. How many does he sharpen?

____

32. Jason had 45 marbles. He gave $\frac{1}{5}$ of them to a friend. How many did he give away? How many does he have left?

____

____

33. Janie's book is 124 pages long. She is on page 63. Is she more or less than halfway finished with her book? Tell how you know.

____

____

34. Michelle has 4 textbooks. Each weighs $\frac{5}{8}$ pound. What is the total weight of her textbooks?

____

35. Label the point for each fraction or mixed number with the corresponding letter.

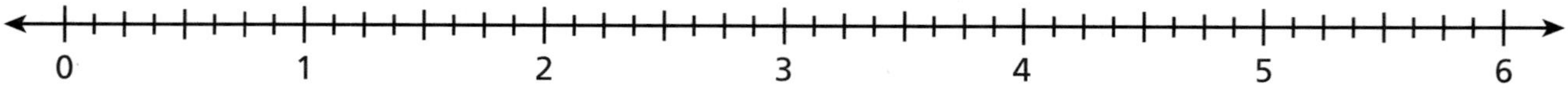

a. $\frac{3}{8}$ b. $\frac{3}{4}$ c. $1\frac{1}{2}$ d. $2\frac{1}{8}$ e. $2\frac{7}{8}$

f. $3\frac{1}{4}$ g. $3\frac{5}{8}$ h. $4\frac{2}{4}$ i. $4\frac{6}{8}$ j. $5\frac{1}{4}$

U5–Test
Unit Test

Name ______________________ Date ____________

Simplify each fraction.

1. $\frac{8 \div}{28 \div} =$

2. $\frac{24 \div}{40 \div} =$

3. Write 5 fractions equivalent to $\frac{1}{3}$.

_______ _______ _______ _______ _______

Write < or > to make a true statement.

4. $\frac{3}{7}$ ◯ $\frac{3}{5}$

5. $\frac{2}{5}$ ◯ $\frac{1}{2}$

6. $\frac{3}{4}$ ◯ $\frac{2}{3}$

7. Label the point for each fraction or mixed number with the corresponding letter.

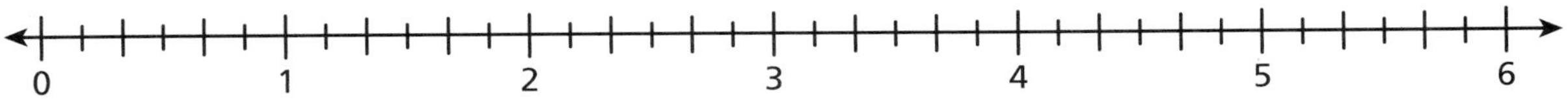

a. $1\frac{2}{3}$ b. $5\frac{1}{6}$ c. $\frac{1}{2}$ d. $3\frac{2}{6}$ e. $4\frac{1}{3}$

Add or subtract.

8. $\frac{3}{7} + \frac{2}{7} =$

9. $\frac{5}{6} - \frac{1}{4} =$

10. $\frac{1}{8} + \frac{3}{4} =$

11. $3\frac{1}{2} - \frac{3}{4} =$

12. $4\frac{3}{5} + 2\frac{4}{5} =$

Name ____________________ Date ____________

Multiply.

13. $4 \times \frac{1}{5} =$ ________

14. $15 \times \frac{2}{3} =$ ________

15. $\frac{1}{6} \times 42 =$ ________

16. $\frac{3}{8} \times 24 =$ ________

Solve.

Show your work.

17. Ryan studied math for 2 hours last weekend. He spent $\frac{1}{4}$ as much time studying as Clair. How much time did Clair spend studying math?

____

18. Tara earns $6 per hour babysitting. Dawn earns $\frac{1}{3}$ as much doing chores. How much does Dawn earn per hour?

____

Suppose you spin this spinner once.

19. What is the probability the spinner will land in a space with stripes?

____

20. **Extended Response** What is the probability the spinner will land in a space with dots? Explain your reasoning.

____

____

____

E–1 Class Activity

Name ______________________ Date ____________

Vocabulary
circle
sphere
radius

▶ Spheres and Circles

Circles are flat and have two dimensions. **Spheres** are round solids and have three dimensions.

Write *circle* or *sphere* for each picture.

1. 

____

2. 
____

3. 
____

4. 
____

5. 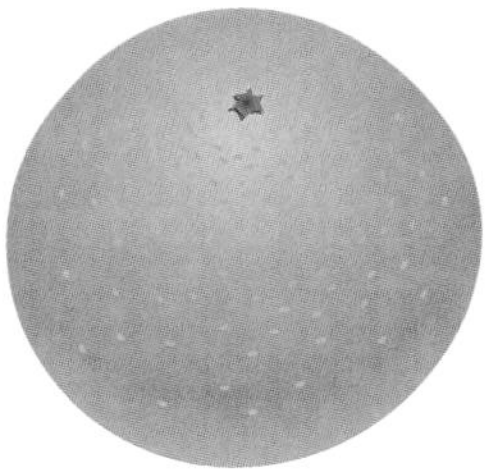
____

6. 
____

7. How are circles and spheres alike? How are they different?

____

____

____

____

8. What is the **radius** of a circle? What is the radius of a sphere?

____

____

____

____

Name ________________________ Date ____________

Vocabulary

cube surface area
face net

▶ Cubes

A **cube** is a solid made of congruent **faces** that are square.

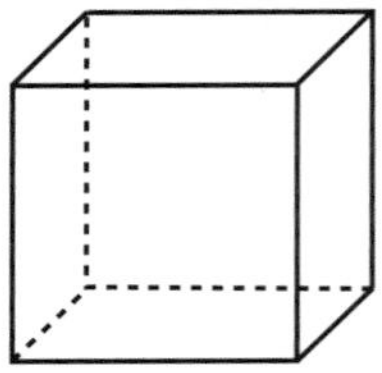

9. How many faces does a cube have? ____________

10. Name a real-world object that is shaped like a cube.

____

____

11. Each edge of a cube measures 3 cm. What is the total area of all of the faces? ____________

12. Why is the total area of its faces called the **surface area** of the cube?

____

A **net** is a flat or plane figure that can be folded to form a solid. The net at the right can be folded to form a cube.

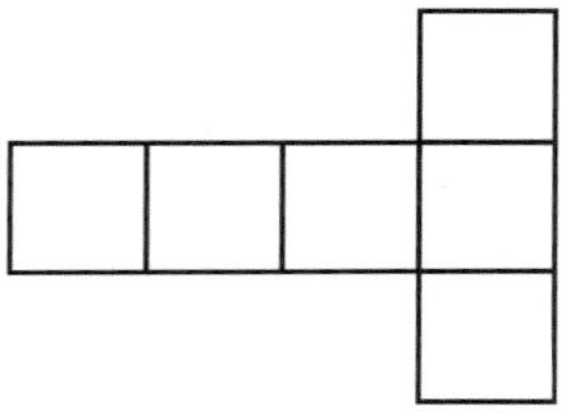

13. On a separate sheet of paper, draw several different nets for a cube.

▶ Make Stacks of Cubes

How many cubes can you see?
How many cubes can you *not* see?
How many cubes are in each stack?

14.

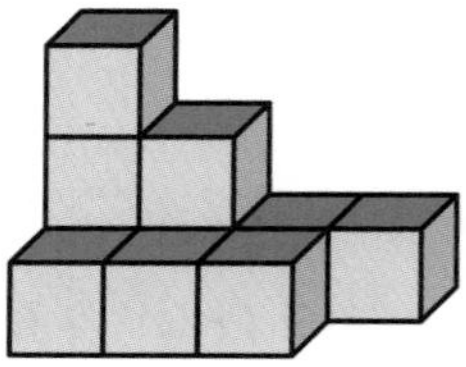

15.

16.

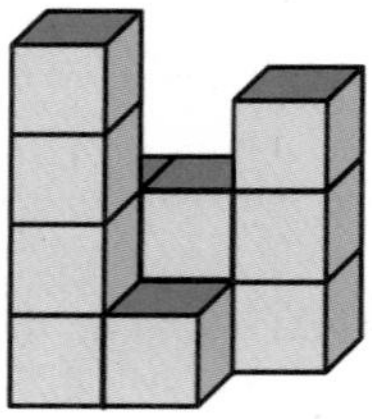

	14.	15.	16.
Cubes you can see:	______	______	______
Cubes you cannot see:	______	______	______
Total number of cubes:	______	______	______

Family Letter

Dear Family,

This unit is about solid figures, such as cubes, spheres, prisms, and cylinders.

During this unit, your child will learn how to recognize and name solid figures, and how to describe their characteristics. Your child will be working with the figures shown below.

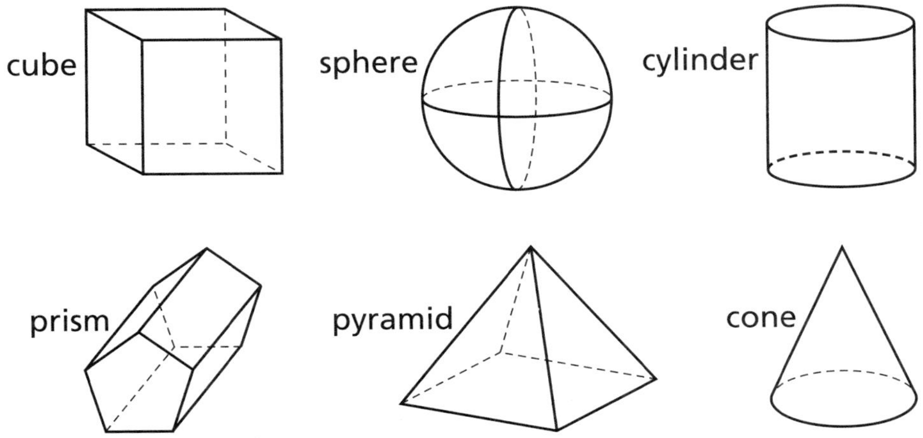

The next unit involves fractions. As students work with fractions, they will need to multiply and divide. If your child needs practice with multiplication and division, you can help by providing him or her with as many opportunities as possible to do so. If you need practice materials or if you have any questions, please call or write to me.

Sincerely,
Your child's teacher

Carta a la familia

Estimada familia:

Esta unidad trata figuras geométricas, como cubos, esferas, prismas y cilindros.

Al estudiar esta unidad su niño aprenderá a reconocer y nombrar figuras geométricas y a describir sus características. Su niño trabajará con las figuras que se muestran a continuación.

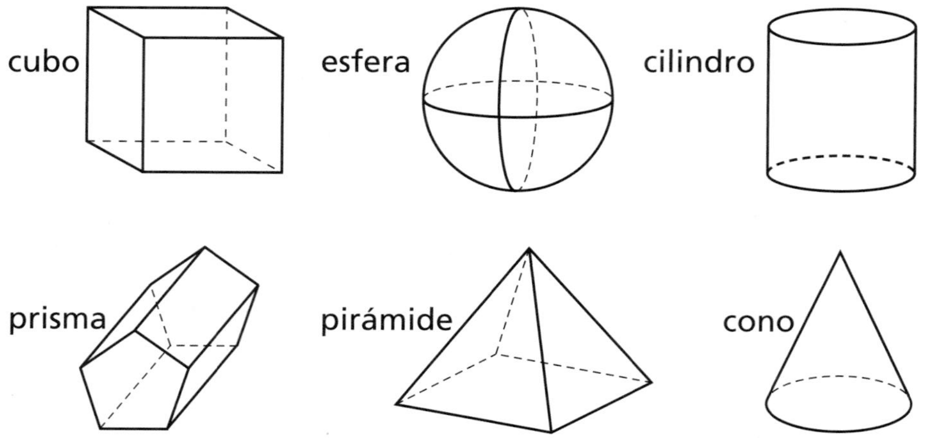

La siguiente unidad trata las fracciones. Cuando los estudiantes trabajen con fracciones, tendrán que multiplicar y dividir. Si a su niño le hace falta prácticar la multiplicación y la división, usted puede ayudarlo ofreciéndole todas las oportunidades de practicar que pueda. Si necesita materiales de práctica o si tiene preguntas, por favor comuníquese conmigo.

Atentamente,
El maestro de su niño

E–2

Class Activity

Name ______________________________ Date ______________

Vocabulary
prism base triangular prism

▶ Make a Prism

A prism is a solid figure with two congruent opposite faces called bases. Follow the steps below to make a triangular prism. The bases of your prism will be equilateral triangles whose sides measure 8 cm.

1. Measure and cut out two congruent bases for your triangular prism.

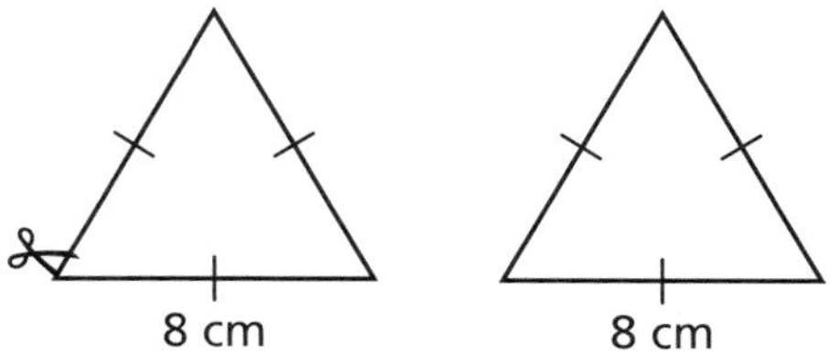

2. Calculate the perimeter of one base.

$$8 + 8 + 8 = 24 \text{ cm}$$

$$3 \times 8 = 24 \text{ cm}$$

3. Cut a sheet of paper so that its length is the same as the perimeter of a base.

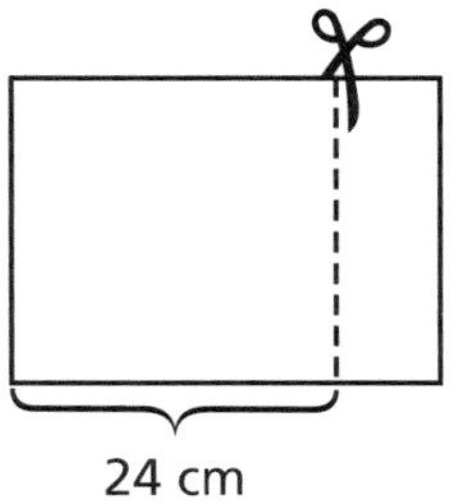

4. Cut the paper to a height of your choice. This picture shows a height of 16 cm.

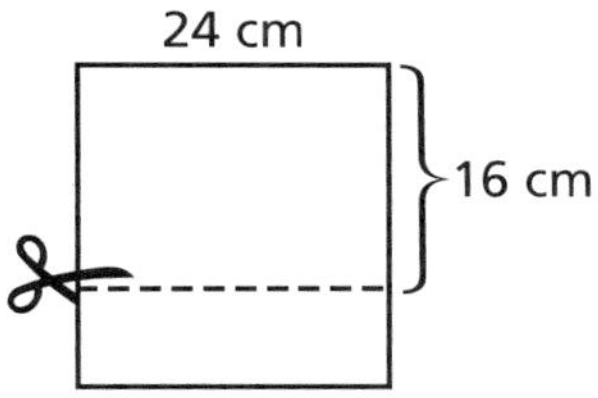

Hint: Don't cut your height too short.

5. Mark lines on the paper that divide the length into three equal parts.

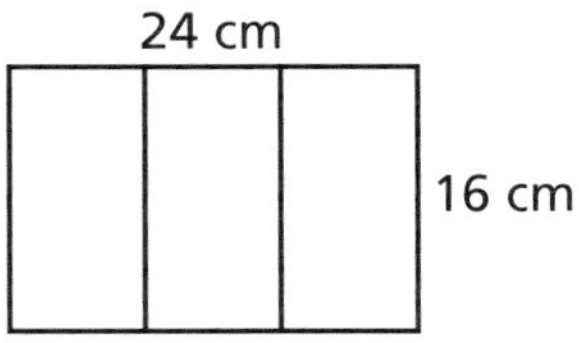

For a length of 24 cm, draw lines at 8 cm and 16 cm.

6. Fold along the lines and tape together the edges to make a prism.

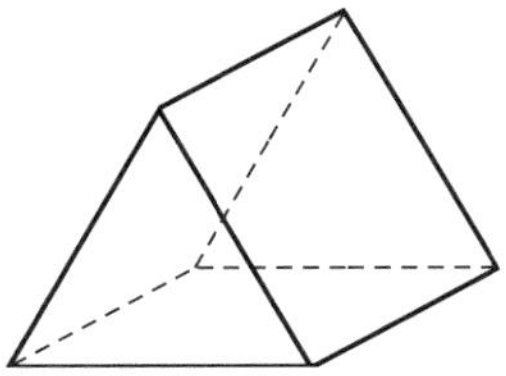

triangular prism

E–2
Class Activity

Name ______________________ Date ____________

Vocabulary
cylinder

▶ Name Prisms

Name the shape of the base and use it to name the prism.

7. 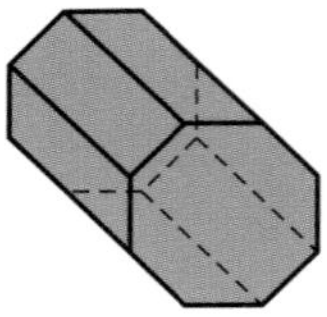

8. 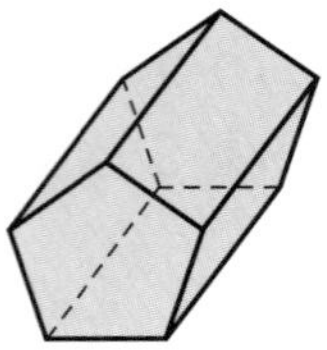

9. 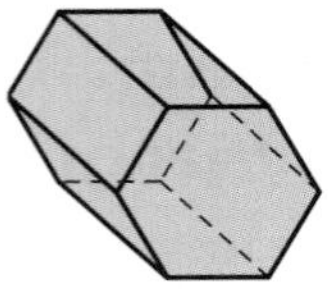

10. 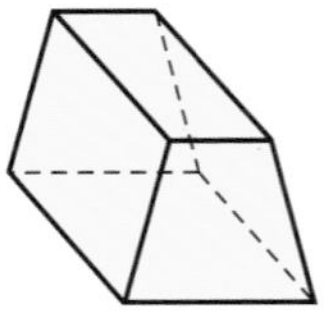

11. 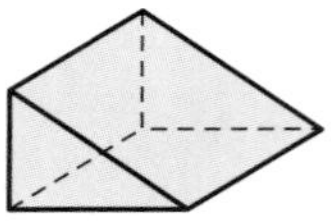

12. 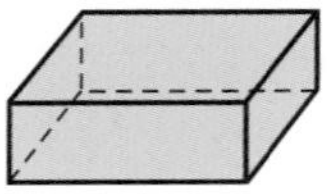

▶ Recognize Cylinders

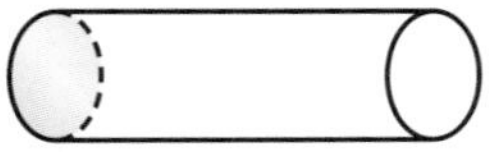

A **cylinder** is another type of solid figure.

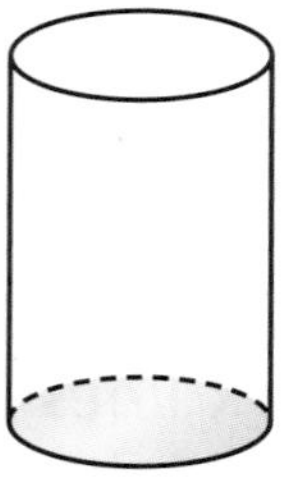

13. List some examples of real-world cylinders.

14. How are cylinders and prisms alike?

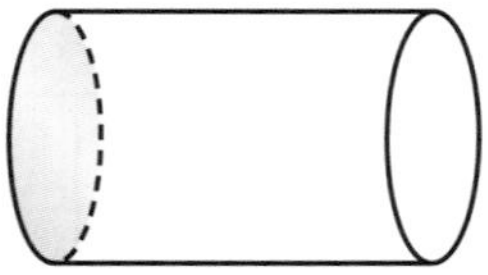

15. How are cylinders and prisms different?

Name ____________________ Date __________

Vocabulary
surface area

▶ Find Surface Area

Name each prism. Write the area of each face on the net. Add the areas to find the surface area of each prism.

16.

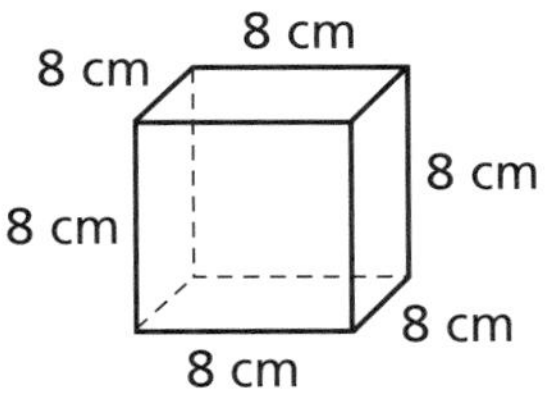

____

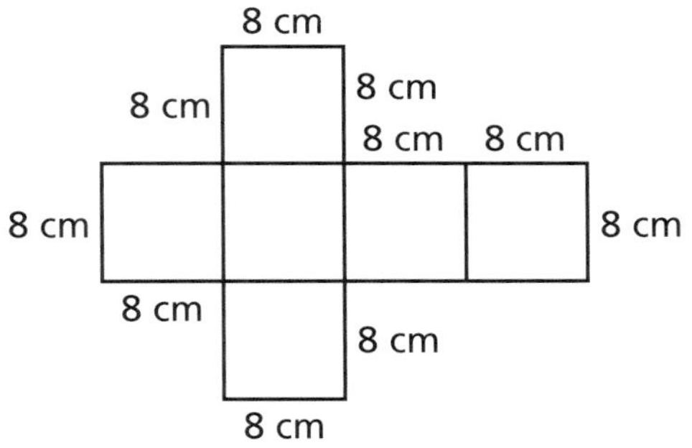

____

17.

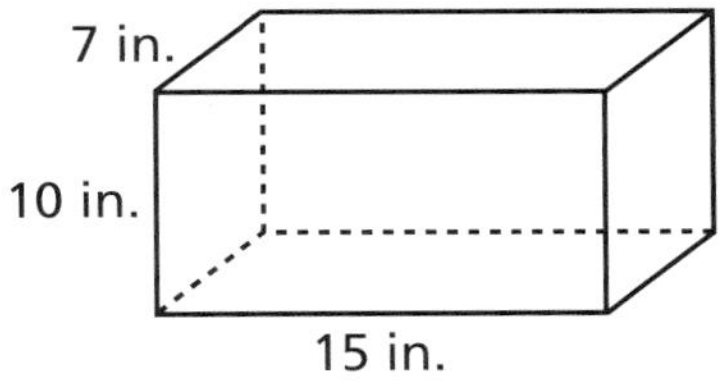

____

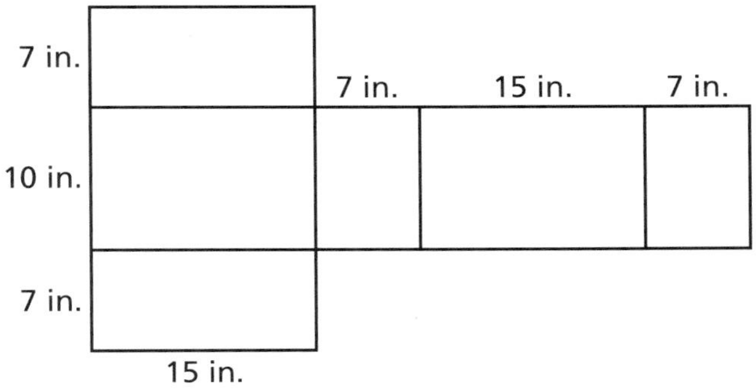

____

18.

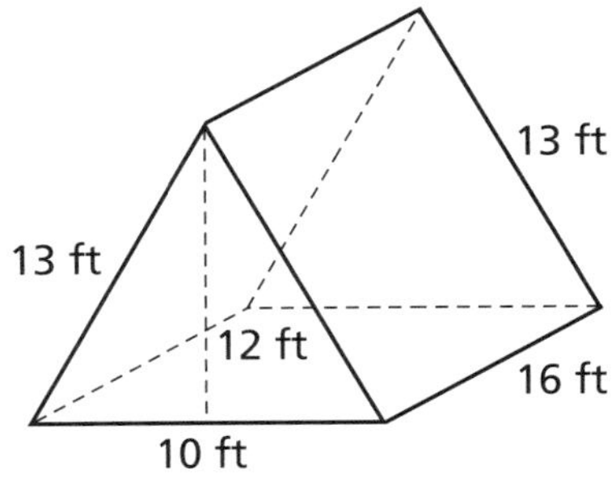

____

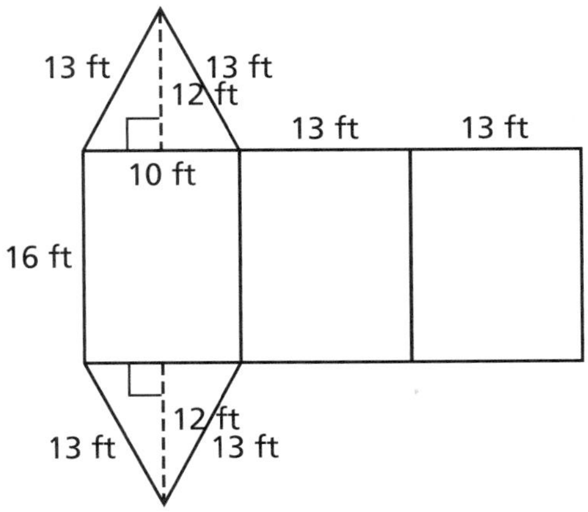

____

19. How can you find the surface area of any prism?

____

____

Name ______________________ Date ______________

Going Further

▶ Match Nets and Solids

Match each net to a solid.

1. 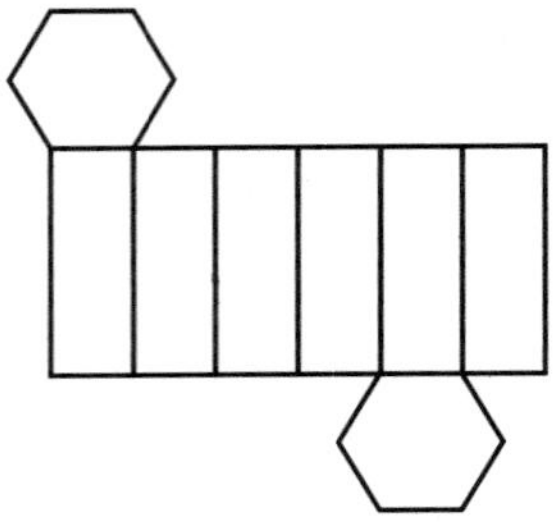

2. 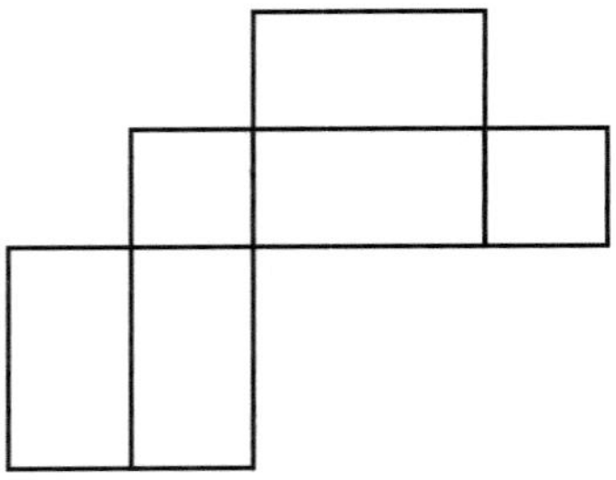

3. 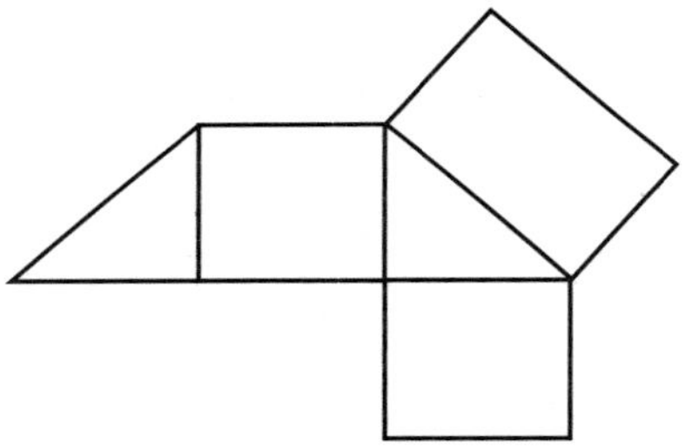

4. 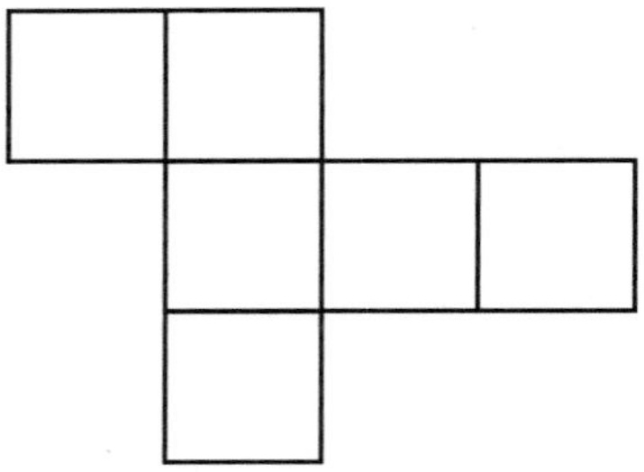

5. 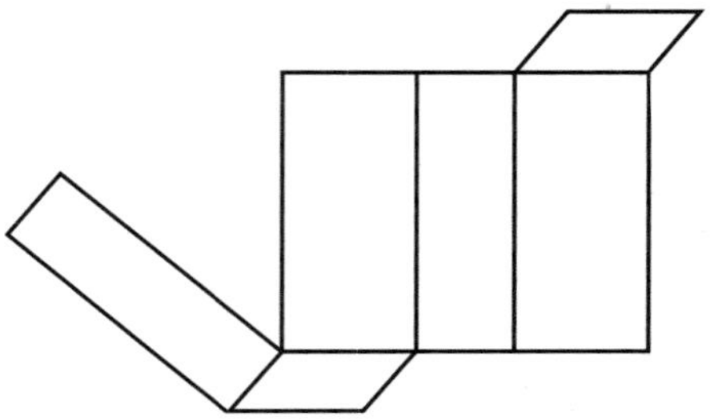

A 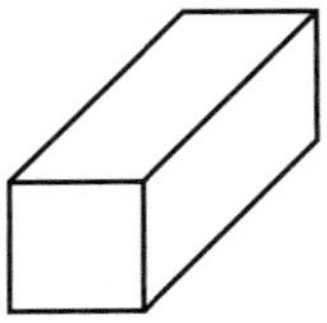

B 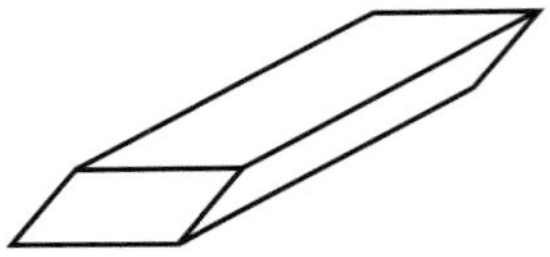

C 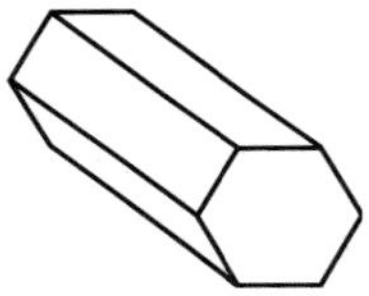

D 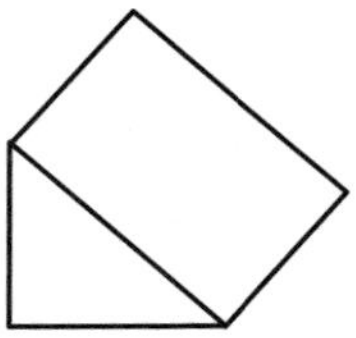

E 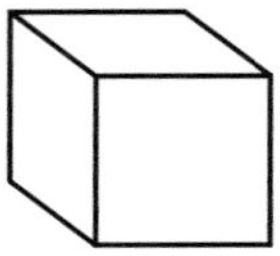

E–3

Class Activity

Name ______________________ Date ______________

Vocabulary
face
edge
vertex (vertices)

▶ Discuss Solid Figures

Name each solid.

1. 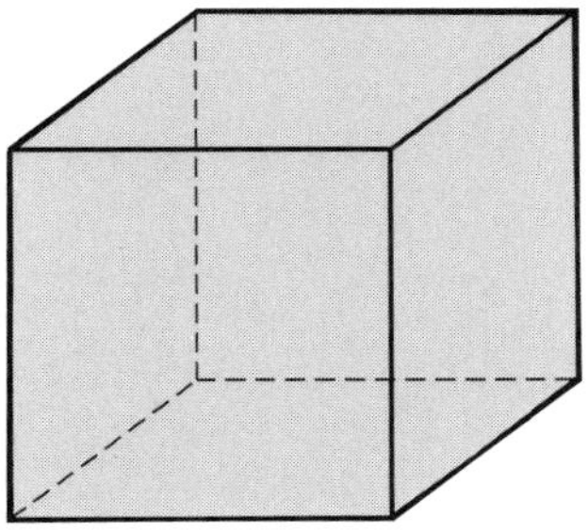

____

2. 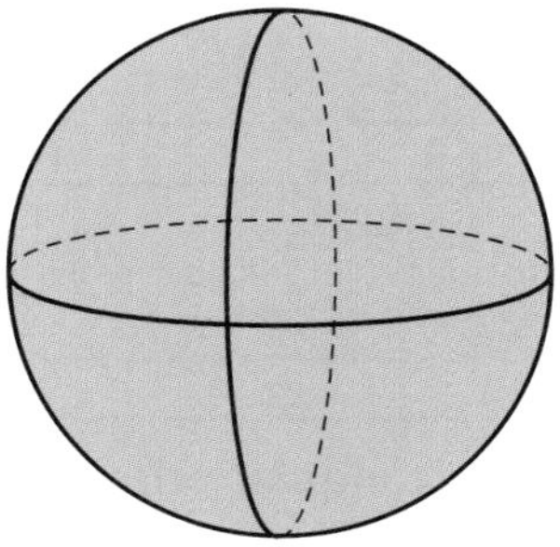

____

3. 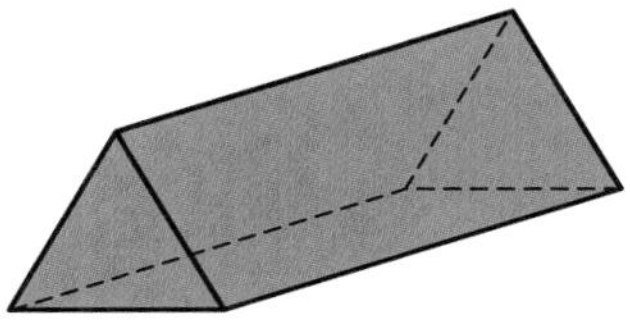

____

4. 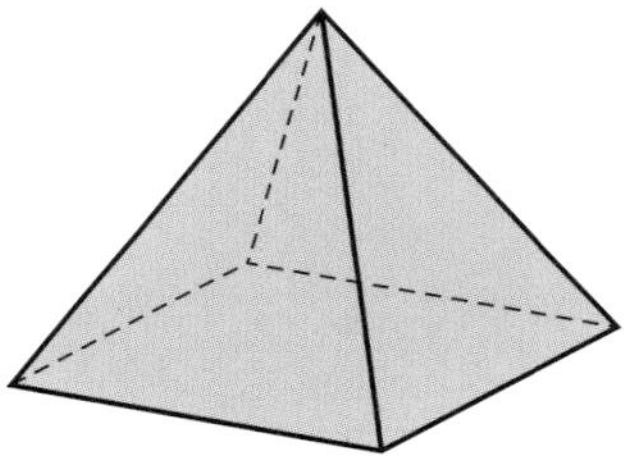

____

5. 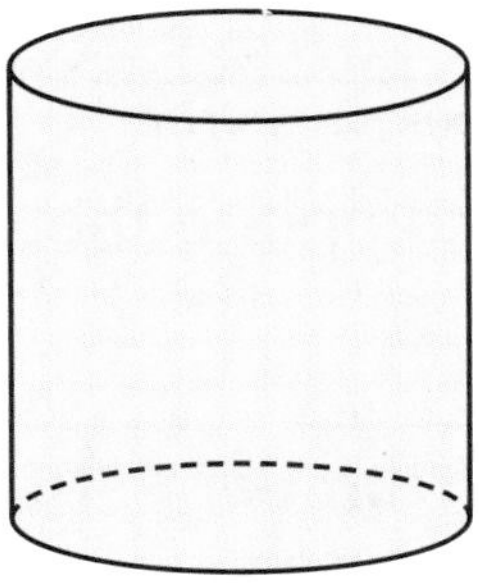

____

6. 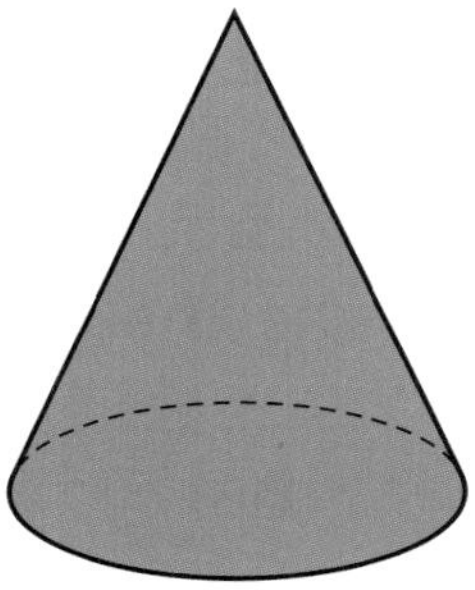

____

▶ Discuss Faces, Edges, and Vertices

Write the number of faces, edges, and vertices for each solid.

7. 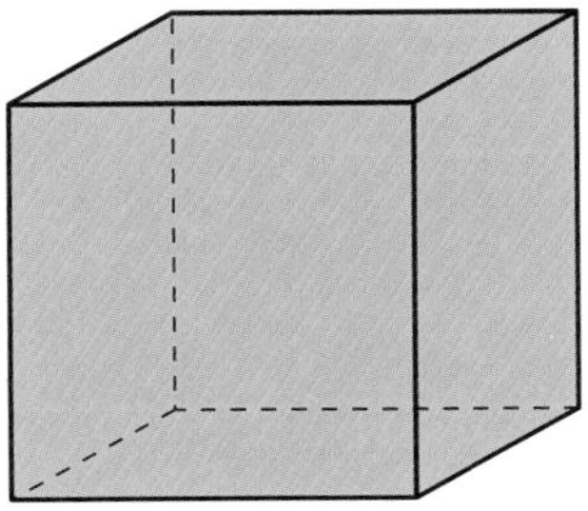

____
____
____

8. 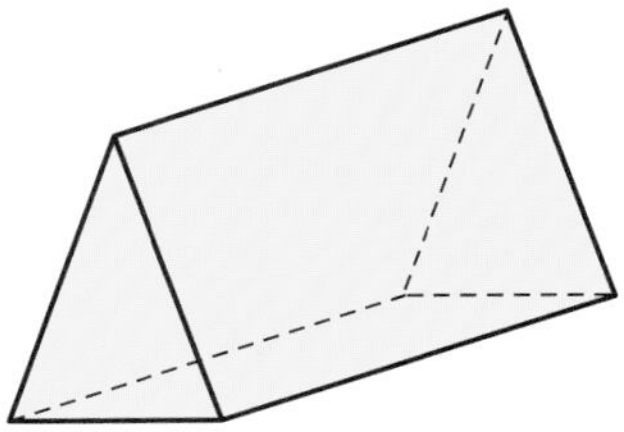

____
____
____

9. 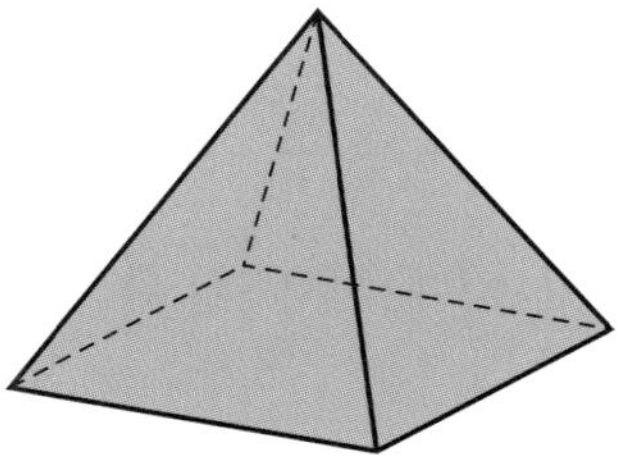

____
____
____

E–3 Name _______________ Date _______________

Going Further

▶ Faces, Edges, and Vertices

A decagon has 10 sides. You can use patterns to predict the number of faces, edges, and vertices of a prism with a decagon as a base.

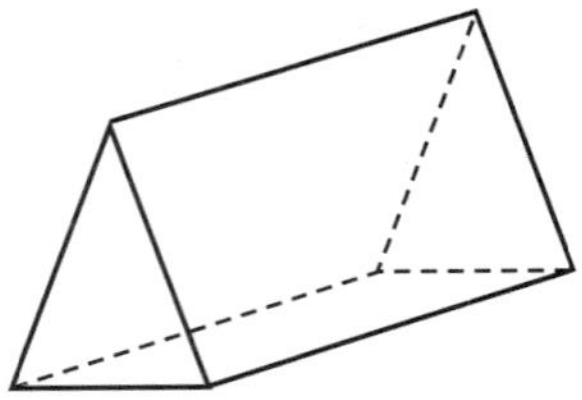

triangular prism

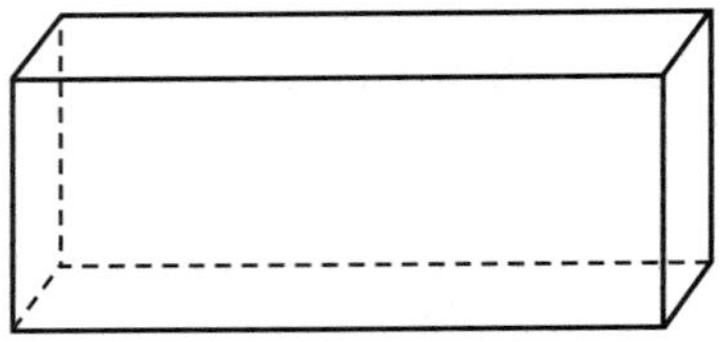

rectangular prism

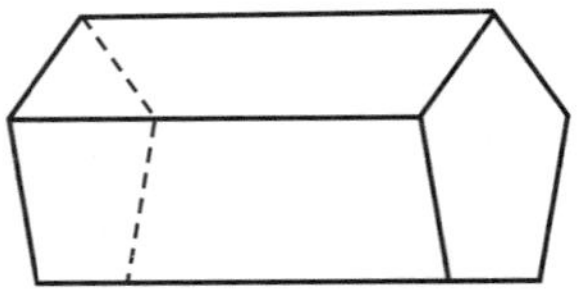

pentagonal prism

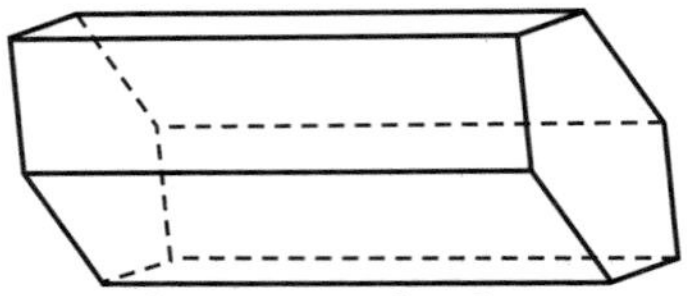

hexagonal prism

1. Use the prisms you see above to complete the next three rows of the chart.

Type of Prism	Number of Sides on Base	Number of Faces	Number of Edges	Number of Vertices
Triangular	3	5	9	6
Rectangular				
Pentagonal				
Hexagonal				
Decagonal				

2. What pattern do you notice in the number of faces?

____

3. What pattern do you notice in the number of edges?

____

4. What pattern do you notice in the number of vertices?

____

5. Use the patterns you noticed to complete the last row of the chart.

Name ____________________ Date ____________

Name the solid.

1.

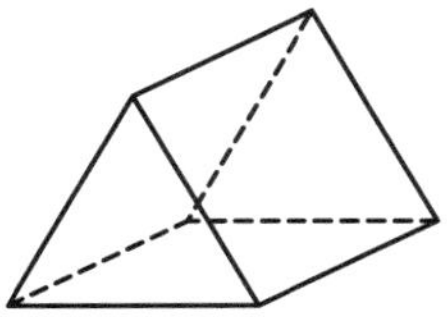

____

2.

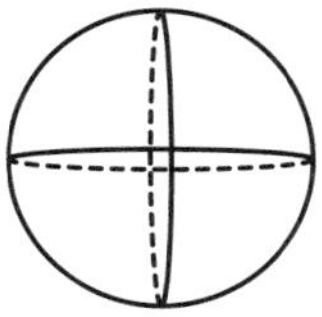

____

3.

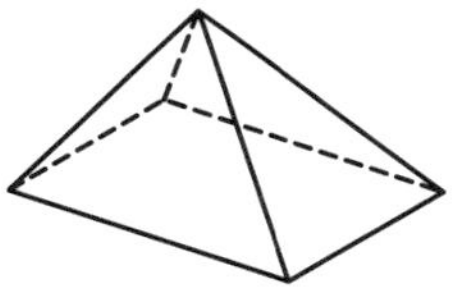

____

4.

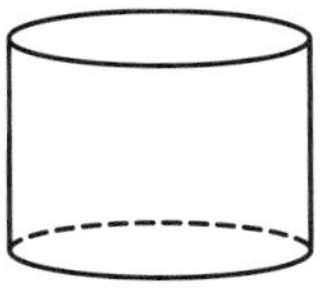

____

Find the surface area of the prism.

Show your work.

5.

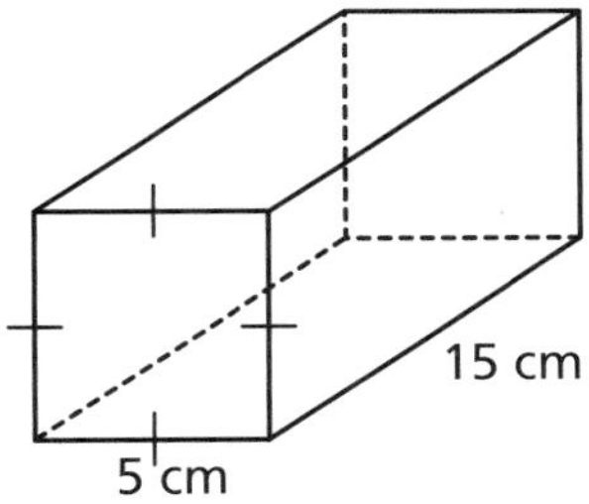

surface area = ______________________

6.

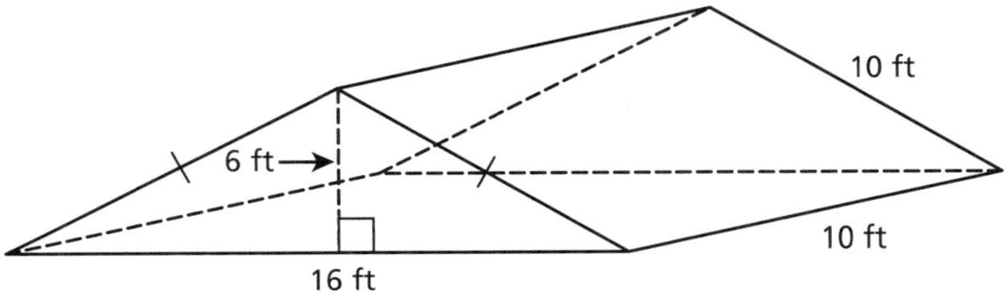

surface area = ______________________

Name ____________________ Date ____________________

Name the solid that you can make from the net.

7.

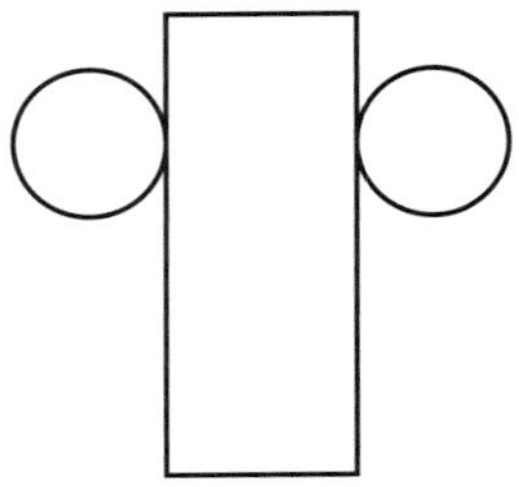

____

8.

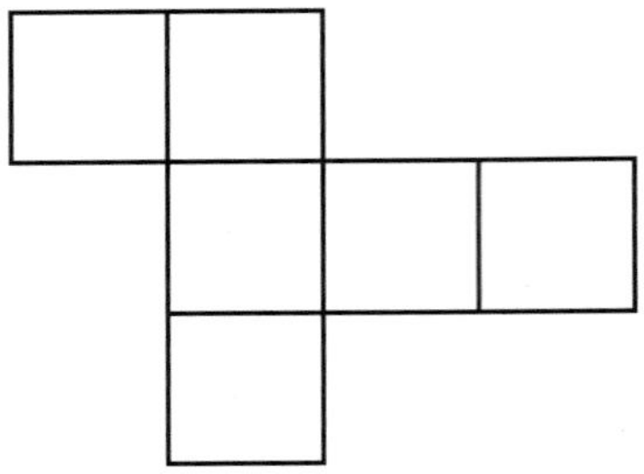

____

9.

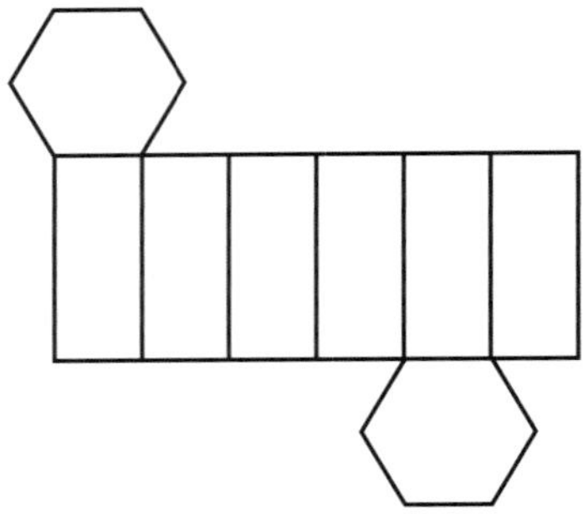

____

10. **Extended Response** How are a cylinder and a triangular prism alike? How are they different? List two reasons for each.

____

____

____

____

____

____

Name ______________________ Date ______

Vocabulary
tenths
hundredths
decimal number

▶ Understand Tenths and Hundredths

Answer the questions about the bars and number lines below.

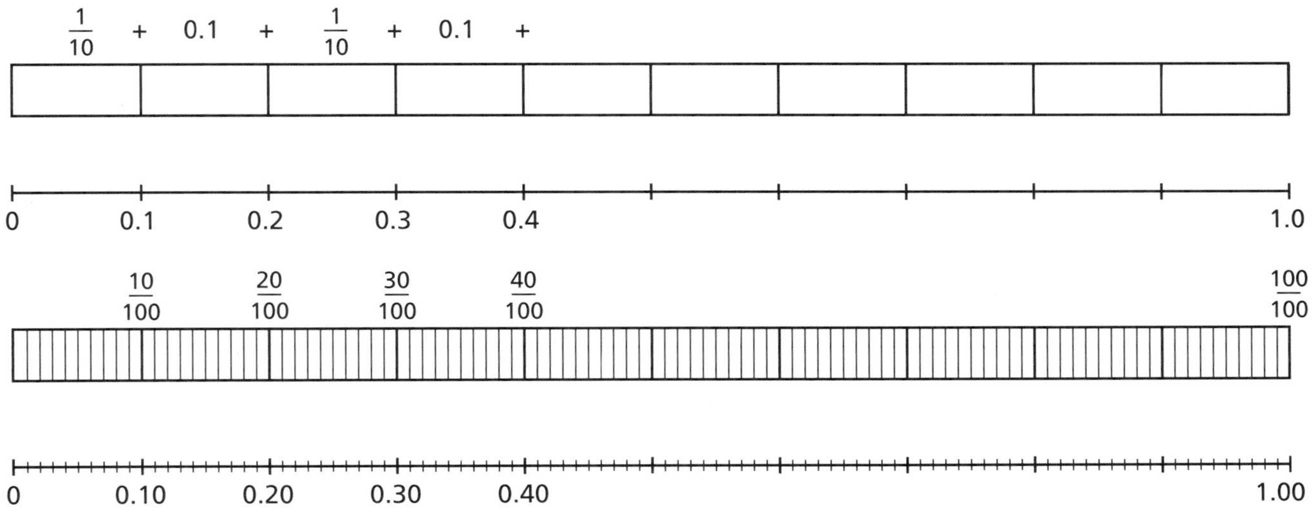

1. The bars show **tenths** and **hundredths**. Finish labeling the bars and number lines using fractions and **decimal numbers**.

2. Use what you know about fractions and about money (a dime = one tenth of a dollar and a penny = one hundredth of a dollar) to explain why 3 tenths is the same as 30 hundredths.

____

____

____

3. Tenths are larger than hundredths even though 10 is a smaller number than 100. Explain why this is true.

____

____

6–1 Class Activity

Name ______________________ Date ______________

▶ Practice Writing Decimal Numbers

Write these numbers in decimal form.

4. 8 tenths ________ 5. 6 hundredths ________ 6. 35 hundredths ________

7. $\frac{92}{100}$ ________ 8. $\frac{2}{10}$ ________ 9. $\frac{9}{100}$ ________

▶ Use Decimal Numbers in Story Situations

Answer the questions below.

In the little town of Silver there are 100 people. Four are left-handed.

10. What decimal number shows the fraction of the people who are left-handed?

____

11. What decimal number shows the fraction of the people who are right-handed?

____

There are 10 children playing volleyball, and 6 of them are boys.

12. What decimal number shows the fraction of the players that are boys?

____

13. What decimal number shows the fraction of the players that are girls?

____

▶ Use Decimal Numbers for Coin Amounts

Complete the table.

	Name of Coin	Fraction of a Dollar	Decimal Part of a Dollar
14.	Penny	$\frac{\quad}{100}$	
15.	Nickel	$\frac{\quad}{100}$ =	
16.	Dime	$\frac{\quad}{100}$ =	
17.	Quarter	$\frac{\quad}{100}$ =	

Family Letter

Dear Family,

In this unit, your child will be introduced to decimal numbers. Students will explore decimal numbers by using bars divided into tenths and hundredths. They will relate decimals to fractions, which are also used to represent parts of a whole.

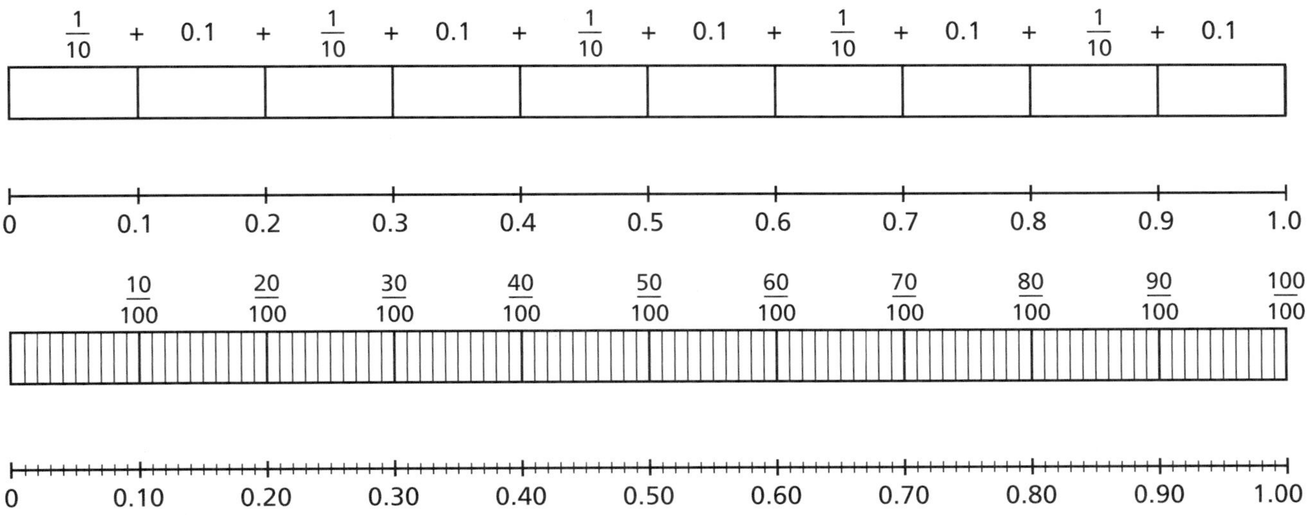

Students will also learn to combine whole numbers with decimals. They will work with numbers such as 1.72 and 12.9. They will round decimal numbers. For example, 0.87 rounded to the nearest tenth is 0.9. Students will also compare decimal numbers with other decimal numbers and with fractions. They will compare decimal numbers with fractions as well.

Students will apply their understanding of decimal concepts when

Adding Decimals

3.9 + 2.21

$$\begin{array}{r} \overset{1}{3}.9 \\ +\ 2.21 \\ \hline 6.11 \end{array}$$

Be sure to remind your child to line up the decimals.

Comparing Decimals

6.8 ◯ 3.42 6.80 (>) 3.42

Adding a zero makes the numbers easier to compare.

they add or compare decimals.

Please call if you have any questions or comments.

Thank you.

Sincerely,
Your child's teacher

Carta a la familia

Estimada familia:

En esta unidad su niño verá por primera vez los números decimales. Los estudiantes explorarán los números decimales usando barras divididas en décimas y centésimas. También relacionarán los decimales con las fracciones, ya que las fracciones también representan partes de un entero.

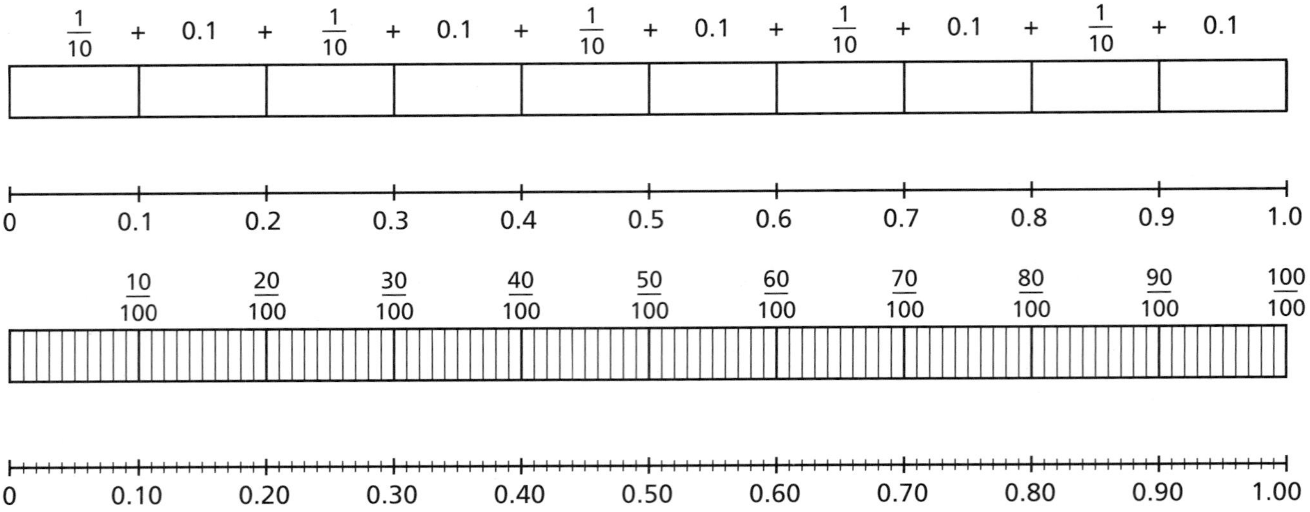

Los estudiantes también aprenderán a combinar números enteros con decimales. Trabajarán con números como 1.72 y 12.9, y redondearán números decimales. Por ejemplo, 0.87 redondeado a la décima más cercana es 0.9. Los estudiantes también compararán los números decimales con otros números decimales. Además, compararán números decimales con fracciones. Por ejemplo, 0.45 es un poco menos de la mitad y $\frac{7}{12}$ es un poco más de la mitad, por lo que $\frac{7}{12}$ es mayor que 0.45.

Los estudiantes aplicarán su comprensión de conceptos decimales al sumar o comparar decimales.

Sumar decimales

3.9 + 2.21

$$\begin{array}{r} \overset{1}{3}.9 \\ +\ 2.21 \\ \hline 6.11 \end{array}$$

Asegúrese de recordar a su niño que debe alinear los decimales.

Comparar decimales

6.8 ◯ 3.42 6.80 (>) 3.42

Añadir un cero facilita la comparación de números.

Si tiene alguna duda o comentario, por favor comuníquese conmigo.

Gracias.

Atentamente,
El maestro de su niño

6–2 **Class Activity**

Name ____________________ Date __________

▶ Word Problems With Decimal Numbers

Solve.

The Cruz family will be on vacation for 10 days this year. So far they have been on vacation for one week.

1. What decimal number shows what part of their vacation is gone? ______________

2. What decimal number shows what part of their vacation is left? ______________

Jeremy spent 3 quarters and a nickel at the school store.

3. What decimal part of a dollar did he spend? __________

4. What decimal part of a dollar does he have left? __________

Dana is planning to run 1 tenth of a mile every day for 8 days.

5. What part of a mile will she have run at the end of the eighth day? ______________

6. How many more days will she have to run to reach a mile?

____

▶ Compare Decimal Numbers

Write <, >, or = to compare these numbers.

7. 0.7 ◯ 0.32
8. 0.14 ◯ 0.6
9. 0.95 ◯ 0.8
10. 0.4 ◯ 0.6
11. 0.08 ◯ 0.8
12. 0.40 ◯ 0.4
13. 0.02 ◯ 0.20
14. 0.5 ◯ 0.49
15. **On the Back** Write a word problem whose answer is 0.18.

Name Date

Name ______________________ Date __________

▶ Discuss the Symmetry Around the Ones

← × 10 **Place-Value Chart** ÷ 10 →

Thousands	Hundreds	Tens	ONES	Tenths	Hundredths	Thousandths
1,000.	100.	10.	1.	0.1	0.01	0.001
$\frac{1,000}{1}$	$\frac{100}{1}$	$\frac{10}{1}$	$\frac{1}{1}$	$\frac{1}{10}$	$\frac{1}{100}$	$\frac{1}{1,000}$

1. Discuss symmetries and relationships you see.
2. Is it easier to see place value patterns in **a** or **b**? Discuss why.

   a. 5,000 500 50 5 .5 .05 .005

   b. 5,000 500 50 5 0.5 0.05 0.005
3. Discuss why **b** might be a safer way to write decimal fractions.

▶ Read Decimals as Fractions

Write each decimal as a fraction or as a mixed number. Then read it aloud.

4. 0.438 5. 0.36 6. 0.04 7. 3.8 8. 0.005 9. 1.72

10. 0.086 11. 2.05 12. 0.018 13. 12.9 14. 0.504 15. 0.316

Name _______________ Date _______________

▶ Write Numbers in Decimal Form

Write each number in decimal form.

16. 3 tenths ________

17. 8 thousandths ________

18. 16 hundredths ________

19. 12 thousandths ________

20. 2 cents ________

21. $\frac{7}{100}$ ________

22. $3\frac{1}{10}$ ________

23. $\frac{81}{1000}$ ________

24. $7\frac{3}{100}$ ________

25. four *and* 56 hundredths ________

26. six *and* 14 thousandths ________

Write each decimal tenth as a decimal hundredth and as a decimal thousandth.

27. 0.3 = ______ = ______

28. 0.9 = ______ = ______

29. 0.1 = ______ = ______

30. 0.8 = ______ = ______

▶ Generate Decimals for Real-World Situations

Answer each question.

31. I ate 2 bags of 100 peanuts plus 23 peanuts from another bag. What decimal number shows the number of bags I ate?

____

32. I ate 3 bags of 100 peanuts plus 8 peanuts from another bag. What decimal number shows the number of bags I ate?

____

33. Of the 1,000 ants in a colony, 35 ants are out walking around. What decimal represents the part of the colony walking?

____

34. Each lot holds 1,000 cars. Two lots are completely full, and there are 19 cars in the third lot. What decimal number shows the number of full lots?

____

6–4 **Class Activity**

Name ______________________ Date ____________

Vocabulary
tenths
hundredths
round

► Round With Decimal Tenths and Hundredths

The number line below shows one whole divided into **tenths**.

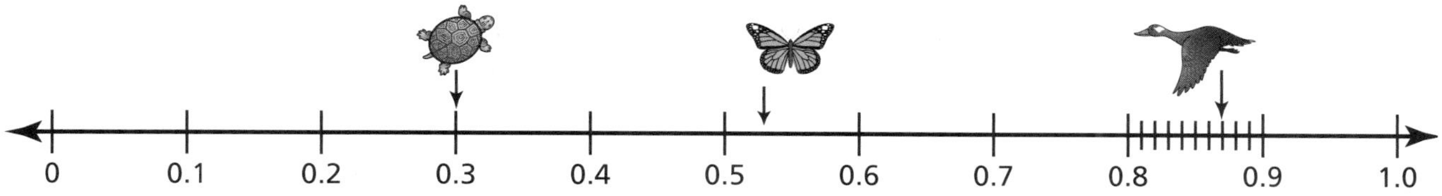

1. What decimal tenth is marked by the turtle? ________

2. The butterfly is between two decimal tenths. To which tenth is it nearer? ________

3. The bird is also between two decimal tenths. The space between these tenths has been divided into hundredths. What decimal **hundredths** are between 0.8 and 0.9?

____

4. What decimal hundredth is marked by the bird? ________

5. To which tenth is this hundredth nearer? (This is the way you **round** a hundredth to the nearest tenth.) ________

Rounding Frames

0.9
0.87
0.8

The number line below shows one whole divided into hundredths.

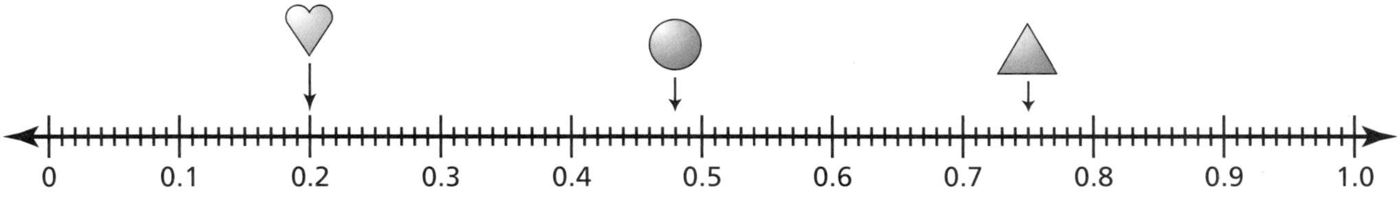

6. What hundredth is marked by the circle? ________

   Round this hundredth to the nearest tenth. ________

0.5
0.48
0.4

7. When you want to round a number that is exactly halfway between two rounding units, round up to the next greater number. What number is marked by the triangle? ________

   Round this number to the nearest tenth. ________

0.8
0.75
0.7

6–4 Class Activity

Name ______________________ Date ____________

▶ Round Numbers Greater Than One

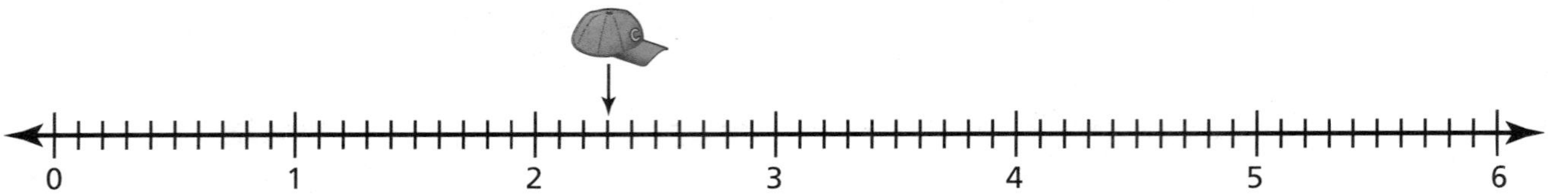

8. Find 4.5 on the number line. Put an arrow there.

   What is 4.5 rounded to the nearest whole number? ________

   What is 4.5 expressed as decimal hundredths? ________

9. What decimal number is marked by the hat? ________

   Round this number to the nearest whole number. ________

The ruler below shows centimeters and tenths of a centimeter.

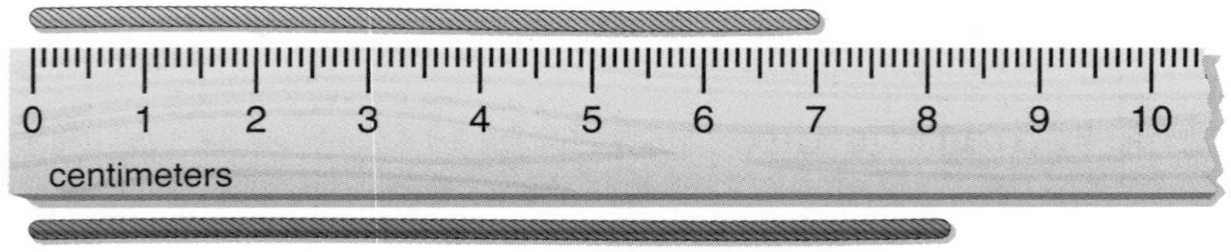

10. How long is the string above the ruler? ________

11. How long is the string below the ruler to the nearest tenth of a centimeter? ________ Round your answer to the nearest centimeter. ________

▶ Practice Rounding

Round to the nearest tenth.

12. 0.72 ________
13. 0.35 ________
14. 0.91 ________
15. 2.09 ________
16. What is $0.56 rounded to the nearest tenth of a dollar (dime)? ________

Round to the nearest whole number.

17. 3.8 ________
18. 32.7 ________
19. 12.5 ________
20. 8.24 ________
21. What is $7.28 rounded to the nearest dollar? ________

Name ______________________ Date ____________

► Zeros in Greater Decimal Numbers

1. What happens if we insert a zero to the right of a whole number?

____

2. What happens if we insert a zero to the right of a decimal number?

____

____

Whole Numbers			Decimal Numbers		
3	30	300	0.3	0.30	0.300
52	520	5200	0.52	0.520	0.5200
67	670	6700	6.7	6.70	6.700

3. What happens if we insert a zero to the left of a whole number?

____

4. What happens if we insert a zero to the left of a decimal number just after the decimal point?

____

Whole Numbers			Decimal Numbers		
3	03	003	0.3	0.03	0.003
52	052	0052	0.52	0.052	0.0052
67	067	0067	6.7	6.07	6.007

5. Are whole numbers and decimal numbers alike or different when it comes to putting in extra zeros? Explain your answer.

____

____

____

____

6. Do the pairs of numbers below have the same value? Why or why not?

0.6 and .6 ________ .25 and 0.25 ________ 0.178 and .178 ________

____

____

Name ______________________________ Date ____________

▶ Adding Decimal Zeros

Cathy had to compare some decimal numbers. She used what she knew about adding zeros to decimal fractions without changing their value. Discuss why her solution is correct.

Problem:

Which of these numbers is the greatest: 0.35, 0.318, or 0.4?

Solution:

0.350
0.318
0.400

With the places aligned and the extra zeros added, we can see which is greatest.

Insert < or > to make a true statement.

7. 0.36 ◯ 0.82
8. 0.405 ◯ 0.62
9. 0.98 ◯ 0.7
10. 2.3 ◯ 0.95
11. 0.626 ◯ 0.65
12. 1.2 ◯ 0.85
13. 0.7 ◯ 0.07
14. 0.54 ◯ 0.504

15. The table below shows the lengths of some common insects in inches. List the insects in order from largest to smallest.

Largest ____________________
____
____
____
Smallest ____________________

Size of Common Insects in Inches

Name	Length
Ladybug	0.25 in.
Aphid	0.062 in.
Mosquito	0.125 in.
Cricket	0.725 in.
Bumblebee	0.8 in.

Circle the number in each group that does *not* have the same value as the others.

16. .29 .290 .209 0.29
17. 0.7 .70 $\frac{7}{10}$ .07
18. .610 .601 0.61 .61
19. 4.8 4.80 4.08 4.800

Name Date

▶ Two Ways to Compare Fractions and Decimals

Decimal numbers and fractions can be compared.

Decimal numbers are special kinds of fractions.
They are another way to write fractions with denominators of 10, 100, 1000, and so on.

Here are two methods you can use to compare $\frac{7}{12}$ and 0.4.

Method 1: Use a fraction for each number.

1. Change the decimal number to a fraction. How is 0.4 written as a fraction?

____

2. Now compare the two fractions.

3. Write a statement using a > or < sign to compare $\frac{7}{12}$ and 0.4.

____

Method 2: Think of a benchmark.

4. For this example, use $\frac{1}{2}$ as a benchmark and compare both numbers to $\frac{1}{2}$. How does $\frac{7}{12}$ compare to $\frac{1}{2}$?

____

5. How does 0.4 compare to $\frac{1}{2}$?

____

6. Write a statement that compares $\frac{7}{12}$ and 0.4 using a > or < sign.

____

6–5 **Going Further**

Name ______________________________ Date ______________

▶ Fractions and Decimal Numbers on a Number Line

Both decimal numbers and fractions can be shown on a number line. You can use a number line to order and compare fractions and decimals.

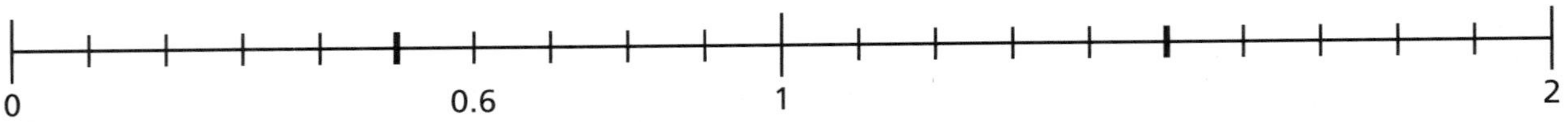

7. Put these numbers in the correct position on the number line above.

   $\frac{1}{2}$ 0.8   0.4 $\frac{2}{10}$ 1.2 $1\frac{6}{10}$ 1.9

8. Put these numbers in the correct position on the number line below.

   2    $\frac{3}{10}$ $\frac{4}{5}$ $1\frac{1}{2}$ 1.4   0.7 $1\frac{1}{10}$ 1.8

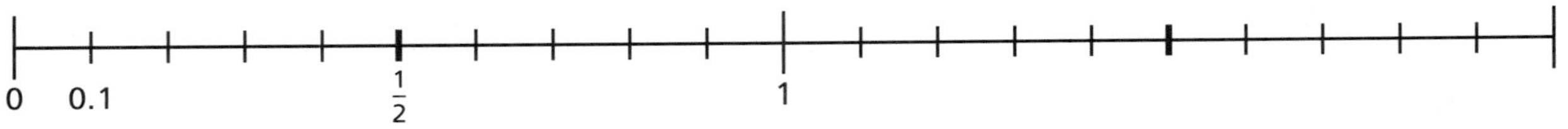

▶ Compare Fractions and Decimals

Insert > or < to make a true statement.

9. $\frac{3}{4}$ ◯ 0.3

10. 0.75 ◯ $\frac{1}{8}$

11. 0.2 ◯ $\frac{5}{10}$

12. 0.7 ◯ $\frac{8}{10}$

13. $\frac{1}{3}$ ◯ 0.6

14. $\frac{1}{3}$ ◯ 0.25

15. 0.04 ◯ 0.1

16. 0.1 ◯ $\frac{4}{9}$

17. 0.1 ◯ 0.01

Name ______________________ Date ______________

▶ Real-World Applications

Solve.

1. Samantha has a quarter, a dime, and 2 pennies in her pocket. What decimal part of a dollar does she have?

____

2. Today the Grade 4 runners ran 0.71 kilometers. The Grade 6 runners ran 0.675 kilometers. Which team ran farther?

____

3. Oliver is building a patio with flat stones. He has decided to use only stones that are between 0.75 and 0.9 meters across. Below is a list of the measurements of the stones he has gathered so far. Check the ones he can use.

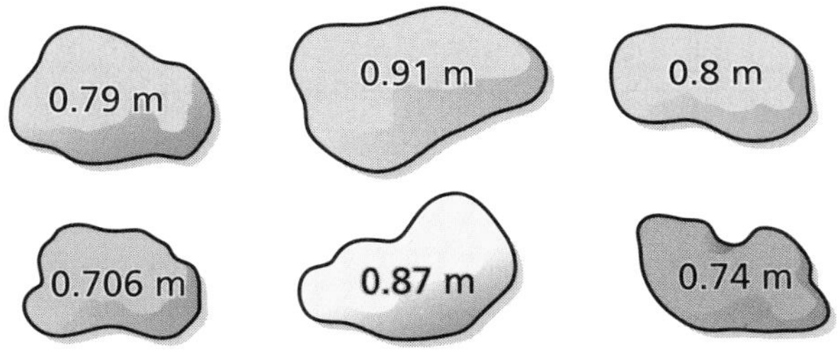

4. Chad is 1.78 meters tall. His friend Rob is 1.8 meters tall, and his friend Brent is 1.735 meters tall. Make a chart showing their heights rounded to the nearest hundredth. List the rounded heights in order from tallest to shortest.

____

____

____

5. **On the Back** Answer the Puzzled Penguin's letter.

Dear Math Students:

I have some squash seeds and tomato seeds to plant, but I don't know which is which. My garden book says that squash seeds are about 0.7 of a centimeter long, and tomato seeds are about 0.25 of a centimeter long. Since 25 is bigger than 7, I would say that the tomato seed is the bigger seed. My friend says that's wrong.

Who is right? Can you explain why?

Thank you.

Puzzled Penguin

Name Date

Name ____________________ Date ____________

▶ Add Unlike Units

The exercises below have *not* been answered correctly. Explain why and correct each answer.

1. \$23 + 10¢ = \$33

2. 5 feet + 12 inches = 17 feet

3. 4 hours + 3 minutes = 7 hours

4. $\frac{2}{3} + \frac{3}{4} = \frac{5}{7}$

5. 0.6 + 0.05 = 0.11

6. 14 + 0.3 = 17

7. Explain what was wrong with 1 through 6 and how to solve them correctly.

____

____

▶ Unlike Units on the Number Line

Use the number line to add the numbers.

8. 4 + 0.8 = ______

9. 2 + 0.3 = ______

10. 3 + 1.9 = ______

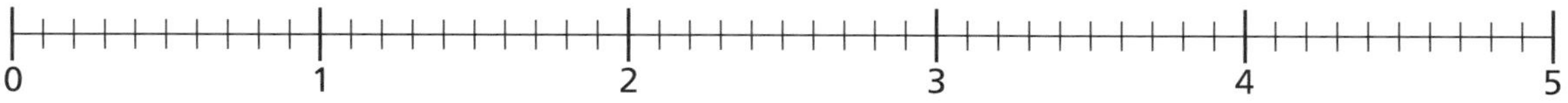

Circle each correctly aligned problem and solve it.

11. A.
```
  1 2.5
+  0.3
```
B.
```
  12.5
+  0.3
```

12. A.
```
   0.9
+ 0.56
```
B.
```
   0.9
+ 0.56
```

13. A.
```
  2.15
+  1.3
```
B.
```
  2.15
+  1.3
```

14. A.
```
  0.734
+  0.68
```
B.
```
  0.734
+  0.68
```

Name ______________________ Date ____________

▶ Align Decimal Numbers to Add

Add.

15. \$48 + 12¢ =

16. 0.3 + 0.03 =

17. 23 + 0.36 =

18. \$32.05 + 63¢ =

19. 0.25 + 0.18 =

20. 87.3 + 0.49 =

21. 16¢ + \$5.27 =

22. 0.006 + 0.07 =

23. 72.17 + 1.5 =

▶ Solve Problems Involving Adding Decimal Numbers

Solve.

24. Roberto grew 0.96 centimeters last year and 0.8 centimeters the year before. How many centimeters did Roberto grow in two years?

____

25. Colleen and Jack both delivered newspapers this summer. Colleen earned \$103.26 and Jack earned \$92.12. How much did they earn together?

____

26. Hannah has 6.721 liters of lemonade. She will mix it with 3.44 liters of raspberry juice to make raspberry lemonade. How many liters of raspberry lemonade will Hannah have?

____

27. Last year Maria's oak tree was 4.5 meters tall. This year it grew 0.41 meters. How tall is the oak tree now?

____

Name ______________________ Date ____________

▶ Order Decimal Numbers to Subtract

Find the difference between each pair of numbers.

1. 0.89 and 0.7
2. 0.09 and 0.23
3. 0.837 and 0.2
4. 0.006 and 0.35
5. 1.04 and 0.7
6. 3.56 and 0.008

▶ Solve Problems Involving Decimal Number Subtraction

Solve.

7. Rosa had a rope 6.5 meters long. She cut off a piece 1.45 meters long to make a jump rope. How much rope does Rosa have left?

   ____

8. A robin's egg is about 1.35 centimeters long. A hummingbird's egg is about 0.6 centimeters long. How much longer is a robin's egg?

   ____

9. A turtle can travel 0.17 miles per hour. A snail can travel 0.032 miles per hour. Which animal can move faster? ____________ How much faster? ______________________

10. Ramona had $26. She spent 35 cents to buy a pencil. How much money does Ramona have now?

    ____

Name ______________________ Date ______________

▶ Decimals on the Map

Use the map to answer the questions 11–13.

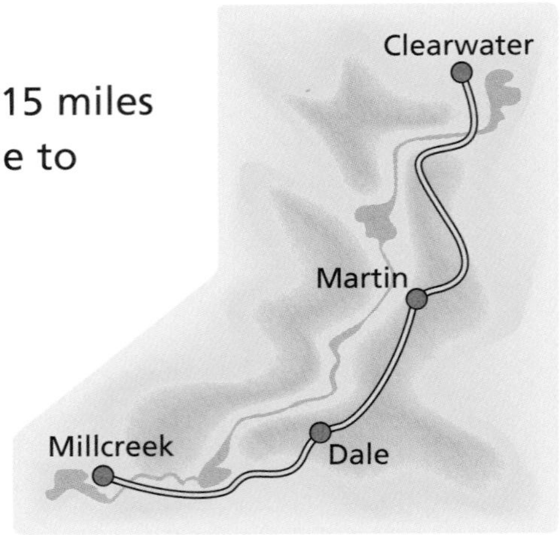

11. If it is 17.5 miles from Millcreek to Dale and 33.15 miles from Millcreek to Martin, how far is it from Dale to Martin? ____________

12. If it is 49 miles from Dale to Clearwater, how far is it from Martin to Clearwater?

____

13. How far is the entire distance from Millcreek to Clearwater? ____________

▶ Decimal Word Problems

Solve.

Show your work.

14. Mr. Kelly raises honeybees for a living. Today he collected 0.28 ounces of dark honey and 0.9 ounces of light honey. How many ounces of honey did Mr. Kelly collect today? ____________

15. Mr. Kelly sells honey in two sizes. There is a 9.5-ounce jar and a 4.75-ounce jar. What is the difference in weight between the two jars?

____

16. Mr. Kelly has collected 0.85 ounces of honey today. How much more will he need to collect to fill a 4.75-ounce jar? ____________

17. Last week Mr. Kelly sold a total of 41.75 ounces of light honey and 18.5 ounces of dark honey. How much honey did he sell last week?

____

Name ______________________ Date ______________

Vocabulary
estimate

▶ Estimate With Decimal Numbers

Estimate the answers by rounding each number to the nearest tenth.

1. 0.83 + 0.121 ____________
2. 0.64 − 0.07 ____________
3. 0.09 + 0.8 ____________
4. 0.75 − 0.18 ____________
5. 3.41 + 1.29 ____________
6. 1.50 − 0.79 ____________

▶ The Puzzled Penguin

Dear Math Students:

I had $0.95 to spend at the store today. I wanted to buy a pen for $0.53 and some stickers for $0.44.

I rounded the price of the pen down to $0.50 and the price of the stickers down to $0.40. I thought I had enough because $0.50 + $0.40 is less than $0.95. But the cashier told me I didn't have enough. What did I do wrong?

Thank you.

Puzzled Penguin

____

____

____

____

Make a safe estimate to solve the problems.

7. Jenna wants to buy apple juice for $0.64 and a muffin for $0.98. She has $1.75. Does she have enough money?

____

____

8. Pedro has 5 quarters. He wants to buy a pencil for $0.34 and a notebook for $0.93. Does he have enough money?

____

____

Name ____________________ Date ____________

▶ Round Different Ways in Different Contexts

The table shows how much money Jahmal earned this month selling newspapers. Use the table to answer the questions below.

Week 1	$19.68
Week 2	$ 8.92
Week 3	$28.95
Week 4	$10.16

9. Estimate Jahmal's total earnings by rounding to the nearest ten dollars.

____

10. About how much more did Jahmal make in Week 1 than in Week 2? Estimate by rounding to the nearest dollar.

____

11. About how much more did Jahmal make in Week 3 than in Week 4? Estimate by rounding to the nearest dollar.

____

▶ Select a Rounding Unit

Select a rounding unit that allows you to estimate the answer mentally. Write your rounded problem and your estimated answer.

12. 0.429 + 0.502 _______________

13. 1.85 − 0.9 _______________

14. 0.88 − 0.283 _______________

15. 0.59 − 0.19 _______________

16. 3.678 + 4.123 _______________

17. 2.69 + 0.3 _______________

Name ____________________ Date ____________

▶ Problem Solving With Metric Measurement

Solve the problems.

Show your work.

1. The length of each side of a square fence is 8.6 meters. Estimate the total length of the fence.

____

2. A quarter has a mass of 5.67 grams. A dime has a mass of 2.268 grams. Estimate the total mass of both coins.

____

3. Kimo bought two jars of juice. One jar had 0.52 liters of juice. The other jar had 1 liter of juice. Estimate the difference in liters between the jars.

____

4. Shawn is painting a fence. He has 5 cans of paint. Each can has 3.784 liters of paint. Estimate how many liters of paint Shawn has in all.

____

5. Nina measured the mass of some apples at 1.34 kilograms. She measured some pears at 1.09 kilograms. Estimate the total mass of the apples and pears.

____

6. The driving distance from Ida's home to Flo's home is 184.19 kilometers. Ida divides the trip into 2 equal parts. Estimate how many kilometers Ida will travel for each part of the trip.

____

7. **On the Back** Arnette put ribbon around a picture frame. The length of the frame is 10.16 centimeters. The width of the frame is 15.24 centimeters. Estimate the total length of ribbon that is needed. Explain how you estimated.

Name Date

6–10 Class Activity

Name ______________________ Date ______________

▶ Find the Difference

Find the difference between the numbers. Use mental math if you can.

1. 0.99 and 0.11 ______
2. 0.006 and 0.356 ______
3. 0.07 and 0.27 ______
4. 1.59 and 0.5 ______
5. 0.835 and 0.1 ______
6. 1.00 and 4.68 ______

▶ Word Problems With Mixed Operations

Solve.

7. David's kite had a tail 1.5 meters long. David made it 0.75 meters longer. How long is the tail now?

______

8. Margarita had $35. She spent 73 cents to buy a bag of peanuts. How much money does Margarita have now?

______

9. Carlos feeds his hamsters 0.09 pounds of seeds mixed with 0.15 pounds of oatmeal every day. How many pounds of food do the hamsters get?

______

10. The Crazy Curl roller coaster travels at 82.03 miles per hour. The Big Drop roller coaster travels at 82.015 miles per hour. Which roller coaster goes faster? How much faster?

______

▶ Neighborhood Map Problems

Refer to the drawing. Estimate each answer by rounding the numbers to the nearest tenth.

11. How far is it from Justin's house to Dana's house? ______

12. How far does Ana have to walk to school? ______

Name _______________ Date _______________

▶ Multiply Decimal Numbers

1. Ernesto is making a bookcase using wood. He cut a piece of wood into 4 equal pieces. Each cut piece was 2.13 meters long. How long was the whole piece of wood he started with?

____

2. $\$0.74 \times 8$

3. 19.7×4

4. 0.37×8

5. $\$5.08 \times 9$

6. 0.982×6

7. $\$6.17 \times 7$

▶ Solve Problems by Multiplying Decimal Numbers

Solve.

8. Ms. Lindy bought 3 rolls of ribbon for wrapping gifts. The price of each roll was $2.16. What was the total cost of the 3 rolls?

____

9. Julie runs 1.35 miles each day. How many miles in all would she run if she ran for 5 days?

____

10. Mr. Cobb wants to buy 6 cartons of juice. Each carton costs $0.89. What would be the total cost of the 6 cartons?

____

11. Donnie can run $\frac{1}{2}$ mile on the track in 4.67 minutes. How many minutes will it take him to run 1 mile?

____

Name ______________________ Date ______________

Write these numbers in decimal form.

1. sixty-four hundredths ________

2. $7\frac{3}{10}$ ________

3. $12\frac{4}{100}$ ________

Write these decimal numbers in words.

4. 23.01 ______________________________

5. 2.178 ______________________________

Insert >, <, or = to make a true statement.

6. 0.727 ◯ 0.75

7. 0.4 ◯ 0.25

8. 0.27 ◯ 0.270

9. Arrange these numbers in order from smallest to largest.

   0.7 0.64 0.09 ______ ______ ______

Round each number to the nearest tenth and to the nearest whole number.

10. 0.87 nearest tenth: ______ nearest whole number: ______

11. 1.318 nearest tenth: ______ nearest whole number: ______

12. 2.67 nearest tenth: ______ nearest whole number: ______

Add or subtract.

13. 7.13 + 2.5 =

14. 8.36 − 4.78 =

15. 1.003 + 0.4 =

16. \$26 − 15¢ =

Name ____________________ Date ____________

Solve.

Show your work.

17. On Monday, the average temperature was 29.7°F. On Tuesday, the average temperature was 37.64°F. How much warmer was it on Tuesday than on Monday?

____

18. Jared's family drove 98.12 km to visit some cousins. Then they drove 85.3 km to visit some friends. How far did they travel altogether?

____

19. Miguel spent $58.93 at the market. He gave the clerk $100.00. About how much change will he get back?

____

20. **Extended Response** Tickets to an amusement park cost $27.99 for adults and $18.49 for children. Mrs. Ramirez has $47.00. Does she have enough money to buy tickets for herself and her 10-year-old son? Use a "safe estimate" to answer this question. Explain how you made your estimate and how you know your answer is correct.

____

____

____

____

____

____

F–1 Class Activity

Name ________________________________ Date ____________

Vocabulary

inch
yard
foot
mile

▶ Units of Length

The inchworm gets its name because its method of crawling helps it move about an inch at a time.

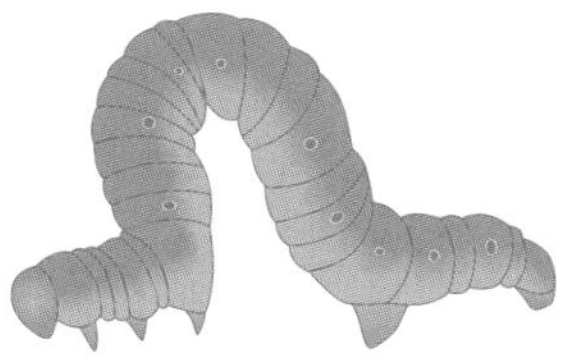

1. This line segment is 1 **inch** long.

   Hold up two fingers 1 inch apart.
   Name an object that is about 1 inch long.

   ____

2. One **foot** is equal to 12 inches. The line segment below is 1 foot long, but it has been folded into two 6-inch lengths.

   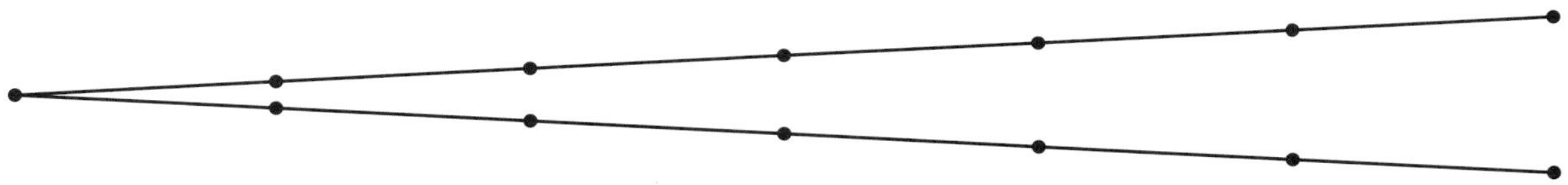

   Spread your hands apart to show 1 foot. Name an object that is about 1 foot long. ______________

3. Many years ago, people considered a distance of 1 foot to be the length of a person's foot. Measure the longest dimension of your classroom using your feet, and compare your results with those of your classmates. Why is using your feet not a good way to measure distance?

   ____

   ____

4. One **yard** is equal to 3 feet or 36 inches. How many 6-inch lengths are equal to 1 yard?

   ____

5. Longer distances are measured in miles. One **mile** is equal to 5,280 feet or 1,760 yards. Why are feet and yards not used as often as miles when describing long distances?

   ____

F–1 Class Activity

Name ____________________ Date ____________

▶ Fractions of Length Units

Since 1 foot = 12 inches, this 6-inch ruler shows a $\frac{1}{2}$ foot.

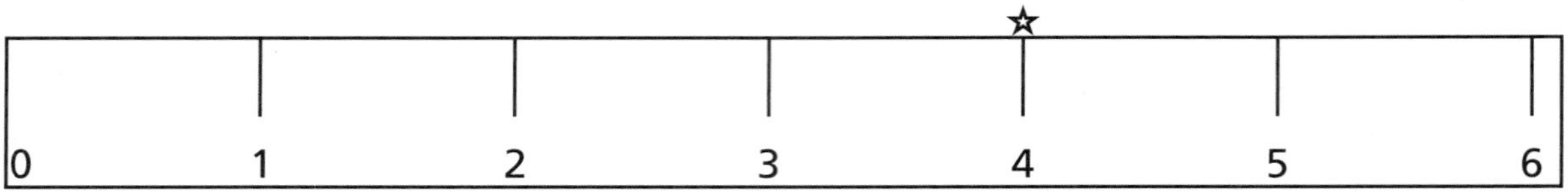

6. How many inches are between 0 and the star? ____________

Use fractions in simplest form to complete the equations.

7. 1 in. = ______ ft
8. 3 in. = ______ ft
9. 4 in. = ______ ft
10. 1 ft = ______ yd
11. 2 ft = ______ yd

The shorter marks between the whole-inch marks represent the fractional parts.

For each ruler below, what fraction of an inch is marked between the whole numbers? What measurement does the star show?

12.

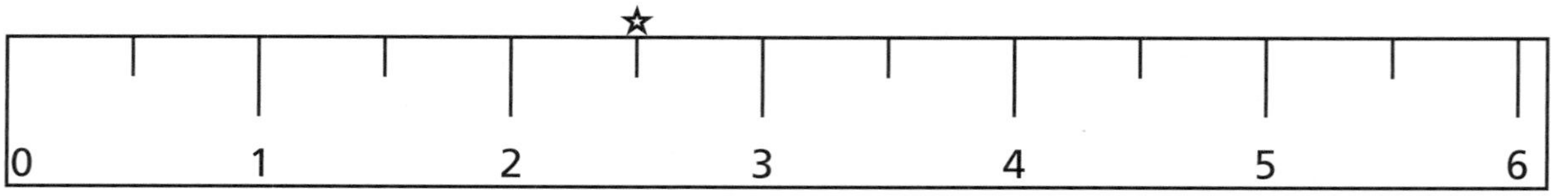

____

13.

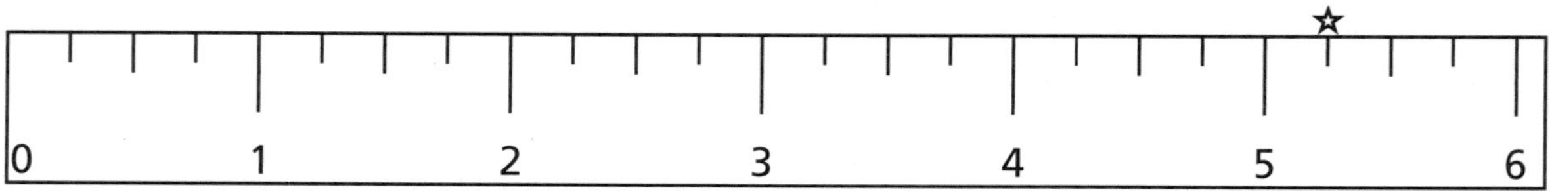

____

14.

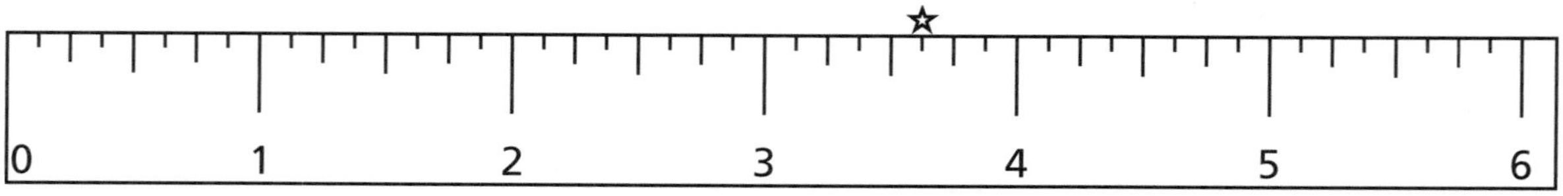

____

15. Some rulers have shorter marks halfway between each $\frac{1}{8}$ mark. What fraction of an inch would these marks represent?

____

Name ____________________ Date ________

▶ Estimate and Measure Length

Estimate the length of each line segment. Then measure it to the nearest $\frac{1}{8}$ inch.

16.

17.

18.

19.

20.

Draw a line segment that has the given length.

21. $3\frac{3}{8}$ in.

22. $1\frac{3}{4}$ in.

23. $5\frac{1}{2}$ in.

24. $2\frac{1}{4}$ in.

25. $7\frac{6}{8}$ in.

Name ______________________ Date ______________

▶ Work Backward

Solve.

Show your work.

1. All of the students in a school are recording how far they ride their bicycles during the summer. They want to discover whether they ride enough miles altogether to equal the distance around the Earth. One day, Lola rode twice as far as Max and Max rode 5 more miles than Meghan. If Meghan rode 2 miles, how many miles altogether did the three riders contribute to the school's total on that day?

   ____

2. Chandra spent half of her allowance for a theater ticket and $2.25 for popcorn. After the movie, she arrived home with $2.75. What was Chandra's allowance?

   ____

3. Shelby's age is one-fourth Allison's age. Mito is 13 years old and 1 year older than Allison. How old is Shelby?

   ____

4. Patrick gave one-third of a length of ribbon to Karin, and then divided the remaining ribbon equally with Jon. If Jon received 12 inches of ribbon, how many yards long was the ribbon Patrick began with?

   ____

Family Letter

Dear Family,

In our math class, we are exploring different ways we measure things using our customary system of measurement.

Some of the units of measurement we will be working with include:

Length and Distance	Capacity
1 foot = 12 inches 1 yard = 3 feet 1 mile = 5,280 feet	1 cup = 8 fluid ounces 1 pint = 2 cups 1 quart = 2 pints 1 gallon = 4 quarts
Weight	**Time**
1 pound = 16 ounces 1 ton = 2,000 pounds	1 minute = 60 seconds 1 hour = 60 minutes 1 day = 24 hours 1 month = 28, 29, 30, or 31 days 1 year = 365 days leap year = 366 days

You can help your child become familiar with these units by finding examples together in your home and work. You might use a calendar to note that the number of days in each month is not always the same. You might use a measuring cup and explore how the cup can be used to make pints, quarts, or gallons of liquid. Or you might use a clock face to find "quarter to," "quarter after," and "half past" various hours. These activities and others will help your child better understand measurement.

If you have any questions, please call or write to me.

Sincerely,
Your child's teacher

Carta a la familia

Estimada familia:

En nuestra clase de matemáticas estamos explorando diferentes maneras de medir las cosas usando el sistema usual de medida.

Algunas de las unidades de medida con las que trabajaremos incluyen:

Longitud y distancia	Capacidad
1 pie = 12 pulgadas 1 yarda = 3 pies 1 milla = 5,280 pies	1 taza = 8 onzas líquidas 1 pinta = 2 tazas 1 cuarto = 2 pintas 1 galón = 4 cuartos
Peso	**Tiempo**
1 libra = 16 onzas 1 tonelada = 2,000 libras	1 minuto = 60 segundos 1 hora = 60 minutos 1 día = 24 horas 1 mes = 28, 29, 30 ó 31 días 1 año = 365 días 1 año bisiesto = 366 días

Será de gran ayuda si usted puede encontrar ejemplos de estas unidades en su casa y puede trabajar con su niño para que se familiarice con ellas. Por ejemplo, puede usar un calendario para hacerle notar que el número de días de cada mes no siempre es el mismo. Puede usar una taza de medir para explorar cómo la taza puede servir para hacer pintas, cuartos o galones. O puede usar la cara del reloj para hallar el "cuarto para" la hora, la hora "y cuarto" y la hora "y media" con diferentes horas. Estas y otras actividades van a ayudar a su niño a comprender las medidas.

Si tiene alguna pregunta, por favor comuníquese conmigo.

Atentamente,
El maestro de su niño

F–2 Class Activity

Name ______________________ Date ______________

Vocabulary

square inch
square foot
square yard

▶ Investigate Area

A square that measures 1 inch on each side is a **square inch**. A square inch is used to measure area. Other units that are used to measure area include a **square foot** and a **square yard**.

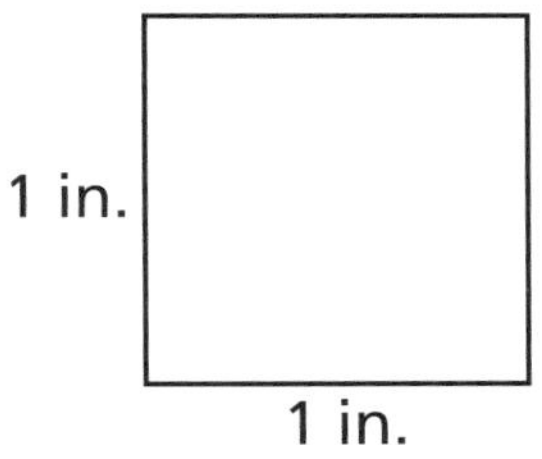

1. How many inches on each side does a square foot measure? How many square inches are equal to 1 square foot?

   ____

2. How many feet on each side does a square yard measure? How many square feet are equal to 1 square yard?

   ____

3. Name something that might be measured in square inches. Name something that might be measured in square feet. Name something that might be measured in square yards.

   ____

   ____

Measure area and show your work.

4. Find the area in square inches of a rectangular shape.

5. Find the area in square feet of the floor of your classroom.

6. Change your answer in exercise 5 to square yards.

F–2 Class Activity

Name ______________________ Date ______________________

Vocabulary
cubic inch
cubic foot
cubic yard

▶ Investigate Volume

A cube that measures 1 inch on each side is a **cubic inch**. A cubic inch is used to measure volume. Other units that are used to measure volume include a **cubic foot** and a **cubic yard**.

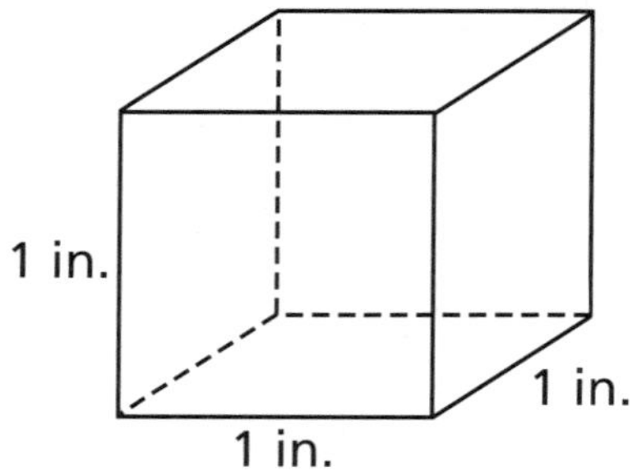

7. How many inches on each side does a cubic foot measure? How many cubic inches are equal to 1 cubic foot?

____

8. How many feet on each side does a cubic yard measure? How many cubic feet are equal to 1 cubic yard?

____

Measure volume and show your work.

9. Find the volume in cubic inches of a small object or a small three-dimensional space.

10. Find the volume in cubic feet of your classroom.

11. Change your answer in exercise 10 to cubic yards.

F–3 Class Activity

Name ______________________ Date ____________

Vocabulary
pound
ounce

▶ Pounds and Ounces

The pound is the primary unit of weight in our customary system. One **pound** is equal to 16 **ounces**.

Fractions of 1 pound are often used to measure weight. For example, butter and margarine are sold in 1-pound packages that contain four separately wrapped sticks.

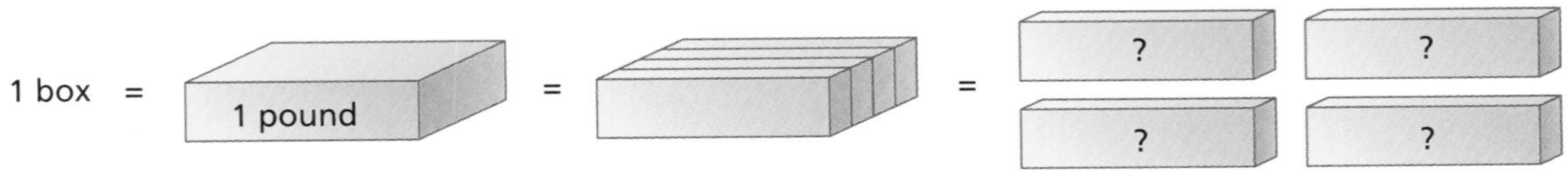

1. In simplest form, what fraction of 1 pound is one stick?

____

2. What is the weight in ounces of one stick?

____

3. In simplest form, what fraction of 1 pound is two sticks?

____

4. What is the total weight in ounces of two sticks?

____

5. In simplest form, what fraction of 1 pound is three sticks?

____

6. What is the total weight in ounces of three sticks?

____

7. A recipe requires 2 ounces of butter or margarine. How many sticks of butter or margarine should be used in the recipe?

____

Name ______________________ Date ______________

Vocabulary

ton

▶ Tons

The weight of heavy items such as cars, trucks, boats, elephants, and whales is measured in **tons**. One ton is equal to 2,000 pounds.

8. The cargo capacity of a small pickup truck is $\frac{1}{2}$ ton. How many pounds of cargo is the same as $\frac{1}{2}$ ton?

____

9. The towing capacity of a vehicle is 2,500 pounds. What number of tons is the same as 2,500 pounds?

____

10. A ship weighs 12,450 tons. In pounds, the ship weighs 24,900,000 pounds. Although either weight can be used to describe the ship, the weight that is most often used is 12,450 tons, not 24,900,000 pounds. Why?

____

____

____

____

11. A container weighs 4 ounces. A shipment of containers weighs 1 ton. How many containers are in the shipment? Show your work.

____

Class Activity

Name ______________________ Date ______________

Vocabulary

cup	pint
fluid ounce	gallon
quart	

▶ Units of Capacity

In the customary system, the primary unit of capacity is a **cup**.

1 cup  = 8 **fluid ounces**

4 cups  = 1 **quart**

2 cups  = 1 **pint**

4 quarts = 1 **gallon**

1. What fraction of 1 cup is 1 fluid ounce?

   ____

2. How many fluid ounces are equal to 1 pint?
   In simplest form, what fraction of 1 pint is 1 cup?

   ____

3. How many fluid ounces are equal to 1 quart?
   In simplest form, what fraction of 1 quart is 1 cup?

   ____

4. How many fluid ounces are equal to 1 gallon?
   In simplest form, what fraction of 1 gallon is 1 cup?

   ____

5. In simplest form, what fraction of 1 gallon is 1 pint?

   ____

6. In simplest form, what fraction of 1 gallon is 1 quart?

   ____

F–4 Class Activity

Name ____________________ Date ____________

▶ Solve Capacity Problems

Solve.

Show your work.

7. Alicia adds 4 fluid ounces of grapefruit juice to $\frac{1}{2}$ cup of orange juice. What fraction of 1 cup of juice does she make?

____

8. Jay has 1 cup of water. He pours out $\frac{1}{3}$ of the water. To the nearest whole fluid ounce, how many ounces of water remain in the cup?

____

9. Sebastian feeds his dog $1\frac{1}{4}$ cups of food each morning, and $1\frac{1}{4}$ cups each evening. How many cups of food does he feed his dog every week?

____

10. Five quarts of motor oil are needed when the oil in Tika's car is changed. Tika purchased two new 1-gallon containers of oil, then changed the oil in her car. What amount of new oil did Tika not use?

____

11. Each bottle of apple juice contains 12 fluid ounces. A shopper purchased 8 bottles. How many quarts of apple juice did the shopper purchase?

____

F–5

Class Activity

Name ______________________ Date ______________

▶ Fractions of an Hour

1. These clocks all show times after noon (P.M.). What time is shown on each clock?

Clock A ________ Clock B ________ Clock C ________

2. In simplest form, what fraction of 1 hour does the minute hand on Clock A show?

____

3. Write the time shown on Clock A using fraction words.

____

4. Write the times shown on Clocks B and C using fraction words.

____

5. How much time has passed from Clock B to Clock C?

____

6. How much time has passed from Clock B to Clock A?

____

7. The school bus arrives in $\frac{3}{4}$ of an hour. If the bus is on time, in how many minutes will it arrive?

____

8. Each day of the week, Molly practices piano for $\frac{1}{3}$ of an hour. How many minutes does she practice each week? How many hours?

____

Name ______________________ Date ______________

Vocabulary
Fahrenheit

▶ Fahrenheit Temperatures

The temperature scale in our customary system is called degrees **Fahrenheit** (°F). Water freezes at 32°F and boils at 212°F.

Answer these questions about temperature.

9. What is a comfortable temperature for the inside of your classroom?

____

10. Suppose the temperature outside your classroom is 52°F. How will you dress to go outside for recess?

____

11. How will you dress for recess if the outside temperature is 85°F?

____

12. The temperature at 6:00 A.M. was 25°F and the temperature at noon was 45°F. During that time, did the temperature increase or decrease? By how many degrees?

____

13. If the temperature outside is 27°F, is it more likely to be raining or snowing? How do you know?

____

14. A thermometer placed in the shade of Andy's backyard reads 105°F. Where in the United States might Andy live?

____

15. The normal temperature for the human body is about 98.6°F. Vanessa's temperature is 102°F. Does she have a fever? How do you know?

____

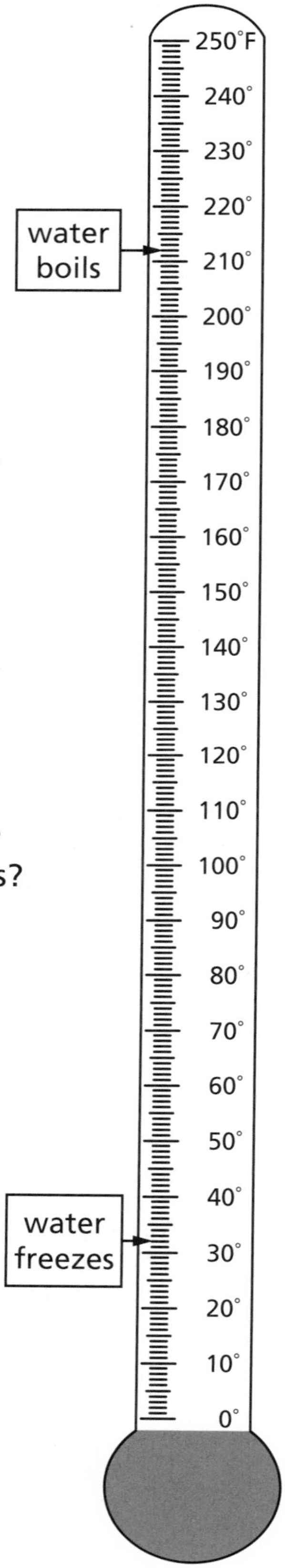

Name ______________________ Date ______________

1. How many inches are in 1 yard?

____

2. Draw a line segment that is $2\frac{3}{4}$ inches long.

3. What is the area of this rectangle in square inches?

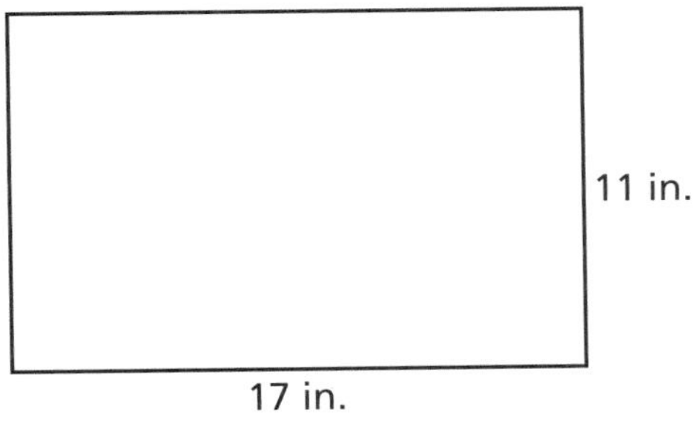

____

Is its area greater or less than 1 square foot?

____

4. How many cubic feet are in one cubic yard?

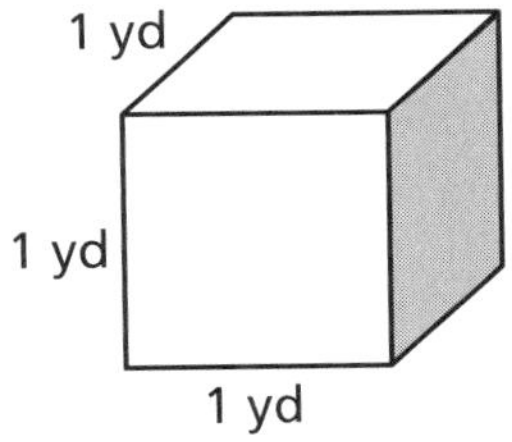

____

Solve.

5. Justine needs 30 ounces of butter. How many pounds of butter should she buy?

____

6. A builder is loading a small truck with 20-lb bags of sand. The truck can carry 2 tons. How many bags of sand can it carry?

____

7. A factory worker needs to pour 8 cups of vanilla into 2-ounce jars. How many jars does the worker need?

____

Name ______________________________ Date ______________

8. Each school day, Alvin rides a bus for $\frac{1}{4}$ of an hour to school and $\frac{1}{4}$ of an hour home from school. How many minutes does he spend on the bus in a school week? How many hours?

____

9. On Tuesday, it was 3 degrees Fahrenheit at 8:00 a.m. and 15 degrees Fahrenheit at noon. How many degrees did the temperature rise?

____

10. **Extended Response** The water in a swimming pool is 6 feet deep. The pool is a rectangle 20 feet by 15 feet. What is the volume of water in the pool in cubic yards? Explain your thinking.

____

____

____

____

Glossary

A

acre A measure of land area. An acre is equal to 4,840 square yards.

acute angle An angle smaller than a right angle.

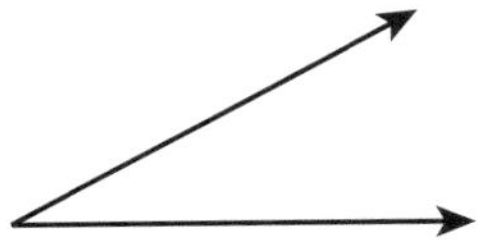

acute triangle A triangle with three acute angles.

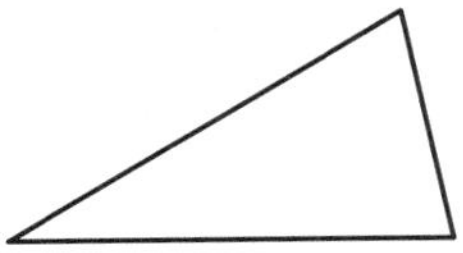

addend One of two or more numbers added together to find a sum.

Example:

7 + 8 = 15

addend addend sum

analog clock A clock with a face and hands.

angle A figure formed by two rays with the same endpoint.

array An arrangement of objects, symbols, or numbers in rows and columns.

area The amount of surface covered or enclosed by a figure measured in square units.

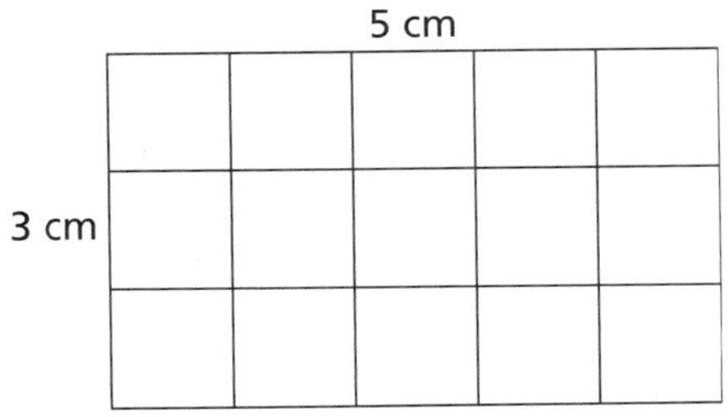

Associative Property of Addition Grouping the addends in different ways does not change the sum.

Example: 3 + (5 + 7) = 15
(3 + 5) + 7 = 15

Associative Property of Multiplication Grouping the factors in different ways does not change the product.

Example: 3 × (5 × 7) = 105
(3 × 5) × 7 = 105

average (mean) The size of each of *n* equal groups made from *n* data values. It is calculated by adding the values and dividing by *n*.

Example: 75, 84, 89, 91, 101
75 + 84 + 89 + 91 + 101 = 440,
then 440 ÷ 5 = 88. The average is 88.

B

bar graph A graph that uses bars to show data. The bars may be vertical or horizontal.

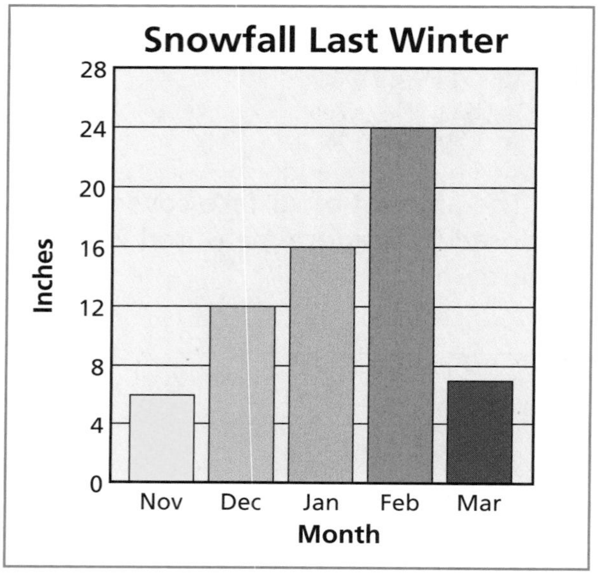

base For a triangle or parallelogram, a base is any side. For a trapezoid, a base is either of the parallel sides. For a prism, a base is one of the congruent parallel faces that may not be rectangular. For a pyramid, the base is the face that does not touch the vertex of the pyramid.

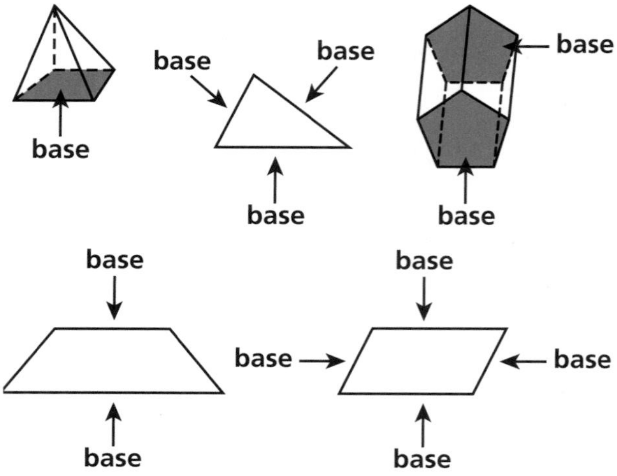

break-apart drawing A diagram that shows two addends and the sum.

C

capacity A measure of how much a container can hold.

Celsius The metric temperature scale.

center The point that is the same distance from every point on the circle.

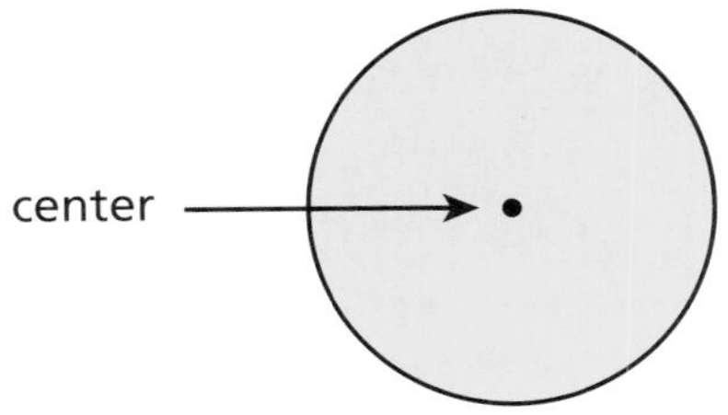

centimeter A unit of measure in the metric system that equals one hundredth of a meter. 1 cm = 0.01 m

change minus A change situation that can be represented by subtraction. In a change minus situation, the starting number, the change, or the result will be unknown.

Example:

Unknown Start	Unknown Change	Unknown Result
$n - 2 = 3$	$5 - n = 3$	$5 - 2 = n$

change plus A change situation that can be represented by addition. In a change plus situation, the starting number, the change, or the result will be unknown.

Example:

Unknown Start	Unknown Change	Unknown Result
$n + 2 = 5$	$3 + n = 5$	$3 + 2 = n$

circle A plane figure that forms a closed path so that all the points on the path are the same distance from a point called the center.

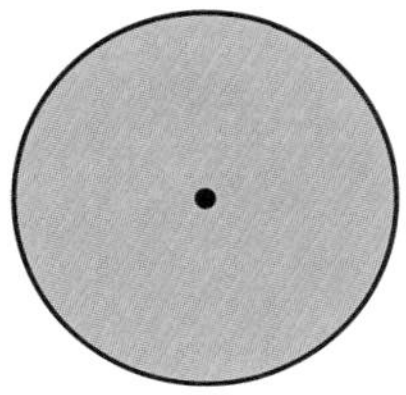

circle graph A graph that uses parts of a circle to show data.

Example:

Favorite Fiction Books

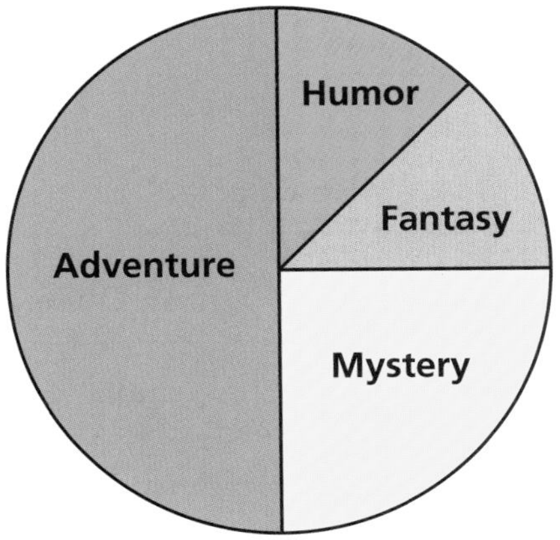

circumference The distance around a circle.

closed Having no endpoints.

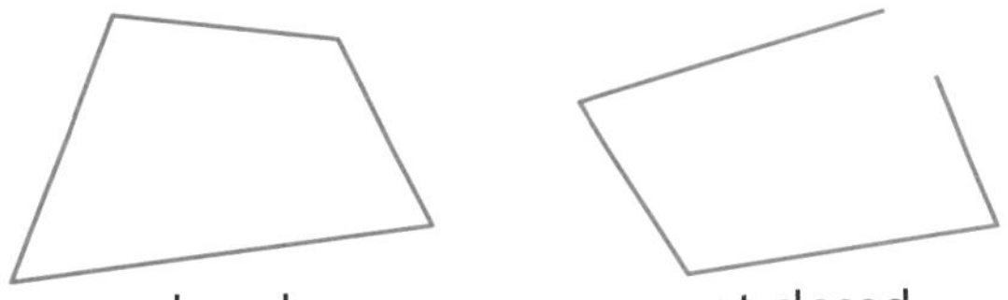

closed not closed

Collection Situations Situations that involve putting together (joining) or taking apart (separating) groups.

column A part of a table or array that contains items arranged vertically.

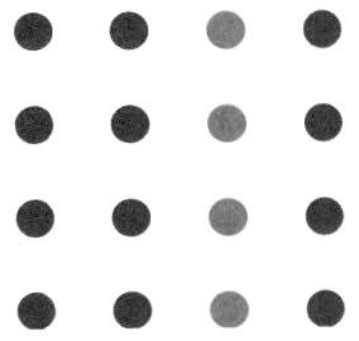

combination situation A situation in which the number of possible different combinations is determined. A table can sometimes be used to show all possible combinations; multiplication can be used to calculate the number of combinations.

Example:

Different Sandwich Combinations

	peanut butter	cheese	turkey
wheat bread	peanut butter on wheat bread	cheese on wheat bread	turkey on wheat bread
white bread	peanut butter on white bread	cheese on white bread	turkey on white bread

Number of combinations = $3 \times 2 = 6$

common denominator A common multiple of two or more denominators.

Example: A common denominator of $\frac{1}{2}$ and $\frac{1}{3}$ is 6 because 6 is a multiple of 2 and 3.

Commutative Property of Addition Changing the order of addends does not change the sum.

Example: $3 + 8 = 11$
$8 + 3 = 11$

Commutative Property of Multiplication Changing the order of factors does not change the product.

Example: $3 \times 8 = 24$
$8 \times 3 = 24$

comparison bars Bars that represent the larger amount and smaller amount in a comparison situation.

For addition and subtraction:

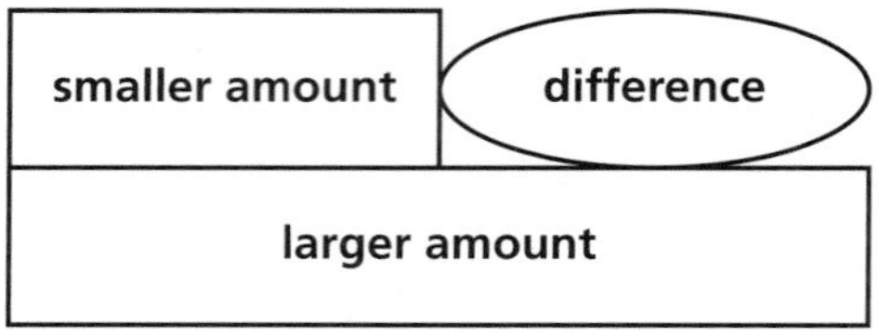

For multiplication and division:

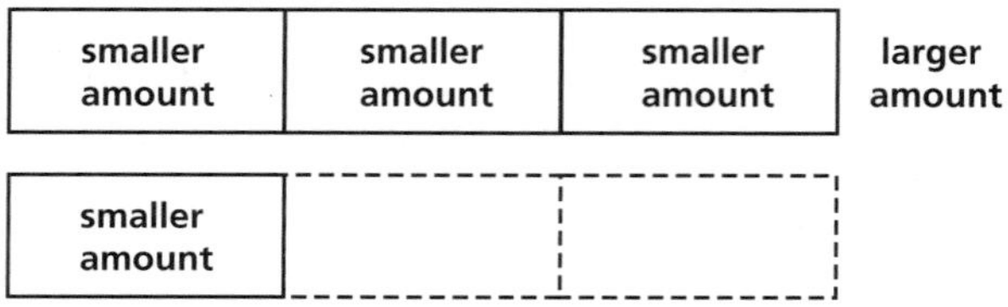

comparison situation A situation in which two amounts are compared by addition or by multiplication. An additive comparison situation compares by asking or telling how much more (how much less) one amount is than another. A multiplicative comparison situation compares by asking or telling how many times as many one amount is as another. The multiplicative comparison may also be made using fraction language. For example, you can say, "Sally has one fourth as much as Tom has," instead of saying "Tom has 4 times as much as Sally has."

complex figure A figure made by combining simple geometric figures like rectangles and triangles. The factor pairs of 18 are 1 and 18, 2 and 9, 3 and 6.

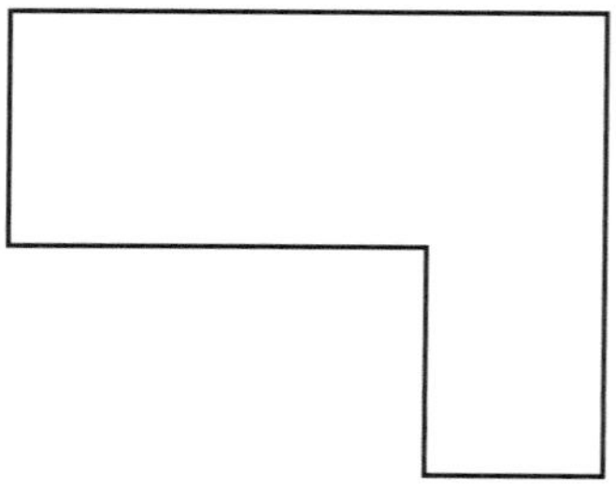

composite number A number greater than 1 that has more than one factor pair. Examples of composite numbers are 10 and 18. The factor pairs of 10 are 1 and 10, 2 and 5. The factor pairs of 18 are 1 and 18, 2 and 9, 3 and 6.

concave A polygon is concave if the inside angle for at least one vertex is greater than 180°.

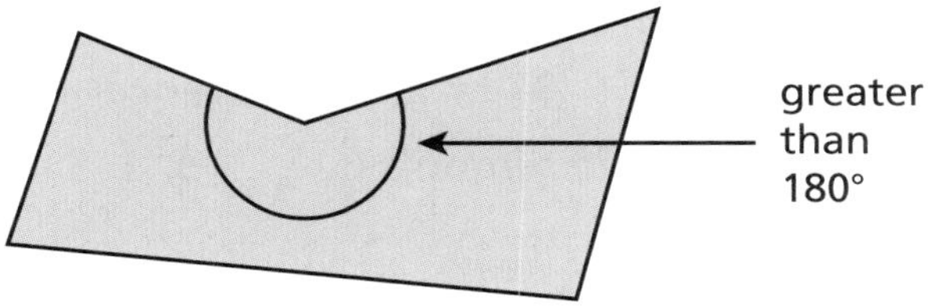

cone A solid figure with a curved base and a single vertex.

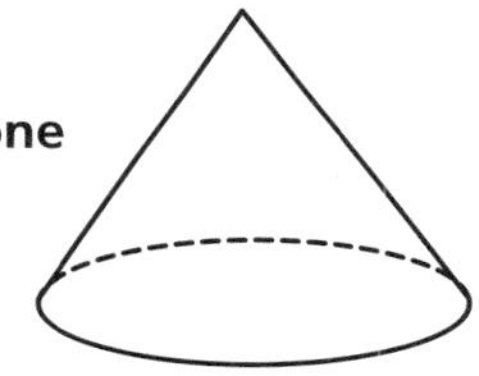

circular cone

congruent Exactly the same size and shape.

Example: Triangles *ABC* and *PQR* are congruent.

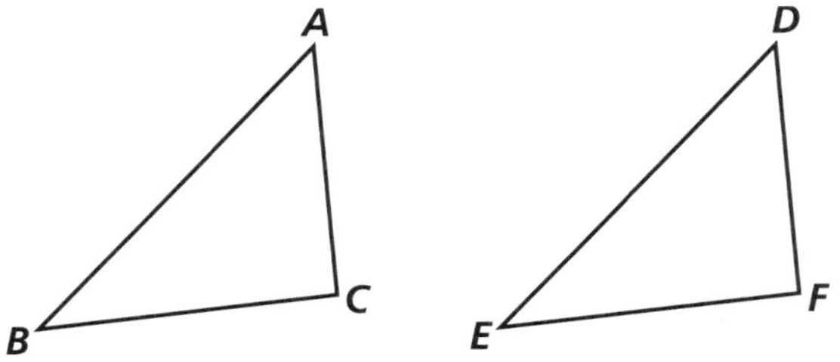

convex A polygon is convex if each inside angle measures less than 180°.

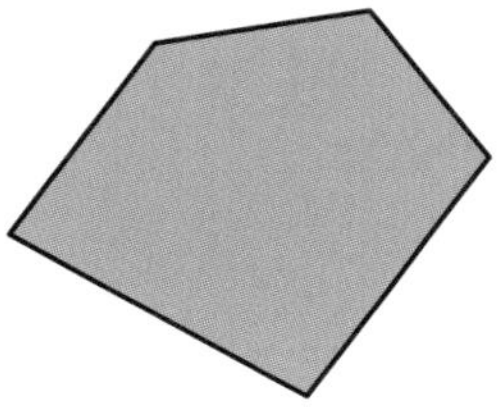

cube A solid figure that has 6 faces that are congruent squares.

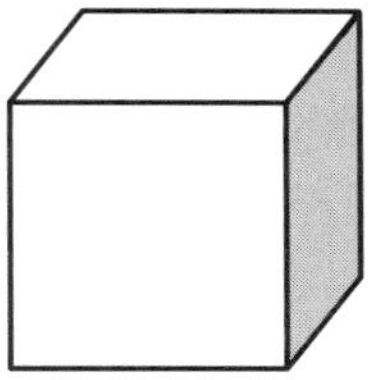

cubic centimeter A metric unit for measuring volume. It is the volume of a cube with one-centimeter edges.

cubic foot A unit for measuring volume. It is the volume of a cube with one-foot edges.

cubic inch A unit for measuring volume. It is the volume of a cube with one-inch edges.

cubic meter A metric unit for measuring volume. It is the volume of a cube with one-meter edges.

cubic yard A unit for measuring volume. It is the volume of a cube with one-yard edges.

cylinder A solid figure with two congruent curved bases.

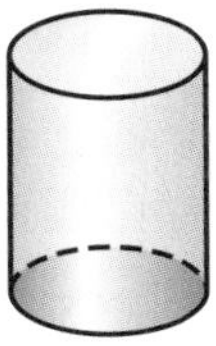

circular cylinder

D

data A collection of information.

decimal number A representation of a number using the numerals 0 to 9, in which each digit has a value 10 times the digit to its right. A dot or **decimal point** separates the whole-number part of the number on the left from the fractional part on the right.

Examples: 1.23 and 0.3

decimal point A symbol used to separate dollars and cents in money amounts or to separate ones and tenths in decimal numbers.

Examples:

\$8.59 1.2

↑ ↑

decimal point

decimeter A unit of measure in the metric system that equals one tenth of a meter. 1 dm = 0.1 m

denominator The number below the bar in a fraction. It shows the total number of equal parts in the fraction.

Example:

$\frac{3}{4}$ ← **denominator**

diagonal A line segment that connects vertices of a polygon, but is not a side of the polygon.

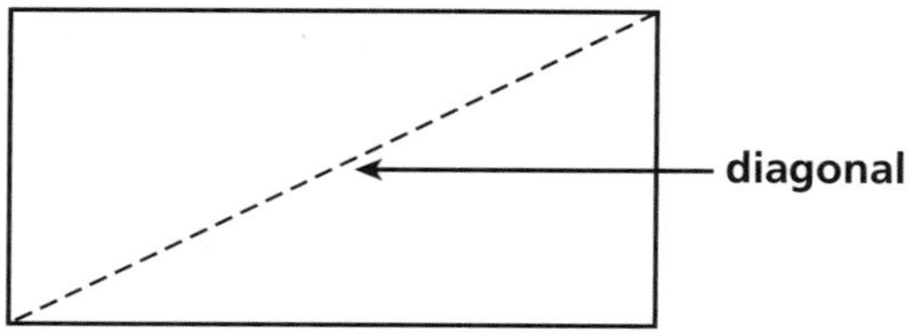

diameter A line segment from one side of a circle to the other through the center. Also the length of that segment.

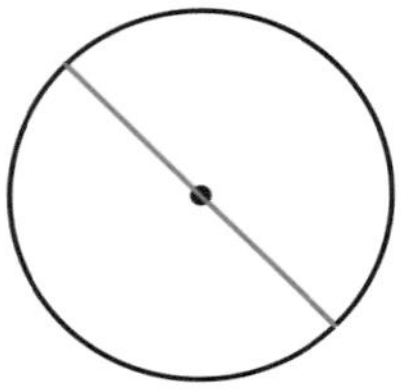

difference The result of a subtraction.

Example: 54 − 37 = 17 ← difference

digit Any of the symbols 0, 1, 2, 3, 4, 5, 6, 7, 8, or 9.

digital clock A clock that shows us the hour and minutes with numbers

Digit-by-Digit A method used to solve a division problem.

Put in only one digit at a time.

```
   5          54          546
7)3,822    7)3,822    7)3,822
 -35        -35        -35
  32         32         32
            -28        -28
             42         42
                       -42
```

dimension The height, length, or width.

Examples:

A line segment has only length, so it has *one* dimension.

A rectangle has length and width, so it has *two* dimensions.

A cube has length, width, and height, so it has *three* dimensions.

Distributive Property You can multiply a sum by a number, or multiply each addend by the number and add the products; the result is the same.

Example:

$$3 \times (2 + 4) = (3 \times 2) + (3 \times 4)$$
$$3 \times 6 = 6 + 12$$
$$18 = 18$$

dividend The number that is divided in division.
Example: $9\overline{)63}^{\,7}$, 63 is the dividend.

divisor The number you divide by in division.
Example: $9\overline{)63}^{\,7}$, 9 is the divisor.

dot array An arrangement of dots in rows and columns.

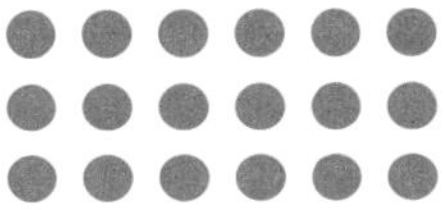

double bar graph Data is compared by using pairs of bars drawn next to each other.

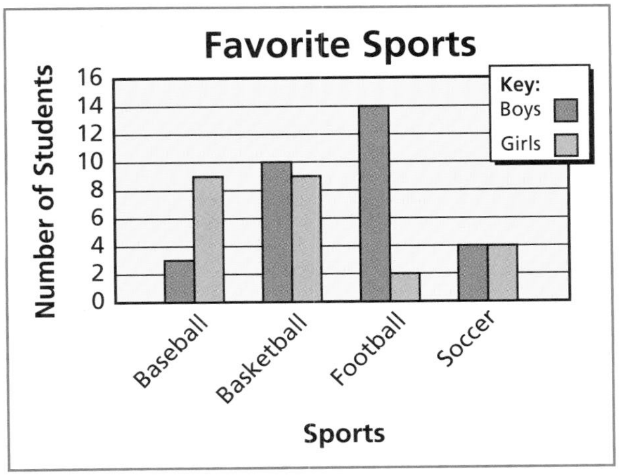

E

edge The line segment where two faces of a three-dimensional figure meet.

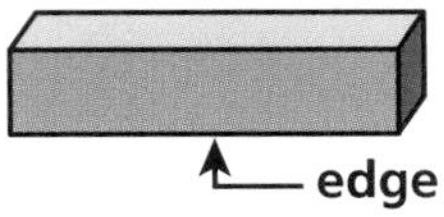

equally likely In probability, equally likely means having the same chance of occurring.

Example: When flipping a coin, the coin is **equally likely** to land on heads or tails.

Equal-Shares Drawing A diagram that shows a number separated into equal parts.

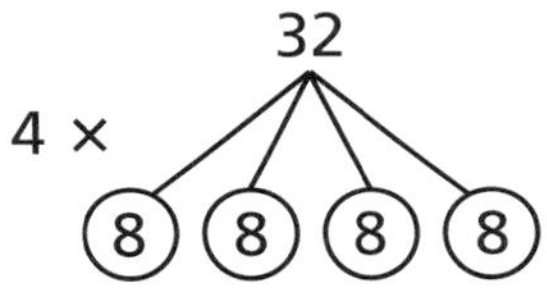

equation A statement that two expressions are equal. It has an equals sign.

Examples: $32 + 35 = 67$
$67 = 32 + 34 + 1$
$(7 \times 8) + 1 = 57$

equilateral Having all equal sides.

Example: An equilateral triangle

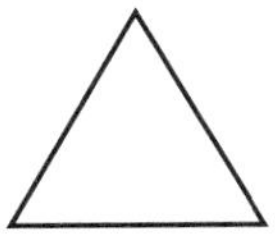

equivalent fractions Two or more fractions that represent the same number.

Example: $\frac{2}{4}$ and $\frac{4}{8}$ are equivalent because they both represent one half.

estimate A number close to an exact amount or to find about how many or how much.

expanded form A way of writing a number that shows the value of each of its digits.

Example: Expanded form of 835:
800 + 30 + 5
8 hundreds + 3 tens + 5 ones

Expanded Notation A method used to solve multiplication and division problems.

Examples:

43 × 67

```
        67 = 60 + 7
      × 43 = 40 + 3
  40 × 60 = 2400
  40 × 7  =  280
   3 × 60 =  180
   3 × 7  = + 21
            2,881
```

3,822 ÷ 7

```
       6 ⎫
      40 ⎬ 546
     500 ⎭
  7 ) 3,822
    − 3 500
        322
      − 280
         42
       − 42
          0
```

expression One or more numbers, variables, or numbers and variables with one or more operations.

Examples: 4
$6x$
$6x - 5$
7 + 4

F

face A flat surface of a three-dimensional figure.

factor One of two or more numbers multiplied to find a product.

Example:

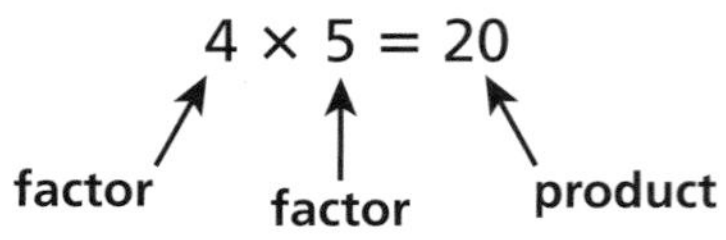

Factor Fireworks Shows how a whole number can be broken down into a product of prime factors.

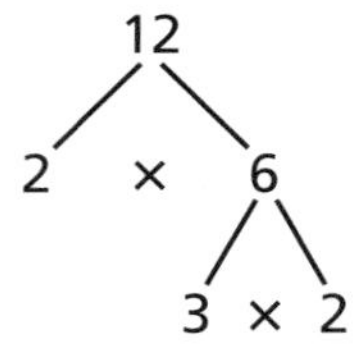

This is also called a **Factor Tree.**

factor pair A factor pair for a number is a pair of whole numbers whose product is that number.

Example:

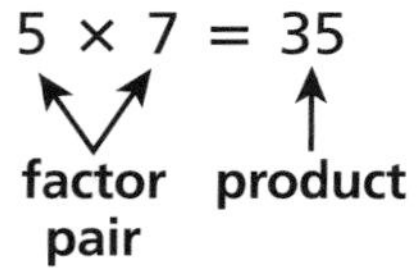

Factor Triangle A diagram that shows a factor pair and the product.

Example:

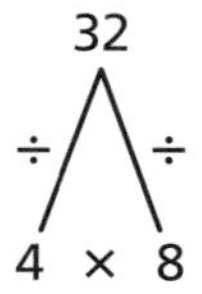

Fahrenheit The temperature scale used in the United States.

Fast Array A numerical form of an array that shows an unknown factor or unknown product.

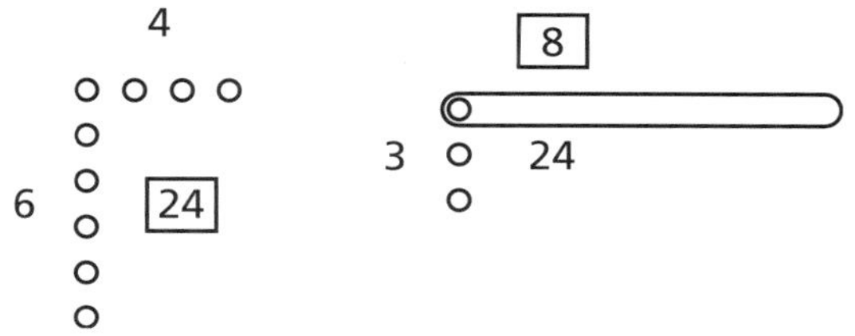

foot A U.S. customary unit of length equal to 12 inches.

fraction A number that is the sum of unit fractions, each an equal part of a set or part of a whole.

Examples: $\frac{3}{4} = \frac{1}{4} + \frac{1}{4} + \frac{1}{4}$

$\frac{5}{4} = \frac{1}{4} + \frac{1}{4} + \frac{1}{4} + \frac{1}{4} + \frac{1}{4}$

frequency table A table that shows how many times each event, item, or category occurs.

Frequency Table	
Height	Frequency
47	1
48	2
49	4
50	3
51	1
52	0
53	2
Total	13

function A set of ordered pairs of numbers such that for every first number there is only one possible second number.

Example: The relationship between yards and feet.

Yards	1	2	3	4	5	6	7
Feet	3	6	9	12	15	18	21

function table A table of ordered pairs that shows a function.

Rule: add 2	
Input	Output
1	3
2	4
3	5
4	6

Heads	1	2	3	4
Legs	2	4	6	8

G

gram The basic unit of mass in the metric system.

greater than (>) A symbol used to compare two numbers. The greater number is given first below.

Example: 33 > 17

33 is greater than 17.

greatest Largest. Used to order three or more quantities or numbers.

H

height The perpendicular distance from a base of a figure to the highest point.

horizontal bar graph A bar graph with horizontal bars.

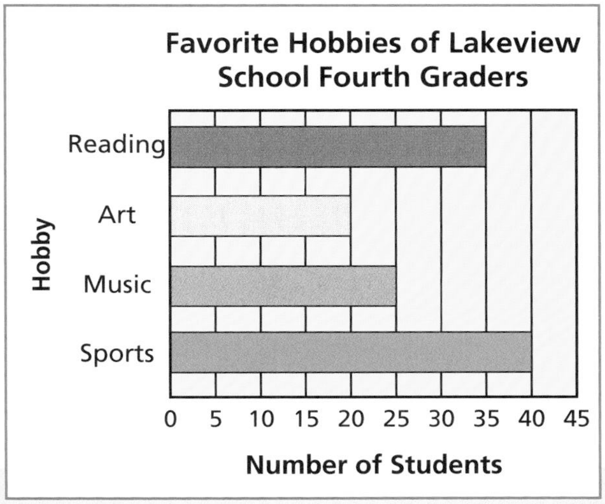

Glossary (Continued)

hundredth A unit fraction representing one of one hundred parts, written as 0.01 or $\frac{1}{100}$.

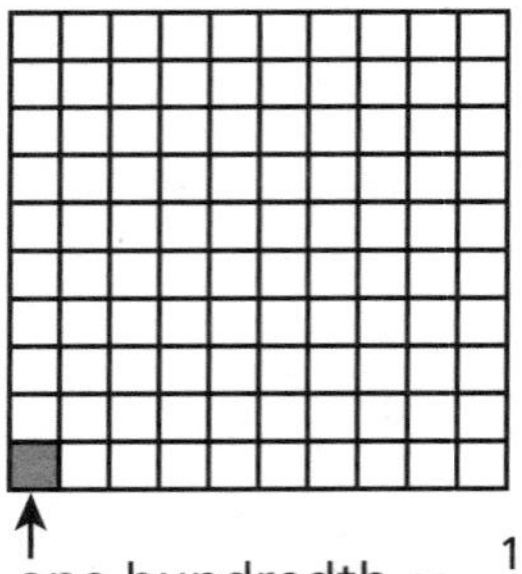

one hundredth = $\frac{1}{100}$ = 0.01

I

Identity Property of Multiplication The product of 1 and any number equals that number.

Example: $10 \times 1 = 10$

improper fraction A fraction that is greater than or equal to 1. The numerator is greater than or equal to the denominator.

Examples: $\frac{13}{4}$ or $\frac{4}{4}$

inch A U.S. customary unit of length.

Example:

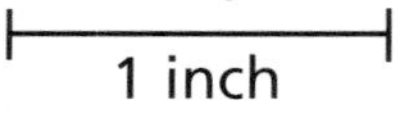

inequality A statement that two expressions are not equal.

Examples: $2 < 5$
$4 + 5 > 12 - 8$

inverse operations Opposite or reverse operations that undo each other. Addition and subtraction are inverse operations. Multiplication and division are inverse operations.

Examples: $4 + 6 = 10$ so, $10 - 6 = 4$ and $10 - 4 = 6$.
$3 \times 9 = 27$ so, $27 \div 9 = 3$ and $27 \div 3 = 9$.

isosceles trapezoid A trapezoid with a pair of opposite congruent sides.

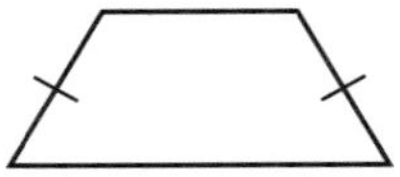

isosceles triangle A triangle with at least two congruent sides.

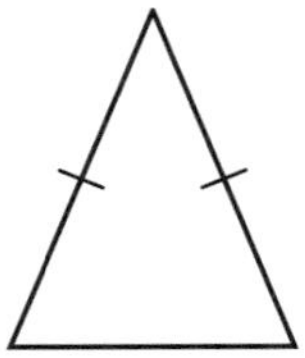

K

kilogram A unit of mass in the metric system that equals one thousand grams. 1 kg = 1,000 g

kiloliter A unit of capacity in the metric system that equals one thousand liters. 1 kL = 1,000 L

L

least Smallest. Used to order three or more quantities or numbers.

least common denominator The least common multiple of two or more denominators.

Example: The least common denominator of $\frac{1}{2}$ and $\frac{1}{6}$ is 6 because 6 is the smallest multiple of 2 and 3.

length The measure of a line segment.

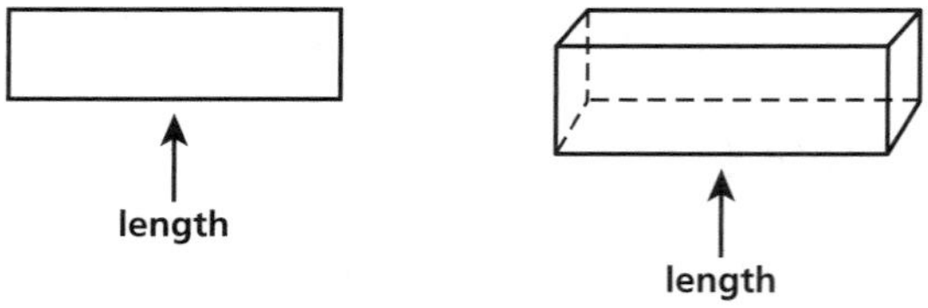

less than (<) A symbol used to compare two numbers. The smaller number is given first below.

Example: $54 < 78$
54 is less than 78.

line A straight path that goes on forever in opposite directions.

Example: line *AB*

line of symmetry A line that divides a figure into two congruent parts.

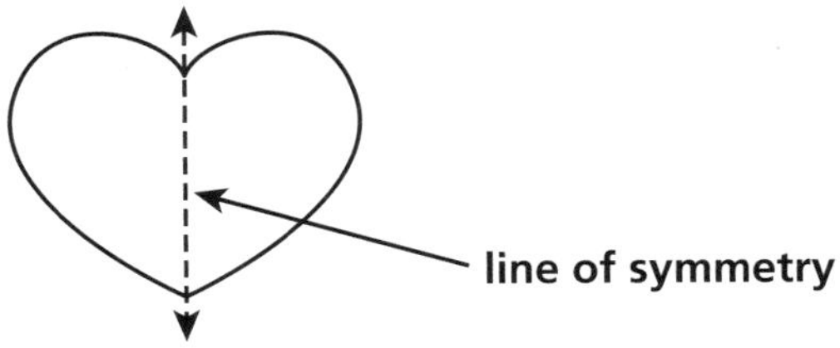

line plot A diagram that shows the frequency of data on a number line.

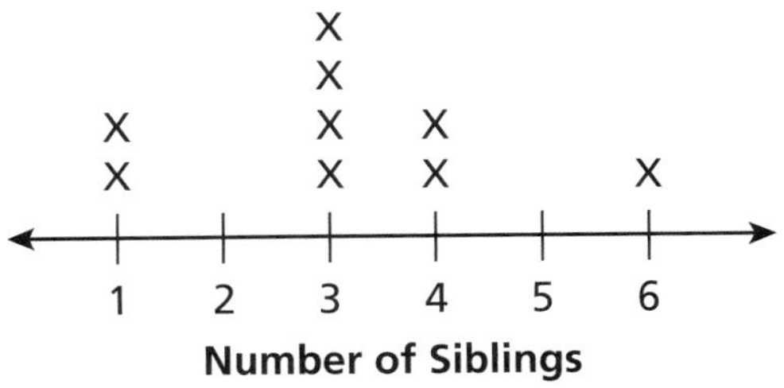

line segment Part of a line that has two endpoints.

line symmetry A figure has line symmetry if it can be folded along a line to create two halves that match exactly.

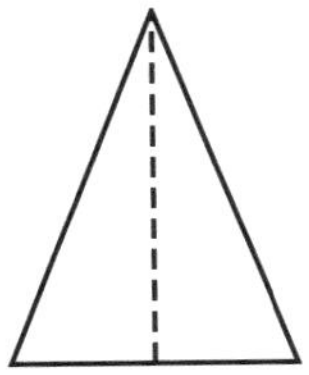

liter The basic unit of capacity in the metric system. 1 liter = 1,000 milliliters.

M

mass The measure of the amount of matter in an object.

mean (average) The size of each of *n* equal groups made from *n* data values. It is calculated by adding the values and dividing by *n*.

Examples: 75, 84, 89, 91, 101
$75 + 84 + 89 + 91 + 101 = 440$, then $440 \div 5 = 88$. The mean is 88.

measure of central tendency The mean, median, or mode of a set of numbers.

median The middle number in a set of ordered numbers. For an even number of numbers, the median is the average of the two middle numbers.

Examples: 13 26 34 47 52
The median for this set is 34.
8 8 12 14 20 21
The median for this set is $(12 + 14) \div 2 = 13$.

meter The basic unit of length in the metric system.

mile A U.S. customary unit of length equal to 5,280 feet.

milligram A unit of mass in the metric system that equals one thousandth of a gram. 1 mg = 0.001 g

milliliter A unit of capacity in the metric system that equals one thousandth of a liter. 1 mL = 0.001 L

millimeter A unit of length in the metric system that equals one thousandth of a meter. 1 mm = 0.001 m

misleading A comparing sentence containing language that may trick you into doing the wrong operation.

Example: John's age is 3 *more than* Jessica's. If John is 12, how old is Jessica?

mixed number A number that can be represented by a whole number and a fraction.

Example: $4\frac{1}{2}$

mode The number that appears most frequently in a set of numbers.

Example: 2, 4, 4, 4, 5, 7, 7
4 is the mode in this set of numbers.

N

net A flat pattern that can be folded to make a solid figure.

net for a cube
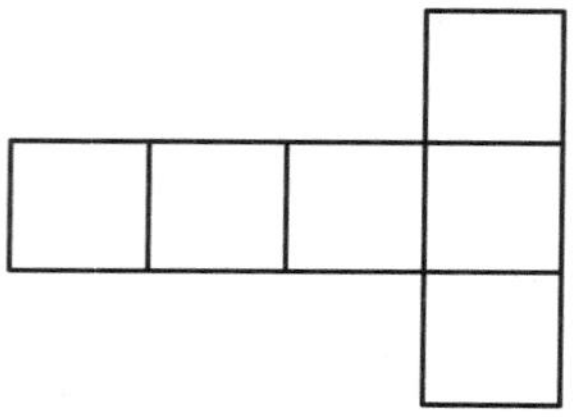

number sentence A mathematical statement that uses =, <, or > to show how numbers or expressions are related. The types of number sentences are equations and inequalities.

Example: $25 + 25 = 50$
$13 > 8 + 2$

numerator The number above the bar in a fraction. It shows the number of equal parts.

Example:

$\frac{3}{4}$ ← numerator $\frac{3}{4} = \frac{1}{4} + \frac{1}{4} + \frac{1}{4}$

O

obtuse angle An angle greater than a right angle and less than a straight angle.

obtuse triangle A triangle with one obtuse angle.

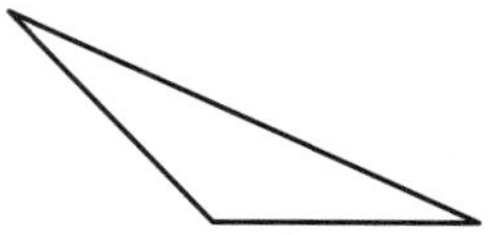

Order of Operations A set of rules that state the order in which operations should be done.

STEPS: -Compute inside parentheses first.
-Multiply and divide from left to right.
-Add and subtract from left to right.

ounce A unit of weight equal to one sixteenth of a pound. A unit of capacity equal to one eighth of a cup (also called a fluid ounce).

P

parallel Lines in the same plane that never intersect are parallel. Line segments and rays that are part of parallel lines are also parallel.

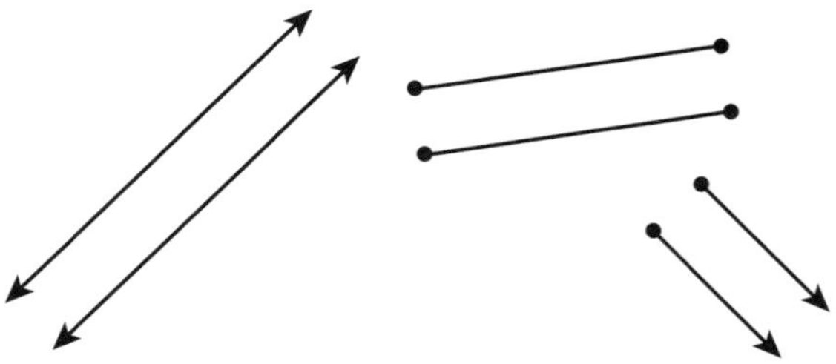

parallelogram A quadrilateral with both pairs of opposite sides parallel.

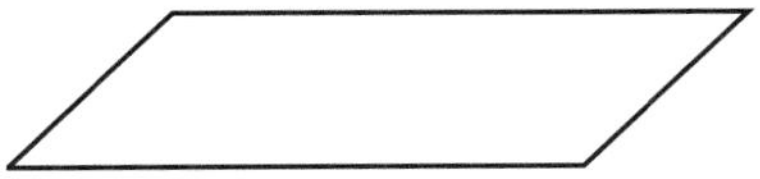

Partial-Quotients Method A method used to solve division problems where the partial quotients are written next to the division problem instead of above it.

Example:

```
8)178
 – 160 | 20
    18 |
  – 16 |  2
     2 | 22
    22   R2
```

pentagon A polygon with five sides.

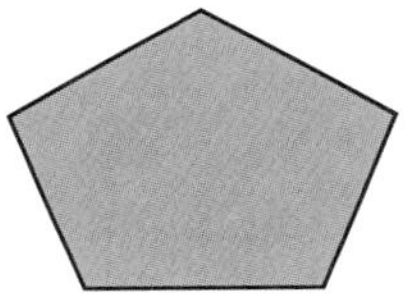

perimeter The distance around a figure.

perpendicular Lines, line segments, or rays are perpendicular if they form right angles.

Example: These two line segments are perpendicular.

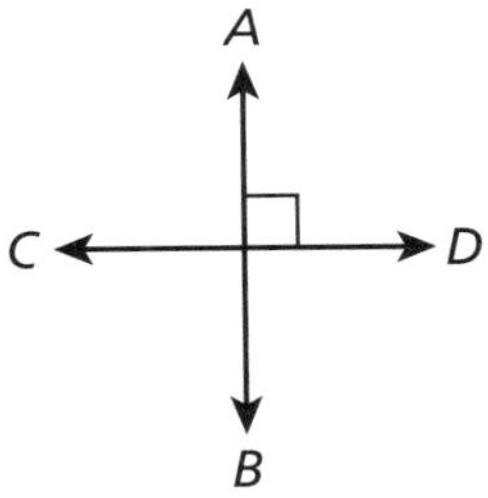

pi A special number equal to the circumference of a circle divided by its diameter. Pi can be represented by the symbol π and is approximately 3.14.

pictograph A graph that uses pictures or symbols to represent data.

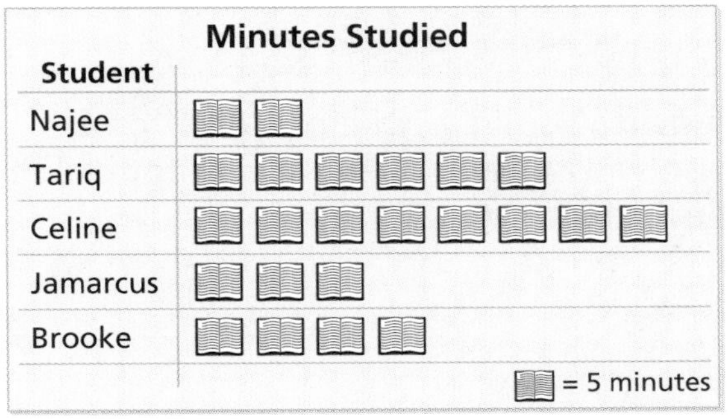

place value The value assigned to the place that a digit occupies in a number.

Example: 235

The 2 is in the hundreds place, so its value is 200.

plane A flat surface that extends without end.

polygon A closed plane figure with sides made of straight line segments.

pound A unit of weight in the U.S. customary system.

prime number A number greater than 1 that has 1 and itself as the only factor pair. Examples of prime numbers are 2, 7, and 13. The only factor pair of 7 is 1 and 7.

prism A solid figure with two congruent parallel bases joined by rectangular faces. Prisms are named by the shape of their bases.

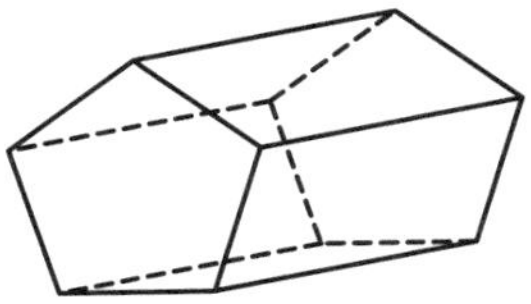

pentagonal prism

probability A number between 0 and 1 that represents the chance of an event happening.

product The answer to a multiplication.

Example: $9 \times 7 = 63$ ↑ product

pyramid A solid with a polygon for a base whose faces meet at a point called the vertex.

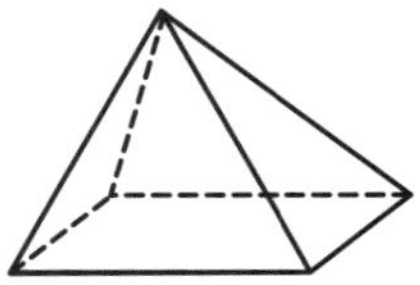

Q

quadrilateral A polygon with four sides.

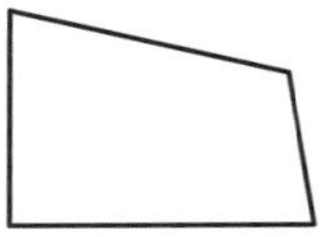

quotient The answer to a division problem.

Example: $\begin{array}{r}7\\9\overline{)63}\end{array}$; 7 is the quotient.

R

radius A line segment that connects the center of a circle to any point on that circle. Also the length of that line segment.

range The difference between the greatest number and the least number in a set.

ray Part of a line that has one endpoint and extends without end in one direction.

rectangle A parallelogram with four right angles.

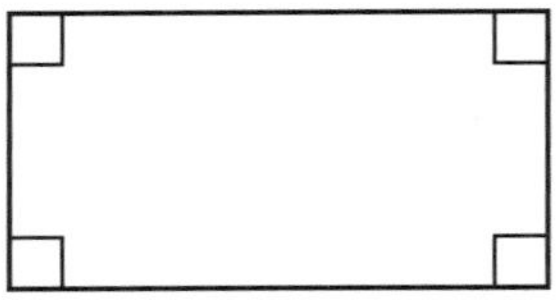

Rectangle Sections A method using rectangle drawings to solve multiplication or division problems.

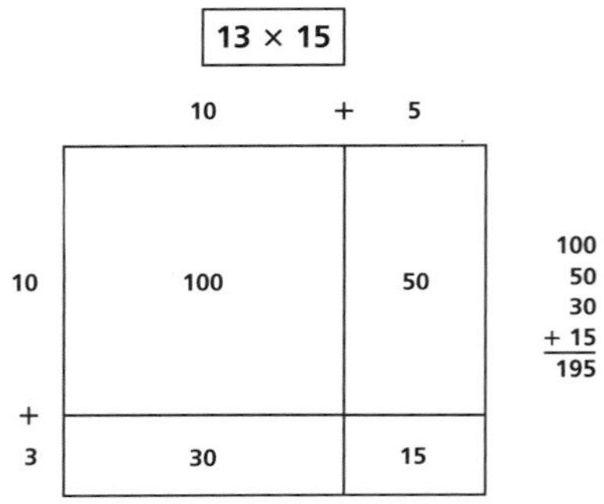

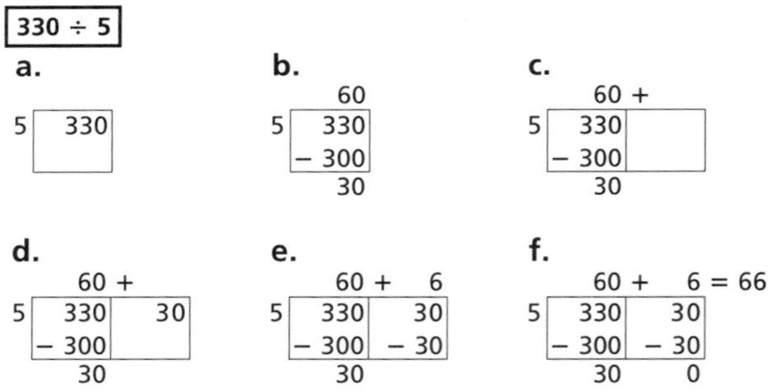

reflection A transformation that flips a figure onto a congruent image. Sometimes called a *flip*.

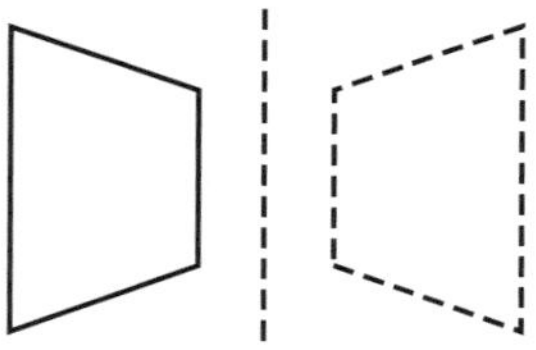

regular polygon Having all sides and angles congruent.

Example: A square is a regular quadrilateral.

remainder The number left over after dividing two numbers that are not evenly divisible.

Example: $5\overline{)43}$ 8 R3 The remainder is 3.

Repeated Groups situation A multiplication situation in which all groups have the same number of objects.

rhombus A parallelogram with congruent sides.

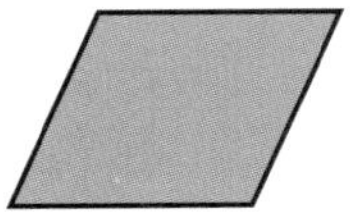

right angle One of four congruent angles made by perpendicular lines.

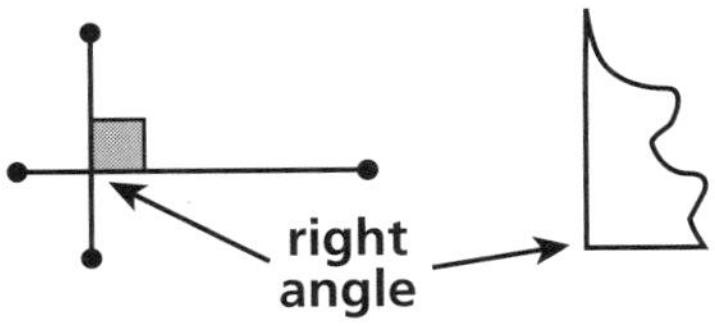

right triangle A triangle with one right angle.

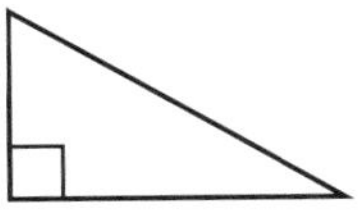

round To find the nearest ten, hundred, thousand, or some other place value. The usual rounding rule is to round up if the next digit to the right is 5 or more and round down if the next digit to the right is less than 5.

Examples: 463 rounded to the nearest ten is 460.
463 rounded to the nearest hundred is 500.

row A part of a table or array that contains items arranged horizontally.

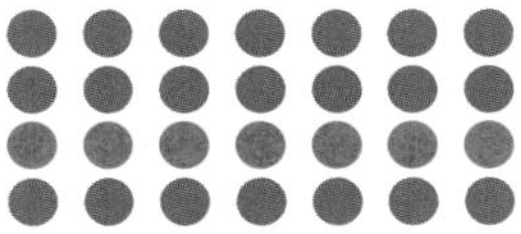

S

scalene A triangle with no equal sides is a scalene triangle.

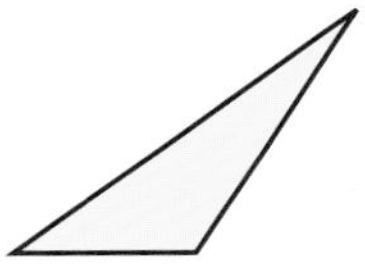

simplest form A fraction is in simplest form if there is no whole number (other than 1) that divides evenly into the numerator and denominator.

Examples: $\frac{3}{4}$ This fraction is in simplest form because no number divides evenly into 3 and 4.

simplify a fraction To divide the numerator and the denominator of a fraction by the same number to make an equivalent fraction made from fewer but larger unit fractions.

Example: $\frac{5}{10} = \frac{5 \div 5}{10 \div 5} = \frac{1}{2}$

situation equation An equation that shows the action or the relationship in a problem.

Example: $35 + n = 40$

slant height The height of a triangular face of a pyramid.

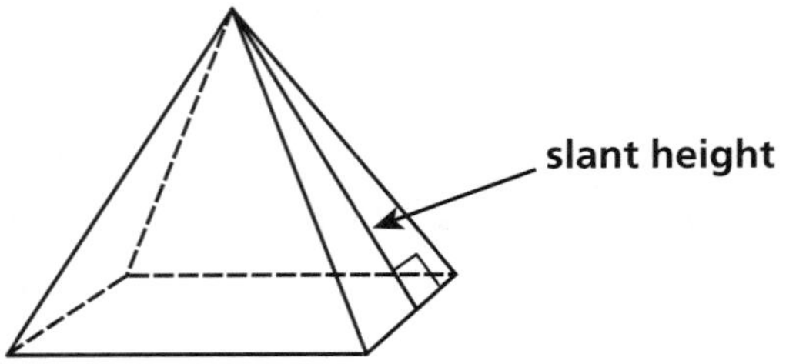

solution equation An equation that shows the operation to perform in order to solve the problem.

Examples: $n = 40 - 35$

sphere A solid figure shaped like a ball.

square array An array in which the number of rows equals the number of columns.

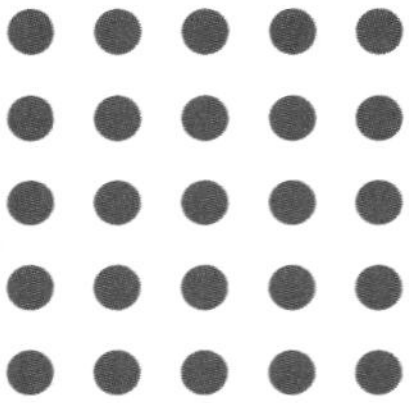

square centimeter A unit of area equal to the area of a square with one-centimeter sides.

square decimeter A unit of area equal to the area of a square with one-decimeter sides.

square foot A unit of area equal to the area of a square with one-foot sides.

square inch A unit of area equal to the area of a square with one-inch sides.

square kilometer A unit of area equal to the area of a square with one-kilometer sides.

square meter A unit of area equal to the area of a square with one-meter sides.

square mile A unit of area equal to the area of a square with one-mile sides.

square millimeter A unit of area equal to the area of a square with one-millimeter sides.

square number The product of a whole number and itself.

Example: $3 \times 3 = 9$
9 is a square number.

square unit A unit of area equal to the area of a square with one-unit sides.

square yard A unit of area equal to the area of a square with one-yard sides.

standard form The form of a number written using digits.

Example: 2,145

sum The answer when adding two or more addends.

Example:

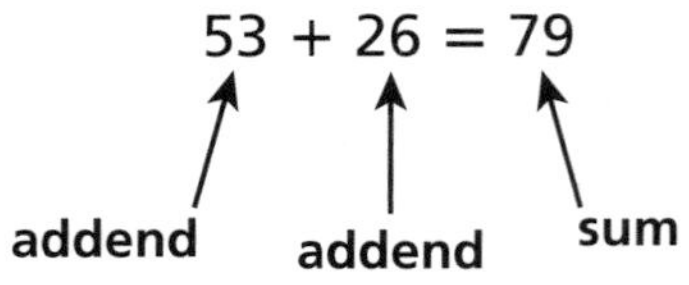

surface area The total area of the two-dimensional surfaces of a three-dimensional figure.

T

table Data arranged in rows and columns.

tally chart A chart that uses tally marks to record and organize data.

Tally Chart	
Height (inches)	Tally
47	///
48	𝍸
49	//
50	
51	𝍸 /
52	////
53	//

/ is 1

𝍸 is 5

tenth A unit fraction representing one of ten equal parts of a whole, written as 0.1 or $\frac{1}{10}$.

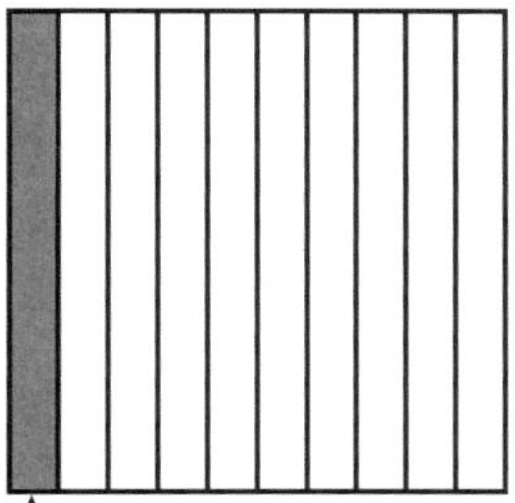

one tenth = $\frac{1}{10}$ = 0.1

12.34

↑

tenth

thousandth A unit fraction representing one of one thousand equal parts of a whole, written as 0.001 or $\frac{1}{1,000}$.

ton A unit of weight that equals 2,000 pounds.

total Sum. The result of addition.

Example:

53 + 26 = 79

addend **addend** **total (sum)**

translation A transformation that moves a figure along a straight line without turning or flipping. Sometimes called a *slide*.

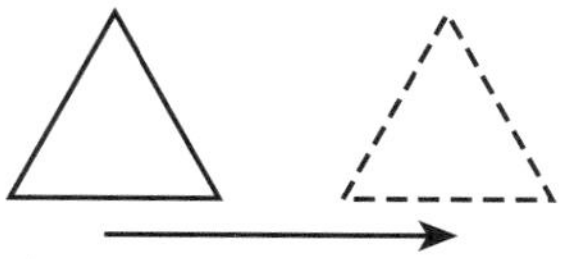

trapezoid A quadrilateral with one pair of parallel sides.

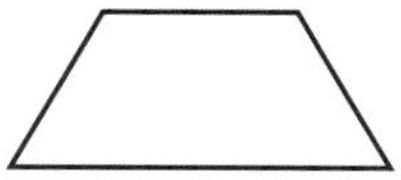

triangle A polygon with three sides.

U

unit A standard of measurement.

Examples: Centimeters, pounds, inches, and so on.

unit fraction A fraction whose numerator is 1. It shows one equal part of a whole.

Example: $\frac{1}{4}$

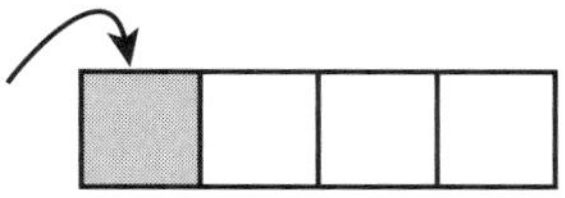

V

vertex A point that is shared by two sides of an angle, two sides of a polygon, or edges of a solid figure.

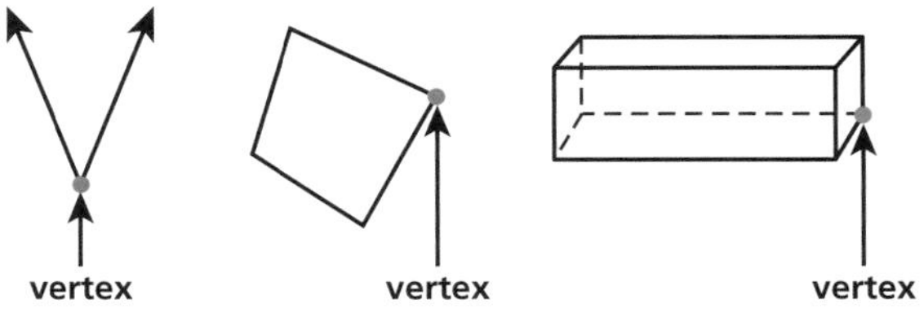

vertical bar graph A bar graph with vertical bars.

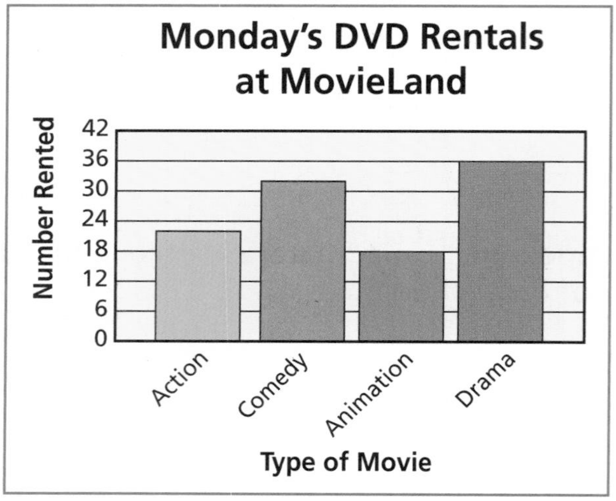

volume The number of cubic units of space occupied by a solid figure.

W

width The measure of one side or edge of a figure.

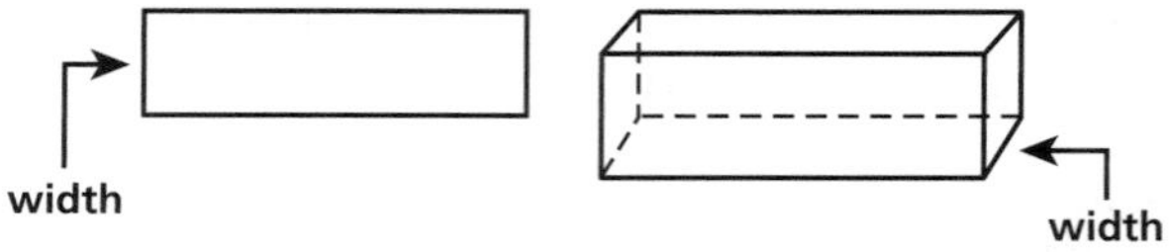

word form The form of a number written using words instead of digits.

Example: Six hundred thirty-nine

Y

yard A U.S. customary unit of length equal to 3 feet.